Making Sense of History

Using High-Quality Literature and Hands-On Experiences to Build Content Knowledge

MYRA ZARNOWSKI

■SCHOLASTIC

NEW YORK • TORONTO • LONDON • AUCKLAND • SYDNEY
MEXICO CITY • NEW DELHI • HONG KONG • BUENOS AIRES

Dedications

This book is dedicated to Maeghan J. Terry, whose interest in women's history continues to grow. She is, indeed, a women's studies specialist!

It is also dedicated to all the teachers and students I have worked with in New York City. Their spunky wit and enthusiasm are truly inspiring. They are a grand group.

✳

Credits

Cover: From *Out of the Dust* by Karen Hesse. Published by Scholastic Press, a division of Scholastic Inc. Jacket illustration copyright ©1997 by Scholastic Inc. Used by permission. Jacket photograph courtesy of Library of Congress Prints and Photographs division, Farm Security Administration collection.

Page 20: From *Give Me Liberty!* by Russell Freedman. Copyright ©2000 by Russell Freedman. All rights reserved. Reprinted from *Give Me Liberty: The Story of the Declaration of Independence* by permission of Holiday House, Inc.

Page 52: From *The Coast Mappers* by Taylor Morrison. Copyright ©2004 by Taylor Morrison. Reprinted by permission of Houghton Mifflin Company. All rights reserved.

Pages 54–55: From *The Voice That Challenged a Nation: Marian Anderson and the Struggle for Equal Rights* by Russell Freedman. Copyright ©2004 by Russell Freedman. Reprinted by permission of Clarion Books, an imprint of Houghton Mifflin Company. All rights reserved.

Pages 111–113: From *Voices from the Fields* by S. Beth Atkin (text and photographs). By permission of Little, Brown and Co., Inc.

Pages 141–142: From *The Birchbark House* by Louise Erdrich. Copyright ©1999 by Louise Erdrich. Reprinted by permission of Hyperion Books for Children.

Page 168: From *Who Were the Founding Fathers?* by Steven H. Jaffe. Copyright ©1996 by Steven H. Jaffe. Reprinted by permission of Henry Holt and Company.

Page 178: Reprinted with permission of Atheneum Books for Young Readers, an imprint of Simon & Schuster Children's Publishing Division from *The Great American Gold Rush* by Rhoda Blumberg. Copyright ©1989 by Rhoda Blumberg.

Cover design by Maria Lilja
Interior design by Sarah Morrow

ISBN-13 978-0-439-66755-5 • ISBN-10 0-439-66755-0
Copyright © 2006 by Myra Zarnowski
All rights reserved. Published by Scholastic Inc.
Printed in the U.S.A.

2 3 4 5 6 7 8 9 10   23   12 11 10 09 08 07

Contents

Part One: If Not Memorizing Facts, Then What?

Part Two: Teaching Sense-Making Concepts: The Antidote to "Why Do We Have to Read This Stuff?"

Acknowledgments

Thank you to the many people who helped me complete this book:

My friend and colleague Debbi Aizenstain, history teacher extraordinaire, worked with me for two years to try out and refine every activity in this book. Thank you, Debbi, for sharing your planning skills, your teaching know-how, and your enthusiasm.

My editor at Scholastic Teaching Resources, Ray Coutu, provided swift, detailed, and thoughtful feedback. Ray, after all that, any "tangled terms" or "shaky syntax" are clearly my own. Thank you for your cheerful support all along the way. Terry Cooper, vice president and general manager, and Margery Rosnick, acquisitions editor, kept me up-beat and energized. Thank you for the professional opportunities you have given me.

My colleagues at Queens College—Penny Hammrich, Lila Swell, Susan Turkel—provided encouragement and good cheer. Thank you, friends, for prodding me to finish.

Finally, my husband, Eddie, gave me this useful bit of advice about how to begin: Just write down Chapter 1. Thank you, Eddie. It worked!

Foreword

By James Cross Giblin

I love history—so much so, in fact, that I write historical nonfiction books and biographies for young people. But this was not always the case. When I was in school I hated most of my history classes. The teachers either read aloud from the textbook or quizzed my fellow classmates and me on dates that we were supposed to have memorized. Rebelling silently, I filled page after page of my history notebooks with doodles—usually unflattering caricatures of those teachers.

Things might have been different if my teachers had had access to an inspiring book like Myra Zarnowski's *Making Sense of History*. Zarnowski knows what bad history teaching looks like. "I've seen it and even done it," she writes. "Students get that glazed look in their eyes. Their minds have fled the scene. . . . They start signing out for the bathroom in record numbers—what another teacher referred to as 'the potty parade.'"

But she also knows what constitutes good history teaching, and she demonstrates it in a clear, lively fashion. Drawing on her own experiences and those of other master teachers, she lays out three essential ingredients for successful instruction: (1) Getting students to think like historians; (2) Blending material from the textbook with relevant historical literature, both nonfiction and fiction; and (3) Involving the students in creative, history-related activities.

To Zarnowski, thinking like a historian begins when the student realizes that the past is familiar—that people throughout history have shared many of the same thoughts and feelings that we do today—and unfamiliar. What would it be like, for instance, to live in a world with no cars or trucks, no movies or television—and no indoor plumbing? How would things be different? How would they be the same? Zarnowski suggests activities to stimulate the students' imaginations and help them travel back to other times and places.

Next on Zarnowski's list of essential ingredients is the use of historical literature to supplement the textbook. For a writer of historical nonfiction like me, this emphasis was particularly gratifying. Zarnowski launches the discussion by citing the basic criteria teachers should employ when evaluating historical nonfiction books: accuracy, clear organization, curriculum connection, and the author's use of primary sources. But she doesn't stop there. Instead, she goes on to mention several other qualities—such as the author's writing style and tone—that can determine whether a historical nonfiction book captures the interest of students or leaves them cold.

Throughout *Making Sense of History*, Zarnowski cites recent and noteworthy nonfiction titles that possess those qualities, such as *Shutting Out the Sky: Life in the Tenements of New York, 1880–1924* by Deborah Hopkinson, *Children of the Dust Bowl* by Jerry Stanley, and *An American Plague: The True and Terrifying Story of the Yellow Fever Epidemic of 1793* by Jim Murphy. "Nonfiction books like these do more than provide facts," Zarnowski writes. "They address issues such as lack of evidence, contradictory evidence, multiple interpretations of the past, and the relevance of the past for understanding the present." In other words, they and nonfiction books like them both enrich and deepen the teaching of history.

Later in the book, Zarnowski focuses on historical fiction, raising intriguing questions about its use in history classes. She asks, "How, I wondered, could a literary work that was part fact and part fiction be helpful in learning history, a discipline rooted entirely in fact? How would students know if they were reading fact or fiction?" She concludes that well-written historical fiction, populated with believable characters and grounded in thorough research, can engage students emotionally and help them identify with people who lived long ago. But she cautions that when using it the teacher must clearly distinguish between fact and fiction—and give students the tools to do that themselves—in order to avoid confusion.

Finally, Zarnowski describes hands-on projects that make students active participants in the learning process. These activities, tested in classrooms around the country, include writing one-page plays about the key events that led up to the American Revolution; learning about mummification for a unit on Ancient Egypt by wrapping fellow students in paper and creating posters explaining the steps; and studying old photos, poems, and books about one-room schoolhouses for a unit on how schooling in America has changed over time.

As I read about these activities, I couldn't help wishing that my teachers had assigned them rather than droning on and on about important dates. It would have been much more fun—and much more instructive. I would have been actually learning instead of doodling idly in my notebook.

Myra Zarnowski urges teachers to "make history happen" in their classrooms. If they use the tools she so generously provides in these pages, and combine them with ideas of their own, there's no reason why that can't happen in history classes everywhere.

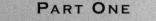

PART ONE
IF NOT MEMORIZING FACTS, THEN WHAT?

PART TWO
TEACHING SENSE-MAKING CONCEPTS: THE ANTIDOTE
TO "WHY DO WE HAVE TO READ THIS STUFF?"

Chapter 1

Reading History

Using Sense-Making Concepts to Join Content and Process

I live and teach in New York, and we New Yorkers are not known for being reserved, passive, or unopinionated. So it's not surprising that when I recently asked teachers in my graduate course for their most pressing questions about teaching history, hands flew up and voices were strong and passionate. Here are some questions they asked me:

* How am I supposed to cover American history from the first settlers to the present in one year?

* How can I use the textbook when the kids groan at the mere sight of it?

* What can I do about the fact that I just don't know enough history to teach it? Where was I when *my* teachers covered all this stuff? Why can't I remember it?

* Are controversial issues appropriate for elementary school? Shouldn't kids be having fun instead of

grappling with difficult social issues? Do I have to bring all the world's problems into my classroom? Shouldn't my classroom be a haven of peace and tranquility?

* How do I—the only white person in the classroom—deal with issues such as segregation and slavery? Books on those issues only make me feel guilty, and the kids sense it.

* What do I say to kids whose answer to ongoing sensitive issues such as racial intolerance is, "I would have beat up those bigots!"?

* What am I supposed to say when most of the kids in my class do not think of the U.S. as *their* country? Their country is where they were born and where they intend to return.

And that was just the first ten minutes. There are probably a lot more questions where those came from. And what's startling to me is that none of these questions is new! They are, instead, stubbornly old. Research has provided us with some answers to these questions, but these answers are often not grounded in specific classroom practices. They are general suggestions, without the reality-based feel of the classroom. Teachers are left wondering, What should my students and I be doing? What does good history instruction look like?

Let's return for a moment to the first question—How am I supposed to cover American history from the first settlers to the present in one year? Research tells us that if covering all of American history in one year means dashing frantically from one topic to the next, then very little will be learned or remembered. You don't need to look much further than Bruce VanSledright's sobering journal article "'I Don't Remember—The Ideas Are All Jumbled in My Head': 8th Graders' Reconstructions of Colonial American History" (1995) for evidence of that. As VanSledright clearly shows us, even after being taught about colonial America during their elementary and middle school years, the junior high school students he interviewed retained very little information. Their heads were full of what he called a "factual stew"—assorted fragments about the people and events of the period. Why? Because

"As many of the [student] responses indicate, the chronological tour through this period—Jamestown to Plymouth to the Middle Colonies—did little to enhance students' understanding. On the contrary, it appeared to produce a type of factual stew. . . .

"A way to offset this would involve focusing on the period from a research-oriented perspective, much the way historians might approach the task."

VanSledright, 1995, p. 339

Making Sense of History

history was taught as an archive of information to be memorized and recalled, and not as information to be questioned, thought about, and debated.

In the article, VanSledright makes a compelling argument for replacing such teaching with an approach that shows students how to think about the past in ways that historians do. This book shows you how to do that, but only if you're willing to abandon the view that teaching history is only about covering content or, as historians jokingly say, covering "one damn thing after another." Teaching history is as much about teaching a process of questioning, investigating, and arriving at conclusions—of "doing history"—as it is about teaching content.

Moving Beyond Content Coverage

If you look again at my graduate students' questions, you will see that many of them deal with content—covering American history, covering a textbook, or covering sensitive issues. A few questions deal with issues related to *what* content to cover—the appropriateness of controversial issues or the adequacy of the teacher's own content knowledge. Still other questions deal with feelings of guilt and anger in response to past events. None of the questions deals with the process of understanding history—how to teach children to make sense of the past. This is a serious omission, but it can be remedied.

You can lay a foundation for the process of "doing history" as early as elementary school, but this requires history-specific teaching. Currently, most content reading is taught by giving students a host of generic strategies such as finding the main idea and identifying related details, predicting outcomes and reading to confirm these predictions, or figuring out words in context. I have never met a teacher who didn't know about using a KWL chart to help students monitor their understanding of content topics. These strategies do support reading comprehension, but they don't provide much help with making sense of history. They are certainly not the most effective strategies for supporting students as they read history.

Instead, I recommend teaching the following historical sense-making concepts along with historical content and general comprehension strategies. In this book, I share my experiences doing just that with fifth-grade teacher Debbi Aizenstain and her class. In Part II, I show how these concepts were brought to the fore and became central to teaching and learning experiences in Debbi's classroom.

Historical Sense-Making Concepts	Instructional Challenges for Teachers
Historical Context	Helping students understand the differences and similarities between the past and the present
Historical Significance	Getting students to recognize historical events that are important to remember
Multiple Perspectives	Helping students understand that people in the past did not all see things the same way
Historical Truth	Encouraging students to use historical fiction to build their understanding of history
Historical Accounts	Showing students that historical accounts are incomplete and require additional facts for the whole story

The Research Behind Historical Sense-Making Concepts

The process of historical sense-making begins with reading about history and then thinking critically about what we have read. Reading history is not just ordinary, everyday reading; it's specialized. To understand what makes it specialized, let's examine the unique aspects of reading history.

According to British researcher Peter Lee (2001), reading history requires following "rules of the game" that historians use to think about content—rules that have not been the focus of instruction in our schools. Lee calls these rules *second-order concepts*. They are not about the content of history—topics like the American Revolution, the Iroquois, or the settlement of the American West. Instead, they are about what historians do with information about these topics. Second-order concepts are the means by which historians make sense of content. They include concepts such as *historical accounts, evidence, change,* and *empathy*.

In addition to Peter Lee, other researchers have found that teaching history has not included teaching second-order concepts. For example, Bruce VanSledright and Lisa Frankes (2000) observed two fourth-grade classrooms studying the same unit on Native Americans and found no instruction related to second-order concepts, such as evidence, point of view, or interpretation. While

Second-Order Concepts	Brief Description of Concepts
Historical Accounts	Historians not only gather and select evidence, they also decide on what it means. Because this meaning is created by the historian, you can find different interpretations of the same facts.
Historical Context	Historians are aware that the past is different from the present and try to understand its unique features. They try not to judge people by today's standards. Instead, they try to understand what it was like to live in the past. At the same time, historians recognize that the past is in some ways similar to the present, not totally foreign. We understand and feel kinship to previous generations because we have had some similar experiences.
Evidence	Evidence is the raw materials used by historians to piece together narratives about what happened in the past. This consists of items such as photographs, letters, diaries, newspaper articles, paintings, and artifacts—primary source materials. An important idea to understand is that we can ask questions about these pieces of evidence that they were not originally designed to answer. What, for example, did the writer of this letter hope to accomplish? What was not included in this photograph?
Empathy/Multiple Perspectives	Historians try to understand the motivations, values, beliefs, and feelings of people in their historical setting—not ours. They try to understand different perspectives in a sympathetic, caring way.
Validity and Reliability	Historians need to determine if the evidence they have is accurate or if it is a forgery, a fake, or deliberately misleading. Evidence can be overly biased or distorted. Is the person writing a letter or an account, for example, telling the truth? How much time has passed between the event and the reporting of the event? One way historians determine this is to corroborate information; that is, they look for several accounts that agree. It's also important to realize that all evidence is naturally biased because it is told from the perspective of the person writing. We need to help students understand that evidence is not either "the truth" or "a lie"—what has been called the "good-bad dichotomy" (VanSledright, 2004). Much of history involves building the strongest case for understanding the past, not eliminating "the lies."
Significance	Significance is called the valuing criterion. In determining significance, historians consider what is important enough to remember and pay attention to. One factor that determines the significance of an event is how many people were affected by it. Another factor is the durability, or long-lasting effects, of an event.

teachers in both classrooms were somewhat successful in introducing information and research techniques such as using the table of contents, neither teacher taught students how to deal with second-order concepts. VanSledright and Frankes suggest that these concepts need to be prioritized—brought to the fore of instruction—if history is to be taught in an intellectually honest way. I agree.

Although this may seem like a lot of concepts to introduce, many of them arise naturally as students are looking up information for reports or projects. For example, if students find contradictory *evidence* in two books, you can discuss why this occurs. If students ask why they have to study a particular topic, such as the Civil Rights movement or the Civil War, you can ask them whether these events affected large numbers of people, whether their effects were deep and long lasting, and whether repercussions from them are still being felt today. If the answer is yes, they are *significant* topics. During class discussions, you are likely to find many opportunities to extend students' understanding of second-order concepts. By addressing students' naturally occurring questions head-on, you stimulate their historical thinking.

The Benefits of Teaching History According to Sense-Making Concepts

In this book, I refer to second-order concepts as *historical sense-making concepts*. Knowing these concepts helps students understand history as a discipline. When you teach these concepts, you

* provide a lasting foundation for historical thinking.

* supply tools for thinking about the present as well as the past.

* combine process and content so that you achieve multiple teaching goals simultaneously.

* offer an authentic purpose for reading the literature of history.

PROVIDES A LASTING FOUNDATION FOR HISTORICAL THINKING

Teaching students to read using historical sense-making concepts provides a foundation for historical thinking that will be useful to them throughout their educational careers. When students question evidence, understand context, and consider multiple perspectives, they are using processes central to the study of history. This is reading according to the "rules of the game," and it shouldn't end at the grade you teach.

In contrast, when students are taught to read history with the sole purpose of remembering, they do not learn what history is all about. Even worse, practices that emphasize remembering "retard the development of historical thinking because they foster the naïve conception that the past and history are one and the same, fixed and stable forever . . ." (VanSledright, 2004, p. 232). This is true not only in elementary and middle school, but at the college level as well, where, according to historian David Pace, "disciplinary thinking is crucial to learning" (2004, p. 1179).

SUPPLIES TOOLS FOR THINKING ABOUT THE PRESENT AS WELL AS THE PAST

The sense-making tools of the historian are useful beyond the study of history. As citizens in a democracy, we need to be able to entertain and evaluate contrasting accounts of current events, question evidence, and think about the perspectives of others. A fifth-grade teacher I know often compares how the *New York Post* and the *New York Times* cover the same event. This activity is a wonderful experience for his students because it shows them that all accounts are not the same. They vary depending on the writer's knowledge and beliefs about the topic. (More on this in Chapter 7.) Sense-making concepts put students on the alert that reading doesn't mean simply pulling out information from any source and giving the same information back on a test or in a report. It means, instead, "detecting spin, hype, snake-oil sales pitches . . ." (VanSledright, 2004, p. 232) as well as differences in opinion and gaps in information.

COMBINES PROCESS AND CONTENT SO THAT YOU ACHIEVE MULTIPLE TEACHING GOALS SIMULTANEOUSLY

Most teachers are expected to cover specific historical content at each grade level. Since using historical sense-making concepts is the best, most authentic process for understanding this content, it makes sense to combine process and content. In doing so, we match our content goals with the best means available for achieving them.

Research and good practice make the case for pairing content and process. Robert Mayer (1998, 1999), for example, argues that when learning history, students need to do two things simultaneously: they need to learn a basic, coherent historical narrative (What happened?) and learn how to critique that narrative at the same time (How do I know this narrative is accurate?). In other words, learning information is just the beginning. At the same time, students need to be doing something with this information. Social studies educator Walter Parker (2001) refers to this dual stance as "knowing and doing." I, too, have found that in order for students to learn history, both *learning and critiquing* and *knowing and doing* are essential (Zarnowski, 2003). It is also essential that the *knowing* matches our curriculum goals and that the *doing* matches the process that historians embrace.

Resources on Teaching Historical Content and Process

The following books and article show teachers and students involved in doing history—learning historical content and process.

Elementary School:

- *Seeking History: Teaching with Primary Sources in Grades 4–6* by Monica Edinger. Heinemann.
    With the help of their teacher, students investigate primary sources in order to learn about Ellis Island and the immigrant experience, the Constitution, and other topics.

- *If This Is Social Studies, Why Isn't It Boring?* edited by Stephanie Steffy and Wendy J. Hood. Stenhouse.
    A number of teachers and researchers show that an inquiry model promotes understanding of the past. Chapter 14, "Exploring Historical and Multicultural Perspectives Through Inquiry," provides a useful explanation of how the model works.

Middle School/High School:

- *Teaching U.S. History as Mystery* by David Gerwin and Jack Zevin. Heinemann.
    Using "mystery packets" consisting of primary source materials, the authors show how evidence can reveal problems in need of solving. Students are encouraged to use the evidence to form their own interpretations of historical events.

- It's Just the Facts, or Is It? Teachers' Practices and Students' Understandings of History by S. G. Grant in *Theory and Research in Social Education, 29*, 65–108.
    One high school teacher, the "master storyteller," presents history as facts, while another teacher presents history as "complex ideas." The students in the second class develop more complex, nuanced ideas because they do more interpreting of historical facts. For a description of these case studies in their entirety, see Grant's book *History Lessons: Teaching, Learning, and Testing in U.S. High School Classrooms* (Erlbaum, 2003), which was awarded the National Council for the Social Studies Exemplary Research Award.

OFFERS AN AUTHENTIC PURPOSE FOR READING THE LITERATURE OF HISTORY

Quality nonfiction literature plays a big part in helping students know and do history. That's because it provides students with factual information and, at the same time, shows how historians think about and interpret that information. For example, in his book *Dr. Jenner and the Speckled Monster: The Search for the Smallpox Vaccine* (2002), Albert Marrin tells how the discovery of a vaccine led to the elimination of smallpox. At the same time, he shows readers that this history is not fixed or well established. Instead, it is riddled with doubt and uncertainty. In the paragraph below, Marrin describes the origins of smallpox. Notice that every sentence contains speculation—what many people think probably happened—not established fact. (Italics have been added for emphasis.)

> Scientists *believe* that smallpox is a fairly young disease. About eight thousand years ago, *they think*, the ancestor of the smallpox virus lived in an *unknown* farm animal *somewhere* in Asia or the Middle East. That virus *probably* made its host animal sick, but not sick enough to kill it. Then *in some way that is still unclear*, the virus crossed over to a person. *Perhaps* the virus's DNA mutated, or changed, in a chance way that allowed this to happen. *Whatever the case*, the virus and its descendants survived in a person by attacking human cells. Because the victim *either* died *or* fought off the disease, the viruses did not attack every cell in the person's body. (p. 13)

This is an amazing paragraph because it shows that doing history requires building the strongest case possible. You might want to examine this paragraph with your students, list the words that show speculation and uncertainty, and then use these words to write about a historical event in history that is still open to debate. For example:

* Who fired the first shot at Lexington, starting the American Revolution?
* Were the colonists right to rebel against Great Britain?
* Did the Declaration of Independence provide "liberty and justice for all"? Or, as teacher James Percoco (2001) asked his students, Is the American Revolution over?

You and your students could also search for other examples of speculation in other history books. You might want to start with *Bard of Avon*, a historical account of the life and times of William Shakespeare, by Diane Stanley and Peter Vennema. Throughout the book, the authors use what they know about the times in which Shakespeare lived to speculate about the events of his life. They use words such as *perhaps, may have been, probably,* and *some people think* to signal their speculation.

Books That Speculate About the Past

Picture Books:

Bard of Avon: The Story of William Shakespeare by Diane Stanley and Peter Vennema, illustrated by Diane Stanley. Morrow.

The Hindenburg by Patrick O'Brien. Holt.

The History of Counting by Denise Schmandt-Besserat, illustrated by Michael Hays. Morrow.

Sybil Ludington's Midnight Ride by Marsha Amstel, illustrated by Ellen Beier. Carolrhoda.

Chapter Books:

Freedom Roads: Searching for the Underground Railroad by Joyce Hansen and Garry McGowan. Illustrated by James Ransome. Cricket.

Hurry Freedom: African Americans in Gold Rush California by Jerry Stanley. Crown.

The Life and Death of Adolf Hitler by James Cross Giblin. Clarion.

The Mystery of the Mammoth Bones by James Cross Giblin. HarperCollins.

Terror of the Spanish Main: Sir Henry Morgan and His Buccaneers by Albert Marrin. Dutton.

York's Adventures with Lewis and Clark: An African-American's Part in the Great Expedition by Rhoda Blumberg. HarperCollins.

Making Sense of History

Concluding Thoughts

As elementary and middle school teachers, we face the unique challenge of dealing with students whose understanding of the past is immature, incomplete, and sometimes inaccurate. We need to help students develop a healthy curiosity about the past which will, in turn, lead them toward a more mature, complete, and accurate understanding of history. Grappling with the questions that arise daily in the classroom—like those at the start of this chapter—can help us shape our teaching so that the things we do promote historical understanding rather than the static thinking that makes history so unpopular with so many students.

In this book, I attempt to align theory and practice by focusing on what good practice looks like. Part One describes an alternative to teaching history as memorization. In this first chapter, we have considered the unique aspects of reading history and why it is important to introduce students to historical sense-making concepts. Chapter 2 considers the crucial role of the teacher. If we are ever to abandon the role of information giver, we need a better role to replace it. This chapter takes a look at what this new and better role might be. You will read about aligning the essential elements of teaching history: historical literature, historical thinking, and hands-on experiences.

Part Two deals with questions that arise when history is considered from a disciplinary perspective—that is, history the way historians think about it. We'll consider how the sense-making concepts such as context, perspective, significance, truth, and historical accounts help students think about historical content. Each chapter addresses an individual concept to show you how to plan for and carry out successful teaching.

Chapter 2

Aligning the Essential Elements of History Teaching

Historical Thinking, Historical Literature, and Hands-On Experience

We all know what bad history teaching looks like. I've seen it and even done it. As one teacher told me, "I lost them within fifteen minutes." Students get that glazed look in their eyes. Their minds have fled the scene. A few might start tapping on the desk with their fingers, or better yet, with a ruler. They start signing out for the bathroom in record numbers—what another teacher referred to as "the potty parade."

In this chapter we'll bypass dreadful history teaching and look instead at examples of good history teaching. First, I'll share how three teachers at different grade levels describe their own best practice. Then I'll discuss what their teaching has in common—namely, the essential elements of good history teaching: historical thinking, historical literature, and hands-on experience. Seeing how these elements work together will help you update and rethink your role in helping students develop historical understanding. It will enable you to take the sense-making concepts discussed in Chapter 1 and apply them in your own classroom.

What Does Good Teaching Look Like?

I asked several teachers to describe in writing their most successful moments teaching history—moments when everything was going right, moments that made them proud. Here are three responses. As you read, consider the following questions:

* What's similar about the way these teachers teach?
* What's making their teaching work?

EXAMPLE #1:

Debbi Aizenstain, fifth-grade teacher at P.S. 24 in Queens, tells about having her students write one-page plays, an idea I first encountered in Tarry Lindquist's book *Seeing the Whole Through Social Studies* (1995/2002):

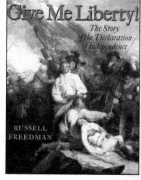

After reading about the events leading up to the signing of the Declaration of Independence and some famous battles of the American Revolution, my fifth-grade class studied Russell Freedman's *Give Me Liberty!* (Holiday House, 2000).

I wanted my students to understand what the American patriots might be feeling and saying. So, as a class, we looked at several illustrations and discussed the events surrounding each one, focusing on how the illustrations either reinforced or extended what Freedman says in the text.

I then divided the class into small groups and assigned each group an illustration. One illustration showed Patrick Henry denouncing the Stamp Tax before the Virginia assembly. Another showed colonists dressed as Mohawk Indians dumping tea into Boston Harbor. Another showed several Minutemen taking leave of their families and going off to fight the British. I asked students to study their illustration, think about what the people in the picture might be saying to one another and script a one-page play. (See sample on the next page.) Then I asked each group to perform the play for their classmates.

Not only did the students have fun writing and performing their plays, but they developed a better understanding of the events leading up to the American

One-Page Play Written by Debbi's Students

Delegate 4: Patrick Henry is making a fool out of himself.

Delegate 2: Why doesn't he just sit down!!!

Delegate 1: Yeah! Sit down, Patrick. You're not going to persuade these delegates to listen to you!!!

Delegate 4: Please Patrick, save your breath.

Delegate 2: This is a waste of time.

Delegate 3: Maybe he is right.

Delegate 4: You agree with him? Why do you even bother to listen to him? He shouldn't even be here.

Delegate 2: I feel like falling asleep at his speech.

Delegate 1: You're never going to get your way.

Delegate 2: I COMMAND YOU TO SIT DOWN!!!!!

Delegate 4: I can't stand that guy. We're going to sit here all day just to listen to him. If Patrick says one more word, we'll probably end up fighting with each other. Aaaghhh.

Delegate 2: That's right. I am so bored.

Delegate 1: I hope he finishes his ridiculous speech very, very soon.

Delegate 2: This speech is as long as a dozen pages.

Delegate 3: Give Patrick a chance. He has a reason for saying this.

Delegate 1: I wish I could get out of this meeting room right this minute!!!

This picture of Patrick Henry addressing the Virginia assembly inspired this dialogue.

Delegate 4: Wait a minute. I am starting to think he is right. We are supposed to be fighting for our colonies. If we just sit here and say he is foolish, then what's the point of fighting for our independence?

Delegate 2: Oh my God! For real? You actually like him all of a sudden?

Delegate 3: We are supposed to be defending our colonies. Listen! Why should we listen to the British, when we could have independence and freedom?

Delegate 1: Hey, that makes a lot of sense. Maybe Patrick Henry is not as foolish as I thought.

Delegate 2: Well, none of you Delegates can convince me Patrick Henry's speech is actually useful. It's just words. It means absolutely nothing to me.

Delegate 4: I think everyone should listen to Patrick Henry because he is right.

Delegate 1: I think he is right.

Delegate 4: Hey! Everyone is fighting for our country. You're the only one who's not. Are you on the side of the British?

Delegate 2: No!!! Well, I guess you're right. He's just so agitated. But independence and freedom are totally what I want. I will agree. Actually, I like the idea very much!!

Delegate 3: WELL!! ALL SHOULD GO ON THE SIDE OF PATRICK HENRY. TELL THE BRITISH HOW WE FEEL!!

Making Sense of History

Revolution and how the colonists felt about those events. They were able to place themselves in a different historical period and think like a colonist.

EXAMPLE #2:

Elizabeth Schneider, sixth-grade teacher, describes her mummy-wrapping project:

When I teach I want to give students experiences they will remember. And our mummy-wrapping project was one of their most memorable experiences. Students worked in groups of three to learn the process Ancient Egyptians used to mummify a body. Then, using toilet paper, students "mummified" each other. The students began by individually researching children's literature and the Internet to come up with a list of steps that were followed by the Ancient Egyptians. In their small groups, they developed a flow chart of the mummification process.

Then we held a mummy-wrapping session: Each group selected one person as the body to be mummified, one person to be the embalmer, and one person to be the priest. The priest and the embalmer followed the process listed on their flow charts. Using toilet paper, they wrapped the "mummy." When each wrapping was complete, the group sent their "mummy" off into the afterlife with a prayer written by group members.

The students got very involved in this project. They enjoyed learning

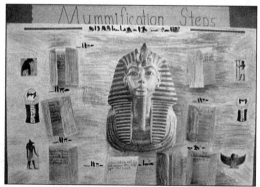

Elizabeth Schneider's mummy-wrapping project

about the mummification process, and some of them even went beyond requirements to create props for their ceremonies, such as replicas of tools used, canopic jars to store the internal organs, and scrolls to hold their prayers. Some groups even created coffins for their "mummies."

It was so wonderful to see my students become involved in this project. For many it did not end with the ceremony, but instead spurred them on to learn more about the ancient world and culture.

Example #3:

Even young children can take an interest in history. Here first-grade teacher Marianne Erster describes how she taught her students about what schools were like in the past, after looking at an old photograph of a school that once stood where their school now stands:

Hanging on a wall in my principal's office was a photograph of a little schoolhouse dated 1898. Below the photo was a poem called "The Little School House Is No More," which explained what going to school was like at that time. (See poem on next page.) According to the poem, the schoolhouse was made of red bricks, had a shingled roof, and had oak floors and steps. Children were greeted at the door each day by the principal as he rang the schoolhouse bell. Inside, students sat on wooden benches and wrote on chalk slates during lessons.

At the end of the poem I was amazed to learn that this was a photo of the former Public School 24, the school where I now teach. This little schoolhouse is no more. In its place is a three-floor building with a concrete playground and transportables that we use for additional classroom space. This incident inspired

P.S. 24 in 1898 and in 2005

Making Sense of History

The Little Schoolhouse Is No More

Signs of the times when the years so keen
To all of us bring changing scene!
The little schoolhouse is no more;
The one with shingled roof, the floor
Of oaken boards, the time-worn seat
Where once we learned our figures neat.
Whose wooden steps, so clean and worn
Were old before we had been born!
Whose lights, though ancient vintage, too,
Shone on dark days as if quite new.
Where every morn the schoolhouse bell
Would sound the laggard's warning knell.
Would still the schoolyard's noise and din,
The signal lessons would begin
When once within its kindly walls
The boys and girls marched through its halls
And there to see that all was right
To greet each one with smile so bright,
Beloved by all, e'en by the boy
Whose chief delight was to annoy,
The kindly principal was seen,
Ever benevolent of mien.
Each day she'd visit every class;
By name she knew each lad and lass!
Each child who tried received her praise,
The bad were warned to mend their ways.
But all went home each day from school
Content and glad, 'neath her wise rule!

The little schoolhouse is no more!
Its passing makes my heart feel sore.
It's gone fore'er, and in its place
A red-bricked giant shows its face.
A friendly giant, who grows more dear
To all of us, as speeds the year.
Whose only fault, if fault there be,
Is in its new formality.
Whose classrooms light and airy halls
Make faces bright, and soon installs
A pride and pleasure quite unknown
Before this giant had been grown.
Where there is space for everyone
To play outside, when school is done.
No need now e'er to use the street
Where dangers lurk from cars so fleet.
And so this giant of modern ways
Deserves its share of thanks and praise.
For still there's fostered in each child
True courtesy, and manner mild.
And still the principal each day
To every classroom goes her way.
To her all yield love and respect,
While happy smiles from hers reflect.
And so there seems to breathe and grow
Transforming thus, as time will show,
The spirit of the schoolhouse small,
Unchanged, unconquered, after all!

Helen B. Thompson, P. S. 24, June 10, 1932

Martha M. Kelly, Principal

me to teach my first-grade class a piece of our history. I wanted the children to be aware of the past and how schools have changed over time.

Eager to begin, I started researching primary-source documents and quality literature to use with my class. I came across a book called *One-Room School* (1999) by Raymond Bial. The book's photographs give historical details that would take my students back in time and make the past understandable. I also found several photographs of old schoolhouses from the library and Internet. When the children arrived Monday morning, the classroom was covered with photographs of schools and schoolhouses, including the 1898 photo of P.S. 24. I thought this would help spark my students' curiosity, and it did.

I gathered the children in the meeting area and began talking about school. We created a KWL chart that would help the children combine new information they learned with any prior knowledge they already had. The next day, I read the book *One-Room School* by Raymond Bial. The children were fascinated by the photographs, which provided them with concrete examples of how things were in the past, and the vivid descriptions of schools and life inside them. I also showed the children the 1898 photo of P.S. 24. We discussed that our school was once a one-room schoolhouse, just like the ones in Raymond Bial's book.

The next day we took a walking tour around the inside and outside of our school. During the tour we discussed the things we noticed that have changed and/or stayed the same over time. We also took new photographs of our school. When we returned to the classroom, the children compared and contrasted their school today with one-room

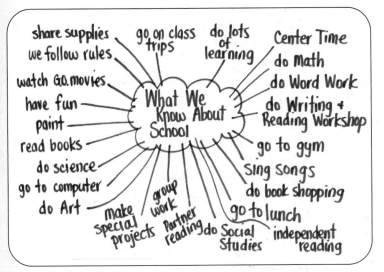

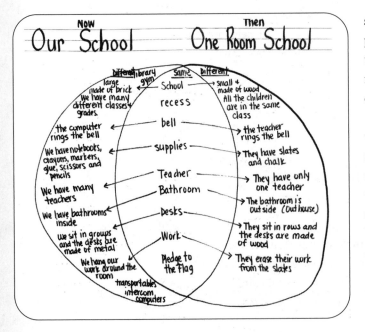

Making Sense of History

schools in the past. I charted their responses on a Venn diagram. From there, the children wrote and drew about their school today and compared it to schools long ago. By analyzing the children's pieces, I could assess whether they understood the similarities and differences between schools of the past and present. To end this study, we completed the KWL chart and made our own book using the photographs we took during our walking tour of the school. The children had a great time.

School then

They use chalk.

They use slate.

They use cart.

They got wood school.

School now

We use pencil.

We use notebook.

We use schoolbus.

We got brick school.

Did you notice that none of these teachers was lecturing, racing from activity to activity, or using a textbook as a single source of information? Did you notice that none of them focused on small bits of information, expected students to memorize names and dates, or hoped for exactly the same response from all students?

Excellent teaching such as this, however, doesn't match the popular conception of history teaching and learning. In the media and even talking to friends and colleagues, you are more likely to encounter hand-wringing laments about how teachers emphasize facts and dates, teach from a textbook, and rely on worksheets (Grant, 2003). Newspapers, radio, and TV constantly remind us that students are ignorant of the facts of history (Paxton, 2003; Wineburg, 2004)—as if knowing a set of random facts (often determined during a telephone interview) equals historical understanding. Yet, as Richard Paxton (2003) points out, students today know just about the same amount of history as did their parents and grandparents. They don't know less.

And some people feel that teachers aren't teaching history at all these days because the math and reading requirements of the No Child Left Behind legislation have, in the words of one observer, "diminish[ed] the role of social studies, especially in elementary classrooms, artificially narrowing the school's curriculum and treating social studies as a 'second class' and 'at risk' discipline" (Howard, 2003, p. 285). Teachers report sacrificing social studies instruction to make more time for standardized test preparation (Staff of Social Education, 2003; Furin, 2003).

Yet amid all this hand-wringing, there is a lot of thoughtful, powerful, ambitious teaching going on in elementary schools and middle schools, such as the teaching I described earlier. Look for other descriptions in journals of the National Council for the Social Studies such as *Social Studies and the Young Learner* for the K–5 teacher and *Middle Level Learning* for middle school teachers. Both journals offer practical articles loaded with ideas and resources. For example, an article entitled "Identifying with Ancestors: Tracking the History of America" by Josephine Barry Davis (2003) describes how using activities such as conducting family interviews, researching family ancestors, mapping countries of origin, and creating time lines that incorporate family history, helps students connect their personal stories to American history. Check out other useful articles in these journals and ask yourself, What are these teachers doing? What's making their teaching work?

You will probably discover, as I did, that teachers are doing a lot more than giving facts and asking students to regurgitate them. Instead, there are common essential elements found in good practice and confirmed by research. Let's turn our attention to identifying and discussing these elements, because they form the basis of good history teaching.

The Essential Elements of Good History Teaching: Historical Thinking, Historical Literature, and Hands-On Experience

I have found through classroom observation, reading, and my own teaching experience (Zarnowski, 1990, 1996, 2003) that for history teaching to "click" instead of "clunk," three essential elements need to be in place in the curriculum:

* Historical thinking

* Historical literature

* Hands-on experience

These three elements are the backbone of teaching history in an active, hands-on way. When we align and combine these elements, we create the right conditions for presenting students with challenges that they can sink their teeth into—challenges that enable students to apply historical sense-making concepts. Because of the importance of these elements, I'll first discuss each one separately. Then I'll consider some of the obstacles teachers face when applying them in the classroom. Some of these obstacles stem from persistent, erroneous beliefs that get in our way (such as the idea that our students are unable to examine the past critically), while others stem from habits that are hard to change (such as relying on a textbook as the ultimate authority). In any case, there's work to be done, since knowing the elements of good history teaching is just the first step. The second and more significant step is putting what we know into practice. Part Two of this book shows ways this can be and has been done.

ESSENTIAL ELEMENT #1: HISTORICAL THINKING

Historical thinking—making use of those historical sense-making concepts explained in Chapter 1—needs to be taught. Why? Because, as researchers tell us, this kind of thinking is "unnatural" (Wineburg, 1999) and even "counterintuitive" (Lee & Shemilt, 2003). Historical thinking is not everyday, walking-around kind of thinking. It won't happen with any level of sophistication just by wishing it would. Samuel Wineburg, a psychologist who studies historical thinking, considers it "neither a natural process nor something that springs automatically from psychological development. Its achievement," he states, "goes against the grain of how we ordinarily think" (1999, p. 499).

This is because historical thinking requires us to recognize that the past is *at the same time* both familiar to us (the people are sort of like us) and foreign to us (their world is quite different from ours). This is a hard job. It requires us to think about people who lived long ago as something between "kissing cousins" and "awesome aliens." That is, we feel kinship with them, but we feel distant from them, too.

Historical thinking is also difficult because, although we know how it all turned out in the end, we don't know what it was like to experience history as it was happening. We can't see the past in a naïve way—see the uncertainty people faced in making decisions because, in hindsight, their decisions seem clear and almost predetermined. We can't see the chaos, confusion, and insecurities people experienced in the past. We can never really fit comfortably in their shoes or see through their eyes, but we can try to understand the conditions in which they lived and the reasons behind their actions and choices.

So, what can we do to promote historical thinking? We can highlight the kinds of thinking that historians do and show our students how to do it. Of course they will not think with the complexity of professional historians, and they will not deal with the same sources of information, but they can begin to uncover the processes that make historical thinking possible.

Students will inevitably turn up inconsistencies in historical facts, dates, and ideas about what's important and what's not. These are all invitations to historical thinking. In the past, I have asked students to deal with a number of questions that promote historical thinking. I have asked:

* Is it important for you to know about what happened to Japanese Americans during World War II?

* What did different people think about Gertrude Ederle, champion swimmer?

* What could have happened—but didn't—when Ben Franklin told his parents he wanted to go to sea?

* What are the similarities and differences between the Black Death, smallpox, and AIDS?

In discussions of these questions, students do more than remember the facts; they begin to think about what the facts mean.

Question Stems That Promote Historical Thinking

* What if . . . ?

* What could have happened when . . . ?

* What is important to know about . . . ?

* Why is it important to know about . . . ?

* What did different people think about . . . ?

* What evidence makes you think that . . . ?

* What did people in the past believe about . . . ?

* What do you think explains why . . . ?

* What are the similarities and differences between . . . ?

Recently, I read a wonderful article entitled "The Rosa Parks 'Myth': A Third Grade History Investigation" (Landorf & Lowenstein, 2004), describing how a third-grade teacher asked her students to deal with this question: "Why did Rosa Parks decide not to give up her seat that day on the bus?" It was certainly not entirely because she was tired at the end of a hard day's work. Answering questions like this is not easy, but it is stimulating because students can sink their teeth into them and puzzle over them before reaching conclusions. In the process of helping students work out answers, we can prompt them to think historically and explicitly teach them how to do it.

ESSENTIAL ELEMENT #2: HISTORICAL LITERATURE

Historical literature consists of historical nonfiction and historical fiction. For now, I'll focus on historical nonfiction, saving historical fiction for later, because nonfiction provides the factual information students need in order to think about the past. Even though historical fiction gives readers a sense of living in the past, it's not always clear where the facts end and fiction begins. This can be confusing to students, especially students who are just beginning to think historically and apply sense-making concepts. When I taught middle school, for example, I had to take a deep breath before responding to one of my students who asked me if Johnny Tremain, the fictional main character of Esther Forbes's famous historical novel *Johnny Tremain* (1943), was real. And when I said he was not, the student followed up that question by asking if Sam Adams, Paul Revere, John Hancock, and a host of other actual historical figures were real. How was he to know? Without help from a teacher or a note from the author, this mix of fact and fiction presents an obstacle to students trying to figure out the simple *Who, What, Where, Why,* and *When* of the past. After doing this sifting, how much stamina is left for thinking critically about what it all means? In my experience, not much. Instead, by starting with historical nonfiction, students build a foundation of understanding they can later apply to reading historical fiction.

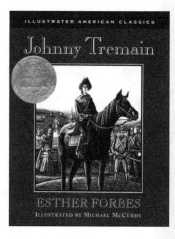

Quality historical nonfiction for children and young adults boosts students' understanding of the past. In addition to the features that define all quality nonfiction—accuracy, organization, access features, visual displays, writing style, documentation, and significance—historical nonfiction supports students by:

* providing background information in a clear and engaging way.
* showing them how to think about history.

Criteria for Choosing Quality Historical Nonfiction

Accuracy Has the author documented the sources of information? Is there a bibliography? Are there source notes? Did experts in the field check the facts?

Clear Organization Does the book have a clear organizational pattern, such as a chronological narrative? Are other organizational patterns, such as cause and effect, comparison and contrast, and description, embedded within the narrative?

Supportive Illustrations Do photographs, diagrams, maps, and other illustrations provide information that helps the reader understand the text?

Engaging Writing Style Is the writing vivid and interesting? Does it contain thought-provoking descriptions, details, and anecdotes?

Enthusiastic Tone Is there evidence of the writer's enthusiasm for and interest in the subject? Does the text explain why the author selected this topic?

Use of Primary Sources Does the book introduce young readers to the "raw" materials that the author worked with? These might be items such as posters, letters, diary entries, newspaper articles, and photographs.

"Visible" Author Does the author speak directly to the reader about the process of "doing history"? Does he or she address such processes as finding, selecting, and questioning the evidence; raising questions and looking for answers; and feeling empathy for people from the past?

Curriculum Connection Does the book support the social studies curriculum that is in place?

Derived from Zarnowski, Myra. (2002). Historical nonfiction and biography. In A. A. McClure & J. V. Kristo (Eds.), Adventuring with Books: A booklist for Pre-K–Grade 6 *(13th ed.). Urbana, IL: National Council of Teachers of English*

Historical Nonfiction Provides Background Information in a Clear and Engaging Way

Students need background information to think about; they can't think about nothing. But they need this background information presented in a way that clearly points out the big ideas and distinguishes them from the small but interesting details—what my students refer to lovingly as the "tidbits" of history. In fact, researchers Margaret McKeown and Isabel Beck (1994) found that coherence in written text—clear causal connections, explicit explanations of big ideas, clear sequencing of events, explicit relationships between main ideas and supporting concepts and details—is much more important than interesting details. Sure, it's interesting to read in *Children of the Dust Bowl* (Stanley, 1992) that the dust storms of the 1930s were so fierce that "families slept with wet washcloths or sponges over their faces to filter out the dust" (p. 7) and that "children were assigned the task of cleaning the nostrils of cows two or three times a day" (p. 7). These are memorable details, but it's essential to know, as author Jerry Stanley tells us, that ". . . in the Panhandle, the dry winds howled for four long years, from 1936 to 1940" (p. 5), causing this terrible suffering. To make sense of history, students need both interesting details and the general context in which these details are set.

Let me give you another example. In *Shutting Out the Sky: Life in the Tenements of New York, 1880–1924*, author Deborah Hopkinson (2003) begins a section entitled "Why Did They Come?" with the statement, "Immigrants came to America for different reasons" (p. 4). As you read the first few paragraphs of this section, notice how succeeding paragraphs provide memorable details—in this case the reasons why specific families left Italy and Romania.

> *Immigrants came to America for different reasons. For Italian families like the Covellos, America offered a chance to escape grinding poverty.*
>
> *In Italy, poor families like Leonard Covello's didn't have their own land, but worked as laborers for others. Toward the end of the nineteenth century, even farmers who did own land were struggling, due to poor economic conditions and changing world markets for goods. Unemployment rose as successful orchards in Florida and California hurt orange and lemon growers in Italy, and high French tariffs disrupted Italy's wine industry.*
>
> *In Romania, young Marcus Ravage was convinced that emigration was his only chance to escape the poverty of his town, and to get an education. Laws in Romania discriminating against Jews made it almost impossible for him to go to a university or start a successful business.*
>
> *For eastern European Jewish families like the Ravages, America offered the promise not only of gold, but freedom from religious persecution. For hundreds of years Jewish people had lived in an area of eastern Europe under the rule of the Russian Empire called the Pale of Settlement. This region included Poland, Belorussia, Ukraine, and Lithuania. (p. 4)*

The balance between the "big idea" (there were several reasons for immigration) and the details (specific examples of people who came) is perfect. People came to own land, to escape poverty, to get an education, to find religious freedom, and to live in safety. There are enough details to make the big idea easy to grasp. And these are only a few. Hopkinson offers many more in the book.

In addition to offering this balance between big ideas and supporting details, historical nonfiction offers readers compelling descriptions of the past that help them visualize what it was like. Here's how Jim Murphy describes Philadelphia during a terrible epidemic of yellow fever in his book *An American Plague: The True and Terrifying Story of the Yellow Fever Epidemic of 1793*:

Saturday, August 3, 1793. The sun came up as it had every day since the end of May, bright, hot, and unrelenting. The swamps and marshes south of Philadelphia had already lost a great deal of water to the intense heat, while the Delaware and Schuylkill Rivers had receded to reveal long stretches of their muddy, root-choked banks. Dead fish and gooey vegetable matter were exposed and rotted, while swarms of insects droned in the heavy, humid air.

In Philadelphia itself an increasing number of cats were dropping dead every day, attracting, one Philadelphian complained, "an amazing number of flies and other insects." Mosquitoes were everywhere, though their high-pitched whirring was particularly loud near rain barrels, gutters, and open sewers. (2003, p. 1)

This description provides an introduction and abundant details that immediately take hold of the reader's senses. The "intense heat," "dead fish and gooey vegetable matter," and "swarms of [droning] insects" create an unavoidably creepy and sinister image. I can just hear the kids shouting—"EEEEUUUU!" After that, though, I would ask them which words caused them to react that way and discuss with them the historical significance of the event. It's no wonder that Jim Murphy won the 2004 Orbis Pictus Award for Outstanding Nonfiction, the 2004 Sibert Informational Book Award, and the Newbery Honor award for this book, *An American Plague*. Among its many, many outstanding qualities is its descriptive and evocative language.

Historical Nonfiction Shows Students How to Think About History

Authors of historical nonfiction can be your "co-teachers" because, like you, they

Orbis Pictus Award-Winning and Recommended Historical Nonfiction

Consider these excellent choices for elementary and middle school teaching.

Elementary:

Confucius: The Golden Rule by Russell Freedman. Illustrated by Frédéric Clément. Scholastic.

Empire State Building: When New York Reached for the Skies by Elizabeth Mann. Illustrated by Alan Witschonke. Mikaya Press.

The Emperor's Silent Army: Terracotta Warriors of Ancient China by Jane O'Connor. Viking.

Leonardo: Beautiful Dreamer by Robert Byrd. Dutton.

The Man Who Made Time Travel by Kathryn Lasky. Illustrated by Kevin Hawkes. Farrar, Straus & Giroux

Tenement: Immigrant Life on the Lower East Side by Raymond Bial. Houghton Mifflin.

To Fly: The Story of the Wright Brothers by Wendie C. Old. Illustrated by Robert Andrew Parker. Clarion.

Saladin: Noble Prince of Islam by Diane Stanley. HarperCollins.

Shutting Out the Sky: Life in the Tenements of New York, 1880–1924 by Deborah Hopkinson. Orchard.

When Marian Sang: The True Recital of Marian Anderson, the Voice of a Century by Pam Muñoz Ryan. Illustrated by Brian Selznick. Scholastic.

Middle School:

An American Plague: The True and Terrifying Story of the Yellow Fever Epidemic of 1793 by Jim Murphy. Clarion.

Getting Away with Murder: The True Story of the Emmett Till Case by Chris Crowe. Dial.

In Defense of Liberty: The Story of America's Bill of Rights by Russell Freedman. Holiday House.

Jack: The Early Years of John F. Kennedy by Ilene Cooper. Dutton.

The Wright Sister: Katharine Wright and Her Famous Brothers by Richard Maurer. Roaring Brook Press.

know the importance of rich, explicit teaching. They do much more than provide facts. They show *how* to think historically about these facts by revealing how it is done. They address issues such as lack of evidence, contradictory evidence, multiple interpretations of the same events, and the relevance of the past to the present as these issues arise in their own work. Instead of brushing these thought-provoking issues under the carpet, authors of historical nonfiction highlight them because they are important to historical thinking. Because the authors are writing for a young audience, they do not assume students know how to read history or critique what they read at a sophisticated level. They provide a helping hand.

Let's see how this is done. Editor Mary E. Lyons tells readers about two important issues to consider when reading her book *Feed the Children First: Irish Memories of the Great Hunger* (2002)—the lack of photographic evidence of the Irish famine of 1845–1852 and the relevance of this famine to us today. First, consider the lack of photographic evidence:

> *The great hunger is hard to imagine. Photographs help us understand the horrors of American slavery and the Jewish Holocaust. Yet no photograph of Ireland's worst famine is known to exist, though pictures taken during later Irish famines show similar conditions. Several Irish newspapermen made sketches when they traveled through the stricken country in 1847. Later, Irish painters told parts of the story on canvas. These are our only images of what the Irish remember as the "hard times."* (p. 7)

Why weren't there any photographs, considering that photography had been invented by 1845? Perhaps no one wanted to see the terrible suffering. Or, no one could afford photographs, a luxury at the time. Or, no one wanted to embarrass the victims of the famine by making their images public. Sketches and paintings done at a later time do exist, but they raise questions about accuracy because they were completed long after the famine occurred.

Now let's look at the issue of relevance. Often students ask us why they have to learn about the past when it's—to be blunt—*past*. The reason is, as Harvard historian Bernard Bailyn explains, because history is "a way of getting out of the boundaries of one's own life and culture and seeing more of what human experience has been" (1994, p. 12). It gives us access to more than just our own lives. Lyons, too, shares her understanding of historical relevance with readers:

> *Irish memories of the great hunger are painful to read, but they have much to teach us about today. From Haiti to Bangladesh, from Afghanistan to Africa, people are still hungry and malnourished. Children suffer most. According to Unicef, six million youngsters under the age of five in 1995 died from lack of nutritious food. The Irish famine is worth remembering when hunger organizations ask us to help them feed the children first.* (p. 9)

Lyons helps readers make a connection between the famine that took place more than 150 years ago and our lives right now. She does this by showing how the Irish famine can help us think about problems of hunger and malnourishment in the world today.

Other authors of historical nonfiction narrate the past and teach students how to think about it. In his author's note that begins *Witch-Hunt: Mysteries of the Salem Witch Trials* (2003), Marc Aronson warns readers that they will most likely have to rethink what they believe to be true about life in Salem, Massachusetts, in the seventeenth century:

> *If you have previously read novels for younger readers or popular adult accounts about those fascinating and frightening times, or if you have visited Salem itself, a good part of what you know is wrong.* (p. x)

Is my so-called knowledge of the Salem witch trials wrong? Am I walking around with a head full of half-truths? I am ready to investigate with Marc Aronson. Learning to think about the past from authors who think about it all the time is energizing. When these authors take us by the hand and point out the pitfalls and pleasures of thinking historically, they invite us to study history the same way they do.

ESSENTIAL ELEMENT #3: HANDS-ON EXPERIENCE

The first time I walked into a New York City public school and had students tell me that history was boring I asked myself, Why? Why did children find history boring, while so many adults found it fascinating and some even dedicated their professional lives to it? After thinking about this for a while, it occurred to me that children and adults were doing very different things when they were studying history. Adults saw history as a lively, living subject, while children saw it as dreary and dead. And they were acting accordingly—adults were asking provocative questions, having lively debates and arguments, and revising and reconsidering how they saw the past, while children were answering someone else's questions, trying valiantly to remember facts, and not even entertaining the possibility that the "facts" could be reconsidered. Adults were active. Children were passive. Adults realized that they could participate in an ongoing discussion about the past. Children didn't.

Want proof? It's easy to find newspapers, journal articles, and books showing that historical questioning, discussion, and debate are alive among adults. Here are three examples.

* In a recent article in the *New York Times*, author James Gleick (2003) discussed the growing list of unresolved questions he raised for himself as he prepared to write a biography about Isaac Newton: Had Newton seen the ocean? When did he first see a clock? What did he look like? These simple yet unanswered questions piqued the author's curiosity and motivated his thinking and research. In other words, for Gleick, Newton's story was unfinished because unanswered questions still remained.

* A recent issue of the journal *History and Theory* featured an article entitled "What Do Historians Argue About?"(Mccullagh, 2004). Yes, argue about. The answer? The validity of their interpretations. They don't mutually agree on a single version of history.

* Historian Eric Foner's book *Who Owns History?: Rethinking the Past in a Changing World* (2003) makes the case for continued discussion and interpretation of history, especially in our current global context as historians try to see local happenings as part of a broader, more wide-ranging panorama of events. Foner tells us that "historians view the constant search for new perspectives as the lifeblood of historical understanding" (p. xvi).

The point is clear. Adults who find history intriguing know the value of questioning, discussing, and debating about the past. It's something in which they can participate—something hands-on that they can do.

Most students, though, are not questioning, discussing, and debating about the past. In fact, they are not sure why they are studying history in the first place or how knowing history can help them. They tell me they study history because "she [the teacher] wants me to." They don't see any difference between learning history and learning any other subject. Requirements for all subjects are the same: read the information, learn it, remember it. And, because remembering is not a popular activity, it should come as no surprise that social studies, and therefore history, too, is an unpopular subject. This attitude tends to begin in elementary school, and by the time students reach high school, any passion they feel for history is largely gone. In 1985, researchers Joan Shaughnessy and Thomas Haladyna reported that "most students in the United States, at all grade levels, find social studies to be one of the least interesting, most irrelevant, subjects in the school curriculum" (p. 694). I haven't seen any more recent research that contradicts these findings, showing a sudden burst of student engagement and enthusiasm. In fact, everything I read seems to confirm this report. But it doesn't have to be this way if we take a hands-on approach to teaching history.

There's evidence that this is so. When Janet Alleman and Jere Brophy (1994) asked adults what they had most enjoyed about history in elementary and middle school (there was *something*, wasn't there?), most said the projects. Maybe it was that diorama they made, the map they drew, the "newspaper from the past" they wrote, or the play they collaborated on and performed. Sifting and shaping historical information makes history memorable. Doing something with facts brings history alive.

Good teachers know this—teachers like Debbi, Elizabeth, and Marianne, whose work I described earlier in the chapter and who all had their students create something using the information they were learning. Professional books by teachers are full of similar descriptions. *History in the Present Tense* (2003) by Douglas Selwyn and Jan Maher, for example, makes a case for project-based learning through "student-centered, meaningful, memorable activities" (p. 7). *Connecting Children with Children, Past and Present* (2004) by Eula Fresch shows how to make this "past-present" connection through hands-on activities that make the past more accessible and promote civic involvement in today's world. *Seeking History* (2000) by Monica Edinger describes how intermediate-grade students can make use of primary sources.

Without hands-on activities, history becomes static—an anthology of "stuff." Students might memorize this stuff, and they might even go through the paces of reading and answering questions about it. But most likely they will forget most of it. I vividly remember the graduate student who looked up from a well-written history book for children that she was reading to ask me, "Where was I when they taught this? Was I sleeping? I don't ever remember learning this!" Thank you, Jerry Stanley, for writing that wonderful book, *Children of the Dust Bowl*.

Does a hands-on approach increase student learning? The research, though sparse, suggests it does. Fred Newmann, Helen Marks, and Adam Gamoran (1996) studied the impact of what they call "authentic pedagogy" on student performance in elementary school, middle school, and high school. One of the essential features of authentic pedagogy is disciplinary thinking such as the historical thinking that I described earlier in this chapter. That means authentic pedagogy promotes

1. **active construction of knowledge**—"producing, rather than reproducing" knowledge (p. 283)

2. **disciplined inquiry**—engaging in inquiry practiced by professionals in the field

3. **value beyond the school**—understanding the relevance of what is being learned to the everyday world

Newmann and his colleagues found that these features had a positive impact on learning. In their words, ". . . authentic pedagogy does pay off in improved authentic academic performance for students at all grade levels and in both mathematics and social studies" (p. 305). (For further discussion of authentic academic pedagogy, see Newmann & Wehlange, 1993 and Scheurman & Newmann, 1998.)

On a smaller scale, Bruce VanSledright (2002b) worked with a class of fifth graders who were taught to think historically. Students engaged in four months of "historical detective work" (p. 141), which included opportunities to weigh conflicting evidence and images, deal with primary and secondary sources, analyze a variety of historical perspectives, and reach tentative conclusions about who fired the first shots at the Battle of Lexington. At the end of the four months, VanSledright found evidence of growth in students' ability to construct evidence-based interpretations, confirm details, judge sources, and apply other skills necessary for thinking deeply about history. In short, his efforts to teach fifth graders to investigate historical sources were successful.

History educators know the value of taking a hands-on approach to history in the early grades. Janet Alleman, Jere Brophy, and Barbara Knighton (2003), for example, describe a first-grade classroom where the students and teacher co-constructed visual displays such as time lines, lists, graphs, posters, and booklets as they learned about cultural universals such as food, clothing, shelter, and transportation. They report that creating these displays made the students feel "energized and involved" (p. 8).

At the college level, Tom Holt (1990) has a similar goal—to make students "active rather than passive readers of historical narratives" (p. 29). This simple, powerful, and widely applicable truth about hands-on experience is worth remembering.

"Good" History Teaching: Obstacles and Opportunities

If good history teaching simply involves putting historical literature, historical thinking, and hands-on experience into place, why isn't it happening all the time in classrooms across the country? Researchers Keith Barton and Linda Levstik took on this question. They asked themselves, "Why don't more history teachers engage students in interpretation?" (Barton & Levstik, 2003). Their answer? Teachers' primary goals are controlling behavior and covering content. These goals, they argue, are not reached by assigning hands-on activities, which require students to talk to one another, move about the classroom, and consider sources in depth. They conclude that, unless teachers' goals match the kind of active involvement required by hands-on activities, historical thinking simply isn't going to happen. They suggest that a more "appealing" approach is to see historical thinking as a necessary requirement for citizenship in a democratic society. That is, learning to think historically is relevant—even essential—for today's citizens.

There is merit in considering what Barton and Levstik tell us, but it's not what I hear from teachers. Instead, I have exchanges like the following:

Teachers Ask Me: How can I teach history well when I don't know all that much about history?

My Response Is: Teaching history isn't about what you know. It's about what you do to help your students think about the past. Certainly, knowing information doesn't hurt, since it provides the raw material for thinking. But you can seek out information along with your students and help them make sense of it. In other words, you can share with them the process of digging into history.

Teachers Ask Me: How can I possibly teach according to the three essential elements and meet curriculum demands and standards?

My Response Is: I know. I feel your pain. However, if you must cover huge spans of time (jokingly referred to by some educators as the curriculum of "Cradle of Civilization to Clinton"), stop at key points along the way to take an in-depth look at what was going on. This might mean making sacrifices—for example, spending more time on the reasons for the American Revolution than on the deciding battles. Part of the art of teaching history is choosing wisely about what to emphasize and what to move over quickly.

In addition, the activities involving the three essential elements of history teaching—historical literature, historical thinking, and hands-on experience— will help you meet the standards set by the National Council for the Social Studies (NCSS) in *Expectations of Excellence: Curriculum Standards for Social Studies* (1994), which calls for teaching that is meaningful, integrative, values-based, challenging, and active. This document states that "powerful social studies teaching emphasizes authentic activities that call for real-life applications using the skills and content of the field" (p. 12). Experiences with hands-on history will also help you meet the standards set forth by the National Center for History in the Schools (1994), which call for chronological thinking, historical comprehension, historical analysis and interpretation, and other important skills.

Above all, you can help students search for meaning about the past, using historical literature to provide both information and thoughtful examples of historical interpretation. Before students deal with document-based questions (DBQs) on state mandated testing, historical literature provides an authentic means of encountering documents. The literature introduces documents and, at the same time, provides the necessary background information required by young readers.

Teachers Ask Me: What you're saying makes sense, but I don't have the literature. How can I get it?

My Response Is: To me, this is the most significant problem. If you are going to teach according to the three essential elements, you need the materials to do the job. A teacher at a conference asked me, "Where am I supposed to get these books?" And a reviewer of my previous book *History Makers* wrote that my ideas for using historical nonfiction literature "validate the effort of teachers who spend personal money on supplementary materials for their students' use" (Evers, 2003, p. 279).

There's no simple way to accomplish this, but here are some suggestions. Many excellent books are available in inexpensive paperback editions. You can buy them at bookstores, online, or through book clubs. I know a number of teachers who share materials with their colleagues. So, at school, make your needs public. You might also work with your colleagues to build a centralized collection of books and related materials on popular topics such immigration, the American Revolution, and westward expansion, as the teachers at P.S. 205 in Bayside, Queens, do. The teachers there started the collection five years ago and each year add to it by referring to annual lists of award-winning books and using funds that principal Susan Sherer puts aside for this important cause.

Concluding Thoughts

If teaching history well was an outrageously impossible idea, I wouldn't be writing this book. It's not. Yes, it requires a lot of planning and active involvement with students, but the payoff is grand—the kind of deep thinking students do when they are given the opportunity. Combining the three essential elements of history teaching—historical literature, historical thinking, and hands-on experience— goes a long way toward answering Part One's guiding question, What am I supposed to be doing? Part Two shows all three elements in action as students dig into history according to the sense-making concepts described in Chapter 1.

PART ONE

IF NOT MEMORIZING FACTS, THEN WHAT?

PART TWO

TEACHING SENSE-MAKING CONCEPTS: THE ANTIDOTE
TO "WHY DO WE HAVE TO READ THIS STUFF?"

Chapter 3

Historical Context

How Can I Help Students Understand the Differences and Similarities Between the Past and the Present?

How can we "know" the past? How can we know how people lived and what their daily lives were like? The truth is that we can never entirely know it. We can only know some of it. And what we do know is pieced together from evidence left behind. This evidence is always incomplete, and sometimes even misleading or misunderstood. So the challenge faced by historians is to assemble evidence into a narrative that people will understand and see as true. At the same time, historians must acknowledge the missing pieces—the information they wish they knew but don't because it isn't available.

Historians cannot escape the fact that they do not completely share the culture or daily concerns of the people they are writing about. As historian David Lowenthal said, the past is a *foreign country* "with the healthiest tourist trade of all" (1985, p. 4). It's this foreignness, though, that makes studying history so appealing.

Understanding historical context means understanding the setting in which the past unfolded. That setting might be colonial America, Renaissance Italy, or (as described later in this chapter) life in the Wild West. In case you are wondering how important understanding context is to historians, and ultimately to you, it is worth keeping in mind Ira Berlin's recent comment: "For the historian, context is all, and to step outside the assumptions of the historical moment violates the fundamental canons of the craft" (2004, p. 1263). This comment reaffirms my commitment to teach history in a way that enables students to develop a sense of historical context for whatever topic I am teaching, whether it's the women's suffrage movement, the Lewis and Clark expedition, or the Vietnam War. It is time well spent because understanding historical context is a major accomplishment for students, not some minor point to touch on lightly.

Knowing how historians work to understand the past holds exciting implications for teaching. This chapter returns to the three essential elements of history teaching described in Chapter 2—historical thinking, historical literature, and hands-on experience—and applies them to the teaching of historical context. It provides strategies for acquainting students with historical context by discussing the following questions:

* What do theory and research say about historical context?
* How does nonfiction literature contribute to an understanding of historical context?
* What activities help students understand historical context?

What Do Theory and Research Say About Historical Context?

Two ideas derived from the work of historians and educational researchers help us, and ultimately our students, understand historical context:

* Building on the tension between the familiar and the unfamiliar
* Finding openings for thought experiments

As you will see, each idea provides a foundation for teaching and learning that stems from historical thinking.

Building on the Tension Between the Familiar and the Unfamiliar

Researcher Samuel Wineburg suggests a powerful way of thinking about how students learn about historical context. According to Wineburg (1999), students think about the past as both *familiar*—that is, the people, places, and events are comfortably recognizable—and *unfamiliar*—that is, the people, places, and events are uncomfortably strange. For example, when Debbi Aizenstain's fifth-grade students studied the Wild West of the 1800s, they learned that some children went to school, a familiar idea. However, the school building, the classroom, the curriculum, and the teachers' qualifications were vastly different and unfamiliar.

Neither the familiar nor the unfamiliar is useful by itself. If we seek only the familiar in history, we miss its unique qualities. If we seek only the unfamiliar in history, we have difficulty connecting with it. But taken together—examining the past for both the familiar and the unfamiliar—these two approaches help students move from a fragile understanding of historical context to a firmer one. Wineburg writes, "I claim that the essence of achieving mature historical thought rests precisely on our ability to navigate the jagged landscape of history, to traverse the terrain that lies between the poles of familiarity with and distance from the past" (1999, p. 490). Our students can begin navigating this jagged landscape in elementary school.

Wineburg calls historical thinking "unnatural," citing examples of adults who have trouble understanding historical context (Wineburg & Fournier, 1994); but this view has been challenged by researchers who work with elementary and middle school students. Keith Barton and Linda Levstik (2004) suggest that understanding historical context and the perspectives of people who lived in the past is manageable—even for young students—when teachers provide experiences that support and extend their understanding. As you will see later in this chapter, teaching students to think about historical context as both *familiar* and *unfamiliar* works, making historical thinking a natural act. It focuses attention on what is important—understanding historical context. In this way, students don't get lost in interesting details and "tidbits" while losing sight of their purpose for reading.

Although historians may argue about whether historical thinking is a natural act, most agree on another point—that students' understanding of historical context varies greatly. That's because one student's fund of background knowledge about historical context is not the same as another's. Bruce VanSledright (1997/1998) advises teachers to pay attention to each student's positionality—his or her frame of reference for understanding the past—because of its impact on

Is Historical Thinking a *Natural* or an *Unnatural Act*?

Compare these two quotes about historical thinking. What's the difference? What are the implications of each position?

Samuel Wineburg:

"Historical thinking, in its deepest forms, is neither a natural process nor something that springs automatically from psychological development. Its achievement, I argue, actually goes against the grain of how we ordinarily think" (Wineburg, 1999, p. 491).

Keith Barton and Linda Levstik:

"Some educators suggest that students find it difficult to use historical perspectives rather than contemporary ones to explain the events of the past; Sam Wineburg cleverly refers to it as an 'unnatural act.' Unnatural it may be, but our work with elementary and middle school students suggests that they are quite capable of using this tool and that they find it a powerful and intuitively sound way of making sense of why people behaved as they did" (Barton & Levstik, 2004, p. 215).

understanding. You will probably find, as I have, that your students' fund of background information about the Civil Rights movement or women's voting rights varies. A student's background knowledge, VanSledright reminds us, serves as "entry-level building blocks of greater expertise in historical thinking and understanding" (p. 6).

Susan Mosborg (2002a, 2002b) made a similar discovery when she studied how adolescents used their knowledge of history to read the daily newspaper. She found that adolescents brought different background narratives—their current understanding of historical context—to their reading. She refers to these background narratives, each composed of different historical events, as "important orienting devices" (2002a, p. 6) because they affected how students connected current events to historical events.

The impact of different background narratives may help explain historians' recent calls to recontextualize, or reexamine, the events surrounding the famous Brown v. Board of Education case, which determined that segregation in public schools was unconstitutional (Gaines, 2004). Now, fifty years later, historians are seeking to understand the Brown case in a wider context that includes the Cold

War, full citizenship participation in government, and racial issues related to groups other than African Americans. Recontextualization helps historians reinterpret the past and direct our understanding of it toward present concerns. It is, as one historian noted, a way to avoid homogenized history (Dudziak, 2004). As each generation of historians applies its ideas about what is familiar and unfamiliar, new understandings emerge.

The familiar/unfamiliar contrast is a tool for thinking, exploring, and challenging our understanding about historical context. Historian Robert Darnton says that "we constantly need to be shaken out of a false sense of familiarity with the past, to be administered doses of culture shock" (1984, p. 4). Surely administering doses of culture shock in your classroom will enliven your study of history! It has worked for me. Later in this chapter, I will show how using the familiar/unfamiliar contrast helped fifth-grade students understand historical context.

FINDING OPENINGS FOR THOUGHT EXPERIMENTS

A second powerful way for students to learn about historical context is through "thought experiments." Doesn't the name alone conjure up an active, mind-expanding experience—one that is just the opposite of the memorizing-names-and-dates model? Thought experiments are precisely what many historians do, and there are two major types: Question → Answer → Question and What If?

Question → Answer → Question

Sometimes thought experiments involve raising questions about information, hypothesizing possible answers, and then raising additional questions based on these preliminary answers. Not surprisingly, this type of thought experiment has been called "Question → Answer → Question."

Let's see how this works. In *Will in the World: How Shakespeare Became Shakespeare* (2004), author Stephen Greenblatt begins by asking questions about the roots of Shakespeare's accomplishments:

Question: "How is an achievement of this magnitude to be explained? How did Shakespeare become Shakespeare?" (p. 11)

Answer: Greenblatt then suggests that Will "almost certainly" (p. 26) attended the King's New School in Stratford, a free grammar school where he would have learned Latin. Greenblatt then considers what else Will would have learned, and notes that in schools at that time students would have read and performed ancient plays in Latin.

Question: That leads him to question whether Will might have developed a passion for drama even *before* going to school. Because he was a bailiff, Shakespeare's father was in a position to decide which plays would be put on in Stratford. As bailiff, he would also decide how much of a reward the Queen's Men were to be given when they performed in Stratford in 1569. As Greenblatt thinks about this performance, he asks, "But would he [John Shakespeare] have taken his five-year-old son to see the show?" (p. 30). And he asks, "What was the play the Queen's Men brought to Stratford?" (p. 30).

Question → Answer → Question enables the author to build a case about how Shakespeare became Shakespeare by using what is known to hypothesize about what is likely, but not definitely known. This is an exciting and challenging process.

Researcher Mimi Lee (2004) describes the questioning process of historian Natalie Zemon Davis, author of *The Return of Martin Guerre*, this way:

> She worked as a detective by assessing her sources and the rules for their composition; putting together clues from many place[s]; and establishing a conjectural argument that made the best, most plausible sense of sixteenth-century evidence. (p. 25)

This view of the historian as a detective solving mysteries is not new, but it is enduring because it suggests that there are puzzles to be solved in order to understand the past. David Gerwin and Jack Zevin's book *Teaching U.S. History as Mystery* (2003) operationalizes this idea by placing mystery at the center of historical inquiry in middle school and beyond.

What If?

Another type of thought experiment is "What If?" When historians apply What If?—or "counterfactual history" as it's sometimes known—they think about what might have happened, but didn't. In *What If? The World's Foremost Military Historians Imagine What Might Have Been* (Cowley, 1999), military historians consider some interesting possibilities. Thomas Fleming, for example, explores many ways the patriots could have lost the American Revolution; Alistair Horn considers what would have happened if Napoleon had won the Battle of Waterloo; and Stephen Sears writes about how the Civil War might have turned out differently if the South had won. Thinking about alternatives to what actually happened helps historians understand historical context, because they see the various decisions that could have been made but weren't. It gives them a comprehensive view of the attitudes, opinions, and struggles of the time. A growing number of counterfactual histories exist. One that is often interesting to teachers is Steve Tally's *Almost America* (2000) which provides several What Ifs? concerning commonly studied topics in American history such as the Constitution, Lee's surrender at Gettysburg, and the Apollo II mission to the moon.

Thought experiments are for students as well as historians. We can use them in the classroom to make learning history more intriguing. VanSledright recommends that teachers provide students with a chance to "cultivate a thoughtful, context-sensitive imagination to fill gaps in evidence trails when they arise" (2002a, p. 1092). Later in this chapter you will see how fifth graders did this—how they reached across time by corresponding with people from the past. Before they began their correspondence, however, they read historical nonfiction to learn about the historical context of the person they were addressing. In the next section, we'll examine how literature supports students' understanding of historical context.

How Does Nonfiction Literature Contribute to an Understanding of Historical Context?

Skilled authors of historical nonfiction make sure their readers bump up against both the familiar and the unfamiliar, and receive that dose of culture shock that Robert Darnton says is necessary for understanding the past. They build on the tension between the familiar and the unfamiliar. At the same time, they show readers that the unfamiliar was appropriate and acceptable for its time. In other words, instead of portraying the unfamiliar as odd, backward, or just plain stupid, they take the time to show it as fitting and reasonable. There are several literary techniques authors use in order to do this:

* The Extended Now-and-Then Contrast
* The Mid-Narrative Jolt
* The Sensory Description of the Unfamiliar
* The Thought Experiment

I explain each of these techniques in the following pages.

THE EXTENDED NOW-AND-THEN CONTRAST

The most common way authors explain the unfamiliar is to contrast it with the familiar. They show that now we do things like this, but in the past they did things like that. Sometimes, authors apply a now-and-then contrast throughout the book. For example, in the beginning of *The Lewis and Clark Trail Then and Now* (2002), a book for grades 4 and up, author Dorothy Hinshaw Patent explains that it took over a month for Lewis to hear from Clark about whether he wanted to join him on the expedition. To give readers a sense of the unfamiliar, she contrasts methods of communication now and then:

> *Today, we get quick answers to our E-mails and phone calls.*
> *But two hundred years ago, the only way to communicate over*
> *distances was by mail carried by wagon or boat. Messages took*
> *weeks or months to reach their destinations.* (p. 8)

Similarly, Patent contrasts the natural fabrics available to the explorers then with man-made fabrics available now:

> *There were no man-made fabrics; everything was made from*
> *natural fibers such as cotton, wool, and linen. That meant cloth*
> *items could easily rot during the trip, and the clothing Lewis*
> *purchased was bit by bit replaced by Indian-style leather clothing.*
> *There was no such thing as plastic back then, so Lewis bought*
> *oilskin bags and metal boxes to carry the precious journals and scientific*
> *instruments.* (p. 10)

The picture book *Century Farm: One Hundred Years on a Family Farm* by Cris Peterson (1999) contains another example of an extended now-and-then contrast. The author describes how the Wisconsin farm on which he lives has operated since it was built by his great-grandparents in the 1890s. He maintains a balance between the familiar and the unfamiliar by describing how things have changed. For example, here are his descriptions of how corn was harvested in his grandfather's time and how it is done today:

> *After the first frost, Grandpa cut the corn by hand and stacked it in tall shocks.*
> *It took ten men and ten teams of horses to haul that corn to the silo and chop it*
> *for winter cattle feed.*

Making Sense of History

Today my wife and I still harvest the corn after the first frost. But we chop it with a forage chopper pulled behind a tractor. Our equipment allows us to do the work of those ten men and their teams of horses. (unpaged)

Photographs show Grandpa cutting the corn by hand and Peterson himself driving a tractor.

There are also examples of how things have remained the same:

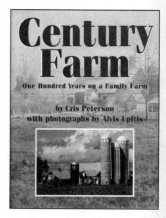

So much has changed in one hundred years, but many things have stayed the same. We still work together when a cow needs help giving birth to a calf. We still grow hollyhocks in the same garden where Grandma grew them decades ago. And we still plant in the same soil that grew the timber for our house and barn and granary. (unpaged)

When reading books like *The Lewis and Clark Trail Then and Now* and *Century Farm*, it's helpful to draw students' attention to words and phrases that signal "now" and "then" because generally the text that follows those words sheds light on the historical context. "Now" is often signaled by words such as *today* or *nowadays*. "Then" is signaled by many different phrases. Here are a few I jotted down while reading *The Lewis and Clark Trail Then and Now* and *Century Farm*:

Then (The Unfamiliar)

* In those days
* No one knew
* Back then
* At that time
* By today's standards
* There was no such thing as
* _____ had not yet been invented
* There was no understanding of
* _____ has been completely transformed

THE MID-NARRATIVE JOLT

While most authors of historical nonfiction do not make extended now-and-then comparisons, many do stop periodically to make sure readers get a healthy jolt of culture shock. It's as if the author is saying, "Wait a minute! Time out! Don't get the wrong idea here. Times were different. Try to understand how people thought.

Try to understand what the conditions were like in the past. Above all, don't judge people from the past by today's standards and expect them to behave as if they lived in the twenty-first century."

In *In Defense of Liberty: The Story of America's Bill of Rights* (2003), author Russell Freedman cautions readers to stop and consider what the writers of the Constitution had in mind when they said "We the people":

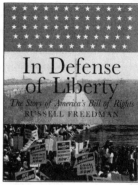

> While the authors of the Constitution were political revolutionaries, they were also men of their time whose vision was filtered through the customs and beliefs of colonial America. When they declared a government in the name of "We the people," they weren't really thinking of all the people. In the 1790s, the liberties guaranteed by the Bill of Rights did not apply to everyone. Whole groups of people were left out. (p. 18)

The author breaks into the narrative, the story of the Bill of Rights, to remind us that the words "We the people" meant something different back then.

Frequently authors provide a mid-narrative jolt to make the case that practices and attitudes that might seem strange or even offensive to us now were commonplace and ordinary for the time. In *Cowboys and Longhorns: A Portrait of the Long Drive* (2003), author Jerry Stanley stops to explain that the methods cowboys used to subdue unruly cattle may seem cruel to us, but they were necessary in order to capture the animals:

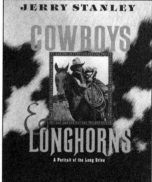

> The cow hunt occurred at a time when the number of longhorns seemed limitless, and there was little regard for the pain and suffering of animals. The cowboys weren't necessarily cruel by the standards of their time. They didn't kill longhorns needlessly but did what was required to secure stock. Longhorns were no docile milk cows. . . . This wasn't the rodeo, where animals are outnumbered and overpowered. (pp. 19–20)

Stanley gives us this mid-narrative jolt so that we can adjust our thinking. "Wait!" he seems to be saying. "Before you jump to conclusions and condemn the cowboys for cruelty to animals, you must understand how difficult and dangerous the cowboy's work was. Understand, too, that this was happening sometime between 1866 and 1885, not today. Think about some of these life-threatening and unfamiliar conditions before you rush to judgment."

TEACHING IDEA

Discuss Mid-Narrative Jolts

You and your students can spot mid-narrative jolts. Use the overhead to share examples during mini-lessons, and challenge students to find more examples during independent reading. Remind students to look for those moments when the author takes time out from the narrative to explain how the past was distinctly different from the present.

One book you could use is Taylor Morrison's *The Coast Mappers* (2004), which describes how George Davidson and his team of cartographers began a survey of the Pacific West Coast waterways in 1850. The survey would provide information so that ship captains could safely navigate in and out of harbors. Morrison "jolts" the reader into recognizing that this was an extremely difficult task since global positioning systems (GPS) of today did not exist:

> A small wooden observatory was built to protect their delicate instruments from the strong winds and dust. Davidson and Rockwell went inside it to work after the sun sank below the horizon.

> Today GPS satellites can instantly pinpoint any place on earth. The same task in 1850 was a major undertaking. Davidson had to patiently observe the stars to find out Point Conception's [their camp's] location.
>
> In the observatory, wisps of smoke puffed out of small oil lanterns that illuminated the telescope sights. . . . (pp. 13, 15)

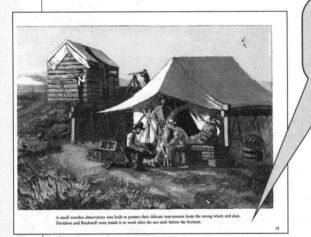

A small wooden observatory was built to protect their delicate instruments from the strong winds and dust. Davidson and Rockwell went inside it to work after the sun sank below the horizon.

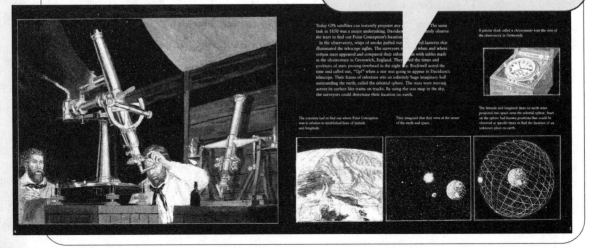

Making Sense of History

Notice the difference between the paragraphs:

- Paragraph one describes how Davidson and fellow scientist Rockwell went to work at sundown. The illustrations in the book show them viewing the stars in order to position themselves.

- Paragraph two jolts the reader to recognize that they had to do this laborious work because modern technology, specifically GPS satellites, did not exist.

- Paragraph three returns to the story of Davidson and Rockwell in their observatory.

When using examples like this, emphasize how the author is helping the reader to understand the unfamiliar aspects of the past.

THE SENSORY DESCRIPTION OF THE UNFAMILIAR

Another way authors help readers understand an unfamiliar historical context is by appealing to their senses. Extended descriptions of sights, sounds, tastes, smells, and textures help readers imagine the past. One of the best examples of this is Russell Freedman's description of traveling west along the Oregon Trail in the 1840s in *Children of the Wild West* (1983). Since travel in a covered wagon is unfamiliar in any real, nitty-gritty, authentic sense to our students, Freedman begins by describing the sights, sounds, and physical discomfort as it would have been experienced by a young boy:

> It was a typical wagon train of the 1840s. The swaying wagons, plodding animals, and walking people stretched out along the trail for almost a mile.
>
> Near the end of the train, a boy holding a hickory stick moved slowly through the dust. He used the stick to poke and prod the cows that trudged beside him, mooing and complaining.
>
> "Get along!" he shouted. "Hey! Get along!"
>
> Dust floated in the air. It clogged the boy's nose, parched his throat, and coated his face. His cheeks were smeared where he had brushed away the big mosquitoes that buzzed about everywhere. (p. 13)

Freedman describes this technique as creating "a vivid, detailed scene that the reader can visualize. . . . The scene is dramatized in order to make it visual, and in order to convey the texture and flavor of the event and the time" (1994, p. 139). The drama and the detail help readers envision the past.

After I read these paragraphs two or three times, I was impressed by the number of details that appealed to the senses, especially the sense of sight (for example, swaying wagons, dust floating in the air), the sense of hearing or sound (for example, mooing and complaining, buzzing mosquitoes), and the sense of touch or feeling (for example, dust-clogged nose, parched throat). By using this excerpt and similar ones from other books, you can work with students to make a list of words and phrases that appeal to the senses and lead to an understanding of historical context.

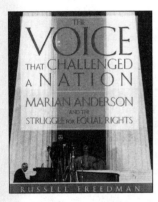

Russell Freedman's book, *The Voice That Challenged a Nation: Marian Anderson and the Struggle for Equal Rights* (2004), begins in a similar way—by presenting a vivid description of Anderson's famous concert from the steps of the Lincoln Memorial. First, we learn about the people arriving to watch her:

Despite cold and threatening weather, the crowd began to assemble long before the concert was to begin. People arrived singly and in pairs and in large animated groups. Soon the streets leading to the Mall in Washington, D.C., were jammed with thousands of people heading for the Lincoln Memorial. (p. 1)

Then, a few paragraphs later, we learn why the concert is being held at the Lincoln Memorial:

She had performed before appreciative audiences in concert halls across the United States. But because she was an African American, she had been denied the right to sing at Constitution Hall, Washington's largest and finest auditorium. The Daughters of the American Revolution, the patriotic organization that owned Constitution Hall, had ruled several years earlier that black artists would not be permitted to appear there. (p. 3)

Finally, Freedman helps us envision how the concert began:

Shortly before the concert got under way, the skies above Washington began to clear. Clouds, which had shadowed the monument, skittered away to the north, and the late-afternoon sun broke through to bathe the reflecting pool and shine on the gaily dressed Easter crowd. Secretary of the Interior Harold L. Ickes appeared on the speaker's platform. He introduced Miss Anderson, and she stepped forward to the bank of microphones.

Making Sense of History

The massive figure of Abraham Lincoln gazed down at her as she looked out at the expectant throng. Silencing the ovation with a slight wave of her hand, she paused. A profound hush settled over the crowd. For that moment, Marian Anderson seemed vulnerable and alone. Then she closed her eyes, lifted her head, clasped her hands before her, and began to sing. (p. 3)

Can't you "see" this happening? Can't you "feel" the anticipation of the crowd? One reviewer described Freedman's success in setting the scene this way: "In the initial chapter, Freedman movingly and dramatically sets the stage for the performer's historic 1939 Easter concert at the Lincoln Memorial" (Gustin, p. 120). Once again, Freedman's use of drama and detail helps readers envision the past.

Other authors of nonfiction use sensory description to bring historical context alive. However, I can't think of any author I would study before Russell Freedman. His craft and style are unparalleled. His books can be read as models for presenting historical context.

TEACHING IDEA
....

Read Books by Russell Freedman to Envision Historical Context

Books by Russell Freedman help students envision what life was like in the past. Use the books listed below for read alouds, group reading, or independent reading. Ask students to identify passages that help them understand the past by providing descriptions that appeal to sight, smell, hearing, touch, and taste.

The Voice That Challenged a Nation: Marian Anderson and the Struggle for Equal Rights. Clarion.

In Defense of Liberty: The Story of America's Bill of Rights. Holiday House.

Confucius: The Golden Rule. Arthur A. Levine/Scholastic.

Give Me Liberty!: The Story of the Declaration of Independence. Holiday House.

Babe Didrikson Zaharias: The Making of a Champion. Clarion.

Out of Darkness: The Story of Louis Braille. Clarion.

Kids at Work: Lewis Hine and the Crusade Against Child Labor. Clarion.

Lincoln: A Photobiography. Clarion.

Students may enjoy drawing pictures of what they "see" in their minds as they read these passages. These pictures can be the basis of group discussions about how descriptive details help them understand historical context.

THE THOUGHT EXPERIMENT

As I said earlier in this chapter, a thought experiment is an active, mind-expanding experience that is just the opposite of the memorizing-names-and-dates model of learning history. It provides students with an imaginative and creative way to think about "the facts" of history. A number of authors provide us with examples of thought experiments by using available information as a jumping-off point for raising questions, making hypotheses, and interpreting information. As they go through the process of reexamining, rethinking, and reinterpreting the past, these authors show how we too can open up new areas of inquiry about the past. Frequently, authors are asking themselves, What if?

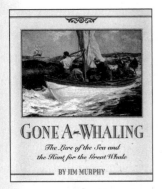

In *Gone A-Whaling: The Lure of the Sea and the Hunt for the Great Whale* (1998), Jim Murphy thinks about whaling from the whale's point of view or at least from the point of view of its defenders. Commenting on the destruction of the whaling ship *Essex* by a whale, and the grisly adventure of the few surviving men, Murphy provides readers with this surprising perspective:

Of course, the whale did not participate in the shaping of the written record of this incident. As a result, the sailors are always presented as the only victims. This could not be just a random accident, one to be expected when hunting a large creature; no, this had to be the work of an evil force. . . .

If the whale could argue its case, it would have insisted it was doing nothing more than defending itself and the rest of the herd against attack. (pp. 134–135)

It's as if Murphy asked himself, "What if the whale could speak?" Murphy goes on to tell us that while Jacques-Yves Cousteau has defended the whale's character as "accommodating to a fault, unfailingly peaceful and forebearing," Cousteau didn't write this until the 1980s! It's up to us, given Murphy's prodding, to imagine the whale's side of the argument in a much earlier context.

Another type of thought experiment involves filling in the gaps—the holes in history—by hypothesizing about what happened. As mentioned before, this is referred to as Question –> Answer –> Question. Using what they know, authors suggest what was possible and *likely* to have happened. Often one question leads to another. In *Shakespeare: His Work and His World* (2001), author Michael Rosen tells us that although little is known about Shakespeare's early life ". . . we can build up a picture of what life was like for someone like Shakespeare who grew up in Stratford at this time . . ." (p. 29). Rosen then begins his thought experiment, speculating about what Shakespeare's schooling might have been like:

> *If Shakespeare went to school, which seems very likely, then he would have gone to the King's New School in Stratford, maybe starting at the age of five. He would have gone six days a week—except for holy days like Easter and Christmas—every week of the year. The school day ran from six in the morning to six in the evening, beginning and ending with prayers. There was a two-hour lunch break. (p. 30)*

Here Rosen is using what he knows about where Shakespeare grew up and what schools were like in Stratford. In the absence of records, he is puzzling out the possible.

Did you notice the similarity between this quote by Michael Rosen and my earlier explanation of Stephen Greenblatt's thought experiment in *Will in the World?*

TEACHING IDEA

Create Thought Experiments

Students can create their own thought experiments. When there are gaps in the information about a person or event, suggest that students make educated guesses. Of course these guesses must be based on what *is* known about life in the past. Here are some questions to get students started:

- Is there a point of view that isn't being told? What would that "silent" person say?

- Is there a gap in the information about a person? What *might* that person have done? What *might* that person have thought? What *might* that person have written?

Here are some words that are useful when creating a thought experiment. These words prompt students to speculate and hypothesize about the past:

might have	possibly	maybe
probably	imagine that	almost certain
could have	perhaps	likely

Both authors are making the same point about schooling, although Greenblatt takes it a lot further. The exciting thing for me is that the kind of thinking done by contemporary historians can also be found in books written for younger readers. It's up to us to identify these books and introduce them to our students.

In the next section, I'll show you how all the theoretical ideas discussed so far inform practice in one exemplary classroom. I'll share what Debbi Aizenstain—a fifth-grade teacher at P.S. 24 in Queens—and I did to build her students' understanding of historical context. Our challenge was to help her twenty-first-century kids understand daily life in the Wild West during the 1800s.

What Activities Help Students Understand Historical Context?

It's easy for us to slip into doing activities that are familiar and appealing, but that fail to help us accomplish our teaching goals. For the sake of your students, don't fall into that trap. Here is how Debbi and I aligned our activities with our goal of helping students understand historical context over a five-week period:

* **Weeks 1 and 2:** Teaching students to read with a focus on the *familiar* and the *unfamiliar*.

* **Weeks 3 and 4:** Guiding students to undertake a thought experiment focused on historical context.

* **Week 5:** Showing students how to write poems of address.

Let's examine each of these activities.

WEEKS 1 AND 2: READING WITH A FOCUS ON THE FAMILIAR AND THE UNFAMILIAR

Tapping what we know from the research on historical context, Debbi and I applied the familiar/unfamiliar contrast to our teaching. If, as David Lowenthal said, the past is a foreign country, we were convinced that this contrast would provide students with a way of understanding it. From the start, Debbi and I focused the students' attention on two questions that would be central to our study:

* What's familiar about the West during the 1800s? (Me, too!)

* What's unfamiliar about the West during the 1800s? (Not me!)

What's Familiar? Past and Present (Me, Too!)	What's Unfamiliar? Past Only (Not Me!)

Figure 3.1: *T-chart for examining historical context*

We suggested that as students learned about life in the Wild West, they would find some aspects of life familiar—that is, similar to the way we live today. Other aspects would be unfamiliar, and they wouldn't recognize them in today's world. We would be thinking about this contrast throughout our study, using a T-chart like the one in Figure 3.1 to collect information. (See page 187 for a reproducible version of this chart.) As they read about the Wild West, students would use the chart to write down their findings about the familiar and the unfamiliar. These findings would form the basis of class discussions that would clarify and solidify students' understanding of the historical context of the Wild West.

We all read *Children of the Wild West* (Freedman, 1983), which provided the basis for mini-lessons, modeling, shared writing, and conversation. Because of its clear, descriptive style and its many photographs, it was just the right book to help students envision the past. Its short chapters on topics of interest to children—for example, traveling to Oregon, going to school, playing, meeting American Indians—provided a rich foundation for discussions and writing.

Read Alouds and Note-Taking Focusing on the Familiar and the Unfamiliar

Children of the Wild West's first chapter, "Frontier Photographers," explains that photography was just coming into use as people were moving west in covered wagons, which is why we have photographs documenting the migration. Debbi used this chapter to demonstrate how to read and take notes using our two questions as guides. After reading the text aloud and examining the accompanying photographs, she began to take notes, going back and forth between the book and the chart. She also encouraged the students to contribute information. When all the familiar and

What's Familiar? Past and Present (Me, Too!)	What's Unfamiliar? Past Only (Not Me!)
• cameras • dark rooms • had to stand still • special occasions	• tripod • picture taken only once in a lifetime • stand still for an hour • equipment weighed more than 5 Caitlins (1 Caitlin = 60 lbs.) • glass plate negatives must be developed immediately • no picture with motion • darkroom was on the wagon
SUMMARY: We still have cameras and darkrooms, and we still have to stand still for special occasions while taking a picture.	SUMMARY: In the 1850s, taking pictures of people emigrating west took a lot of work and time. The equipment weighed between 200–300 pounds and carrying it was hard.

Figure 3.2: *Debbi's chart of Chapter 1 of* Children of the Wild West

unfamiliar items were listed, she demonstrated how to write a one- or two-sentence summary of the information in each column. This would be the procedure that we followed while reading the remaining six chapters of the book—a consistent focus on historical context. As you examine Debbi's chart for the first chapter (Figure 3.2), notice that she helped her students understand the weight of photographic equipment in the 1800s (the unfamiliar) by comparing it to the weight of Caitlin, a girl in her class (the familiar).

Encouraging Independent Work

In the days following Debbi's modeling of how to read with a focus on the familiar and the unfamiliar, students tried out this approach. Using the T-chart with its two columns, they worked independently to read and take notes on each chapter of *Children of the Wild West* before meeting as a class to discuss it. That way, they had time to think about the familiar and unfamiliar aspects of the context. When Debbi brought the class together, they brought their notes with them and they were ready for conversation. She followed this procedure as the students completed each chapter in sequence, giving them a day or two to read and prepare for class discussions.

Convening the Class to Discuss Findings

During class discussions, Debbi and her students constructed a class chart, pooling the information and clarifying points of confusion about the chapter. Among other things, these discussions helped students see that some of their classmates, many of whom came from countries outside the United States, had different ideas of familiar and unfamiliar. For example, a boy who spent his earlier life in India was familiar with some of the farm chores and daily experiences from the past, while most of his classmates were not. Creating the T-chart wasn't simply a matter of pulling information from Freedman's book. It was also a matter of relating that information to our experiences in order to make sense of it.

To see how the children's individual charts contributed to the cumulative class chart, take a look at Figure 3.3, which shows three students' notes about "Going West," Chapter 2 in *Children of the Wild West*, and then compare these notes with the cumulative class chart shown in Figure 3.4. Pooling information was wise since it yielded a much more complete set of notes.

Although the summary statements the class generated may seem like simple, even naïve generalizations, they aren't! Why? First, these statements rest on a firm foundation of knowledge. Students had to know a great deal in order to generalize. Second, each is an original distillation. As teachers, you are probably well aware of how much students resist summarizing. They want to tell you *everything* they know. They don't want to tell you one thing—the most important thing. Being able to formulate that single most important idea—the idea that crystallizes all the facts they know—can be difficult. So give these statements the awe they deserve, even when some of them have, what I like to call, "shaky syntax," or phrasing that is a bit clumsy. Shaky syntax is a sign that students are moving beyond the comfort zone in reading and writing to do something challenging with new content. This is an act to applaud, while gently nudging students to refine and reshape their ideas. Figure 3.5 shows the summary statements students made for the six chapters of *Children of the Wild West*.

Extending the Work

Debbi and I extended this work by having students focus on the familiar and unfamiliar in book clubs, in partner reading, and in their independent reading. A list of the books they read appears on page 65. Students particularly enjoyed reading different books and sharing with classmates new information they discovered about the Wild West.

What's Familiar? Past and Present (Me, Too!)	What's Unfamiliar? Past Only (Not Me!)
• Children also played tag. • Like us, pioneers didn't like to travel in bad weather like rainstorms. • Families traveled together.	• Traveled by covered wagons. • Most pioneers walked the whole trip. • Pioneers only traveled 15 miles a day. • The United States ended at the banks of the Missouri. • They had to lift the wagon off its wheels and float it across the river if it was a deep river. • Many people died during the trip because they were either injured or sick.
• The children would play tag. • They would bring some of the same stuff like blankets. • Make fires • Use maps	• They would pick up their wagons to cross a river. • People got sick easily. • Children got caught in stampedes. • They traveled on the same path. • Fired rifles
• Whenever I go on trips, the adults stand in small groups talking. • People cook over fires when they go camping. • We take our possessions when we are moving.	• They started the day by firing a rifle. • There aren't grave markers along the trail. • The wagons aren't locked together. • We don't find abandoned wagons on our way when we're traveling. • Some pioneers had to abandon their wagons and walk barefoot.

Figure 3.3: *Three students' notes about "Going West," Chapter 2 of* Children of the Wild West

What's Familiar? Past and Present (Me, Too!)	What's Unfamiliar? Past Only (Not Me!)
1. Girls like to stay with girls. 2. Families traveling together 3. Getting up early 4. Vehicles 5. Moving—We bring our possessions (furniture, dolls, video games, blankets). 6. Leaving behind items not able to take with you 7. Children playing tag 8. Camping—people cook on open fires. 9. Planning their trip 10. Stopping to rest and eat 11. These places still exist. 12. Still have leaders (like a ship's captain) 13. Maps 14. Gold and silver 15. Moving for similar reasons 16. Don't like to travel in bad weather	1. Traveling involved caring for animals. 2. Don't always travel in big groups 3. Medicines have changed. 4. Don't have to pose for 1 hour 5. U.S. is bigger. 6. Firing rifles (sentries) to wake up 7. Don't walk for long trips 8. Fording rivers 9. Long time traveling (6–8 months) 10. Don't bury people beside the road 11. When we move we stay [travel?] indoors not outdoors. 12. No tombstones, no names on markers of dead 13. No circle for wagon train
SUMMARY: From the 1840s till now, families travel together from place to place, and it's still a hassle.	SUMMARY: In the 1840s traveling required more hard work, like crossing rivers and surviving storms, than it does today.

Figure 3.4: *Cumulative class chart about "Going West"*

WEEKS 3 AND 4: CREATING A THOUGHT EXPERIMENT

When you believe students have read enough to understand the historical context—a hard but necessary decision—stop them and encourage them to apply the information in a hands-on activity. Entering into a thought experiment is one way to do that. When we engage in thought experiments, we push the possibilities. We wonder. We reason. But a thought experiment is not a free-for-all. It is reined in by what we know about historical context. The possibilities we come up with need to be true to the times, past and present.

As I mentioned earlier, authors of adult and children's historical nonfiction provide examples of thought experiments all the time. Children can participate in thought experiments too.

What's Familiar? Past and Present (Me, Too!)	What's Unfamiliar? Past Only (Not Me!)
Going West	
From the 1840s till now, families travel together from place to place, and it's still a hassle.	In the 1840s traveling required more hard work, like crossing rivers and surviving storms, than it does today.
Settling Down	
Many cities developed and people lived in them. Like now, there were general stores and people from all around the world.	In the old times people used to make their houses out of sod, raw material from the earth, and most houses had one room.
American Indian	
The way the American Indians lived is similar to the way we live today. For example, the games and toys, the cooking, sewing, songs and dances, and clothes.	In the 1840s the Native Americans' way of living in tepees, hunting for buffalo, and using bows and arrows was very different from the present.
Frontier Schools	
Just like back then, in the 1840s we have reading, writing, and arithmetic in school.	In the 1840s, children walked several miles to get to a one-room schoolhouse, where many teachers were not very educated and taught children of all age groups.
Building the West	
Children then and now are expected to do daily chores like cooking, doing dishes, cleaning house, and laundry.	In the West, families did most things on their own like gathering anything that burned for the stove and girls helping to construct their homes.
Games, Parties, and Celebration	
Now and then, our celebrations are similar, like Christmas and the 4th of July, picnics, games, theaters, and churches.	In the 1840s the celebrations of the same holidays were different because they decorated and celebrated in schoolhouses, courthouses, and stables, with the whole town, and parades were different.

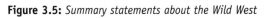

Figure 3.5: *Summary statements about the Wild West*

Books About the Wild West

Children of the Trail West by Holly Littlefield. Carolrhoda.

Conestoga Wagons by Richard Ammon. Illustrated by Bill Farnsworth. Holiday House.

. . . If You Traveled West in a Covered Wagon by Ellen Levine. Illustrated by Elroy Freem. Scholastic.

Life in the Old West Series created by Bobbie Kalman. Crabtree. Titles include:
Life on the Trail, Homes of the West, The Gold Rush, The Wagon Train, Who Settled the West?, and *Women of the West.*

People of the West by Dayton Duncan. Little, Brown.

A Pioneer Farm Girl: The Diary of Sarah Gillespie, 1877–1878 edited by Suzanne Bunkers. Blue Earth Books.

Pioneer Girl: Growing Up on the Prairie by Andrea Warren. Morrow.

Pioneers: A Library of Congress Book by Martin Sandler. HarperCollins.

The West: An Illustrated History for Children by Dayton Duncan. Little, Brown.

Window on the West: The Frontier Photography of William Henry Jackson by Laurie Lawlor. Holiday House.

Words West: Voices of Young Pioneers by Ginger Wadsworth. Clarion.

Deciding on the Thought Experiment: Letters to People of the Wild West

The thought experiment we introduced to fifth-grade students was writing a letter to a person living in the Wild West. It was inspired by an article I found in the *New York Times*, "A Woman's Worth: 1857 Letter Echoes Still" (Cohen, 1998). This article reports how three modern-day women—a columnist and author, the wife of the president of the Southern Baptist Church, and a university scientist—were asked to "speak . . . across the years" (Cohen, 1998, B7) to respond to an 1857 letter from Susan B. Anthony to Elizabeth Cady Stanton, a women's rights advocate from the mid-1800s. What would these women have to say to Susan B. Anthony? How would they manage to address the past from the perspective of the present?

To correspond with Anthony, the writers had to address both the familiar and the unfamiliar—the same goal I had for Debbi's students. I gathered some useful phrases from their letters:

Familiar	Unfamiliar
some things haven't changed	in your day
still	from my perspective
we agree/we disagree	how I wish you could see
	for me

All three writers responded to the letter, paying attention to the familiar and the unfamiliar. For instance, Katha Pollitt, the columnist, began her letter by pointing out the unfamiliar:

> Dear Susan B. Anthony,
> How I wish you could see the way the women's movement you helped to start has transformed our society—for the better. The life patterns of men and women have altered unrecognizably since your day. (In Cohen, 1998, B9)

With this opening she was able to launch into a discussion of what Anthony would find unfamiliar in today's world. Four paragraphs later, she switched her focus to the familiar and wrote, "Some things haven't changed, though" (B9). She then launched into a discussion of the many things that have remained the same.

Developing a Planning Sheet

I tried the thought experiment myself, but instead of writing to Susan B. Anthony, I wrote to a pioneer boy. I wanted to get a sense of the challenge involved, and I wanted a sample letter I could share with students. (See Figure 3.6.)

Here are some phrases I used to address the familiar and unfamiliar:

Familiar	Unfamiliar
like you/unlike you	it's hard for me to imagine
knowing about your life	it might seem odd to you

Using my letter as a basis, I prepared a planning sheet so that Debbi's students could try out this thought experiment too. (See Figure 3.7.) The sheet would first help students to decide whom to address and what to write about and then provide a list of useful words and phrases, and a structure for the writing. I was confident that the students would enjoy this activity and would produce interesting, varied results. Most important, it would maintain their focus on historical context. They would be able to use information from *Children of the Wild West* and the other books and materials they had read.

At the end of the sheet, I suggested that students plan a decorative border for their letters, containing illustrations of objects they were writing about. This idea

February 18

Dear Pioneer Boy:

I admire the stamina you had for travel. Getting up at 4 a.m., walking a good part of the day along a dusty trail, prodding the slow-poke animals to move—it all sounds like hard work to me.

Like you, I have also traveled. I moved to Boston when I went to college. I left my family and friends behind and went to live in an unfamiliar place. Like you, I also left most of my belongings behind and started a new kind of life. We both traveled to find new opportunities. I moved to have the opportunity to go to a good school, and you moved to find land and opportunity. We both looked forward to good times.

Unlike you, I only traveled for one day, whereas you spent six to eight months on the trail. Your red, white, and blue prairie schooner was crowded with everything you needed. You would have been really surprised to see my parents' car as it sped across the highway taking me to Boston! Everything I needed was in the trunk or had been sent ahead. My family traveled alone; no other families or guides came with us, but my father used a map. We stopped for snacks, but instead of the cold lunch you would have had, we had hamburgers and soup. Our trip was comfortable. The only danger we faced was bad weather and bad drivers. It might seem odd to you that we had no big worries like you did about drowning, epidemics, snake bites, or heat exhaustion. I had smooth sailing, not the daring adventure you had.

It's hard for me to imagine traveling to a new destination for months instead of days. Knowing about your life makes me appreciate modern transportation, but I still admire your courage and hard work moving west. Many books have been written about you and your trip out west. We haven't forgotten about what you did.

Sincerely,

Myra Zarnowski

Figure 3.6: *Myra's sample letter*

was inspired by *A River Ran Wild: An Environmental History* (1992) by Lynne Cherry, in which the running text is framed with illustrations that provide extra information about the historical setting. When Cherry describes how the Nashua River was first settled by Native Americans, for example, she includes a border showing many of the tools they used such as arrowheads, mortar and pestle, and stone ax. Like Cherry, I invited students to extend their writing through illustration.

Planning Sheet

1. Circle the person your letter is addressed to:
   - pioneer girl (If it's a specific girl, give the girl's name.)
   - pioneer boy
   - Indian girl
   - Indian boy
   - teacher

2. What topic(s) will you be writing about? Circle one:
   - going west
   - settling down
   - American Indians
   - frontier schools
   - games, parties, and celebrations

Dear _____,

Paragraph #1: Introduce yourself. Consider one or more of these ideas:
   - Tell who you are and how you learned about him or her.
   - Tell what you admire about the person.
   - Tell something unusual you learned about the person.

Paragraph #2: What's **familiar** about his or her life? Useful words and phrases:
   - I understand . . .   I, too . . .
   - Like you, I also . . .   Another thing that hasn't changed . . .
   - My family also . . .   similar
   - You and I both . . .   same
   - I agree . . .   resembles
   - We both . . .   alike

Paragraph #3: What's **unfamiliar** about his or her life? Useful words and phrases:
   - Nowadays . . .   We no longer . . .
   - It might seem odd to you . . .   Unlike you . . .
   - You might be surprised to learn . . .   different
   - In my day . . .   unusual
   - In your day . . .   strange
   - The way I see it . . .   From my perspective . . .

Paragraph #4: Final Comment: What do I want to say? Useful Words and phrases:
   - How I wish you could see . . .   • Knowing about your life . . .
   - If I could show you . . .   • In the future . . .
   - I agree . . .   • It's hard for me to imagine . . .
   - I disagree . . .   • Although things have changed since you . . .
   - surprising

Plan the border of your letter. Show what it will look like by making a sketch.

Figure 3.7: *Planning sheet for writing letters to people of the Wild West*

Making Sense of History

Modeling the Process and Getting Started

To begin, I read the students my letter, and then Debbi took over. She introduced the thought experiment to the students by choosing a person to address— a frontier photographer inspired by Chapter 1 of *Children of the Wild West*— and drafting a letter on the overhead projector. Her letter began as follows:

> *February 27*
>
> *Dear Frontier Photographer:*
>
> *I recently read a wonderful book entitled* Children of the Wild West *and was fascinated by the beginning of photography. I am currently a teacher at P.S. 24 in New York City and use photographs as teaching tools. Photography is still popular today. I even have a photograph of my husband on my desk.*
>
> *I was especially interested in why a photographer would want to travel with a wagon train to the West. . . .*

This was enough to get the students started. Using the planning sheet, students made decisions that would shape their letters. They each selected a person to address and a topic. They then proceeded to introduce themselves and deal with the familiar and the unfamiliar aspects of the person's life. In the final paragraph, they made comments and observations about their choice.

As they drafted their letters, students frequently referred to the books and illustrations about the Wild West. They also shared their drafts with other students and conferenced with Debbi and me.

Examining Student Letters to People From the Past

So, how did the students do? Extraordinarily well. Every student was able to address the familiar and unfamiliar aspects the life in the Wild West. While I have many samples to share—more than you probably want to see—I have selected two because they allow me to point out some interesting qualities. Please keep in mind that these letters went through several drafts before they appeared in the shape they are in here. They are the result of hard work—the students', Debbi's, and mine.

Krishna's letter is addressed to Martha Ann Morrison, a pioneer girl who Russell Freedman tells us in *Children of the Wild West* traveled west from Missouri to Oregon when she was thirteen. At the age of fifteen, she married a hired hand who worked for her father. Marriage at an early age is familiar to Krishna, since her great-grandmother wed at twelve. Krishna wonders how much of Martha Morrison's

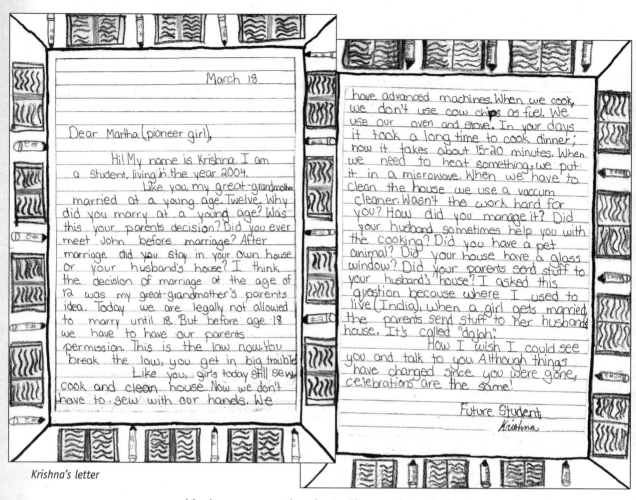

Krishna's letter

Left page of letter:

March 18

Dear Martha (pioneer girl),

Hi! My name is Krishna. I am a student, living in the year 2004.

Like you, my great-grandmother married at a young age. Twelve. Why did you marry at a young age? Was this your parents decision? Did you ever meet John before marriage? After marriage did you stay in your own house or your husband's house? I think the decision of marriage at the age of 12 was my great-grandmother's parents idea. Today we are legally not allowed to marry until 18. But before age 18 we have to have our parents permission. This is the law now. You break the law, you get in big trouble.

Like you, girls today still sew, cook and clean house. Now we don't have to sew with our hands. We

Right page of letter:

have advanced machines. When we cook, we don't use cow chips as fuel. We use our oven and stove. In your days it took a long time to cook dinner; now it takes about 15-20 minutes. When we need to heat something, we put it in a microwave. When we have to clean the house we use a vaccum cleaner. Wasn't the work hard for you? How did you manage it? Did your husband sometimes help you with the cooking? Did you have a pet animal? Did your house have a glass window? Did your parents send stuff to your husband's house? I asked this question because where I used to live (India), when a girl gets married, the parents send stuff to her husband's house. It's called "dajah."

How I wish I could see you and talk to you. Although things have changed since you were gone, celebrations are the same!

Future Student,
Krishna

experience was like her great-grandmother's. She wonders, "Did your parents send stuff to your husband's house? I ask this question because where I used to live (India), when a girl gets married, the parents send stuff to her husband's house. It's called 'dajah.'" Most of the other students were unfamiliar with the idea of early marriage. Some even found it unthinkable. Imagine getting married as a high school student! No way! Yet Krishna's letter proved to us that not everyone comes to class with the same background experiences.

Paarth writes to teacher Tom Clay, who is also described in *Children of the Wild West*. He points out a number of differences between Tom Clay and his teacher. One idea that really amazed him was how Clay began class the first day by laying his six-shooter on the desk. That was one way to prevent fooling around! Another striking idea was that teachers boarded at their students' homes. These were startling ideas not only for Paarth, but also for the rest of the class. Paarth goes on to state that he "didn't think there were teachers till the late 1800s." Did

Making Sense of History

March 16

Dear Tom Clay,

My name is Paarth and I just read a book entitled Children of the Wild West and the book had a little about you. I was surprised that on the first day of school you took out a six shooter and put it on your desk! I understand that on the first day of school you need quiet so you can explain things to the pupils, but teachers today don't take out a six shooter. They just calm the pupils down by talking. Nowadays teachers don't bring guns to school because thats the law.

Now about me. I currently am a pupil at public school 24 in Flushing, New York. I love reading and math and thats how I got to know you — by reading.

Mr. Clay I noticed some things familar about your life and my life now, like there are still teachers. I didn't think there were teachers till the late 1800's. Now teachers live in their own houses but in your time they went to the pupils houses.

In your day the schools used to be one room for children of all ages, but now the

schools are huge. We don't drink from the same bucket of water and schools last for ten months not four. If I can show you the school I study and learn, you would be amazed. Now schools are so big about 500-1000 people can come.

We now have cars to take us around. They are big and small and most people have them. You might be wondering what a car is so I'll tell you. Cars are like wagons but are more high-tech. They run from fuel and their normal speed is 35 miles per hour.

Sincerely,
Paarth

Paarth's letter

he think that teaching was a relatively recent profession? If so, writing this letter prodded him to rethink and reassess his assumption.

This thought experiment raised language-related challenges. For example, several students wrestled with explaining television, radio, cars, buses, and video games to pioneers. The challenge, of course, is that words such as *electricity*, *gasoline*, and *miles per hour* aren't useful. Some resorted to including pictures, which helped somewhat. But in general, students struggled to explain what was familiar to them yet unfamiliar to the person they were addressing. Other than that, the activity was manageable and fun—a fitting way to extend their knowledge of historical context.

There are strong reasons this activity succeeded:

* Students had enough background information to apply it in a thought experiment.

* The familiar/unfamiliar contrast was a useful way to sort information.

* Students found the activity challenging and interesting, but also manageable.

This thought experiment is about a lot more than the Wild West. It is about becoming aware of historical context and can be used to connect students to other time periods and phenomena commonly taught in elementary and middle school—ancient civilizations, colonial America, the American Revolution, immigration, and so on.

WEEK 5: WRITING POEMS OF ADDRESS

Writing poems of address was another activity that helped Debbi and me reach our goal of teaching about historical context. Paul Janeczko, author of *How to Write Poetry* (1999), describes these poems as "written to somebody or to something" (p. 59). Our study of the Wild West suggested many audiences students could address.

To introduce poems of address, I shared a list of phrases I had gathered from the chapter in *Children of the Wild West* dealing with travel in a covered wagon:

wagon train of the 1840s	*splintered wreck*
prairie schooner	*wooden grave markers*
crammed with the family possessions	*foothills of the Rockies*
food, clothing, furniture	*treacherous deserts of Utah and Nevada*
top-heavy wagons blown over	

Then I showed how some of these words could be incorporated into a poem of address. Here's a poem that I wrote:

Covered Wagon

Hold on to our possessions
Don't break down
You've got everything we own:
Our food, clothing, furniture
Our tools, bedding, kitchenware
I have heard of wagons becoming splintered wrecks
I need you to hold on.
Be our place of rest, our protection, our sturdy schooner
Climb the Rockies
Cross the deserts of Utah and Nevada
Hold on.

Debbi and I then asked students to select an audience (e.g., Indians, pioneer teacher, pioneer child) or an object (e.g., a covered wagon, school, or sod house)

Making Sense of History

and to brainstorm of list of words and phrases to use. We also encouraged them to skim books on the Wild West. After creating their lists, students began writing their poems. These poems are excellent models to share with your students.

Writing poems of address provided an additional opportunity for students to think about historical context. In "Indian Boy," Vaishnavi expresses interest in wanting to know more about the subject of the poem. In fact, she asks him for information about himself: "I am really anxious to hear . . ."; "Tell me . . ."; "Share all your adventures. . . ." This is followed by a series of questions about school and family life. Clearly, Vaishnavi is eager to learn more about the unfamiliar.

Areeba's poem "On the Wagon Trail" is a collection of sensory details—what she believes she would have remembered if she had traveled west in a covered wagon. She reports on the heat and the dust she would've felt, the creaking and groaning she would've heard, and the change in the wagon's appearance she would've seen over time. She concludes with a vision of a circle of wagons chained up for the night. This poem is a powerful depiction of a scene Areeba knows only from books, photographs, and conversation.

Tochukwu's poem "Covered Wagon" emphasizes the yearning he would have felt as a pioneer traveling west, "hoping to make it all the way." The ending shows the ups and downs of "starting a new life." Tochukwu puts himself into that wagon,

Indian Boy
by Vaishnavi

I am really anxious to hear what you have to say.
Tell me about your customs, and your way of living.
You play so many familiar games;
Acorn tops, one-legged hopping races.
Will you play them with me?
Share all your adventures as an Indian boy with me.
Your precious tribes and bands scattered all over the West.
Is your new school taught by the white settlers comfortable for you?
Do you have a sister that takes care of the family?
Do you hunt?
Do you farm?
Your life is filled with many exciting things
But before you experience them,
You're gone with the wind in a blink of an eye.

On the Wagon Trail
Areeba   Class 5-328

Traveling out west in the summer heat,
But while on you, we can roll up the canvas for a breeze.
While walking along your side, there was a lot of dust.
It's smeared over my face and it makes me sneeze.

You creak and groan, yet you're still sturdy.
I remember when you were new, red wheels, blue body and white canvas.
Now you're crusted with mud and are very dirty,
Your paint has faded and your top is stained.

You can't take much load,
So some of our possessions were left behind.
Every two miles, there are grave markers made from others like you,
For people laid to rest is all we find.

When we stop for the night,
We lock you with chains.
You only go 15 miles a day,
So there's more traveling, more pain.

> ### Covered Wagon
>
> #### Tochukwu
>
> I'm traveling, going out west,
> With your brand new red wheels, and a painted
> blue body, with your new, fresh, white canvas
> top,
> Pulled by oxen or mules, Carrying my younger
> brothers and sisters
> With my family's treasured belongings, Hoping
> to make it all the way.
> As your wheels slowly move across the plains,
> You get to a river,
> Fording across it.
> Nighttime has come.
> Your wheels are no longer red.
> Your body is no longer blue
> And your canvas top is no longer white.
> Now, we are on our way,
> Starting a new
>
> ## L I F E.

referring to "*my* family," "*my* younger brothers and sisters," and "*my* family's treasured belongings." Having come to New York from Nigeria, Tochukwu knows about starting a new life and the hopes people have for new beginnings. I have seen, again and again, how students like Tochukwu tap their background experiences to connect to events in history.

Copies of all the poems of address were collected in a class book. Throughout the year, the collection served as a reminder of the importance of understanding historical context.

Concluding Thoughts

When Ira Berlin wrote "For the historian, context is all . . ." (2004), I believe he meant that looking at the past means acknowledging the unfamiliar and not trying to change it into something comfortably familiar. He meant that understanding history means paying attention to the unique qualities of the past.

Yet even when we do our best to see the past as somewhat unfamiliar, history doesn't lie down dead so that we can wrap up all its loose ends, write it down, and be done with it. No, not at all. We may agree on the facts, but not on what they mean or how they impact our lives. So for anyone who wants to understand history, there is more to think about. In Chapter 4, we'll think about historical significance—why we consider some facts to be more important than others.

Historical Significance

How Can I Get Students to Recognize Historical Events That Are Important to Remember?

Recently, while I was meeting with a group of sixth-grade social studies teachers, a teacher told an all-too-familiar story. After being introduced to the topic of the American Revolution and while discussing the Battle of Lexington, a student asked that question we've all heard: Why do we have to know this?

This question has always made me uncomfortable because I haven't had a good answer for it. And the answers often suggested in professional literature (for example, in *Building a History Curriculum* published by the National Council for History Education, 2003) are unconvincing to students—answers such as, "Because knowing it will help you understand yourself better." Or, "It will help you deal with change." Or, "It will provide you with a sense of identity." Or, "It will help you become an effective citizen." All of these answers may be true, but they are lofty and vague. They have never helped me win over any skeptical students.

Instead, I have had much more success teaching history by turning the tables on students and asking them, What do *you* think is important to know? How could you decide? I've even asked students if, in their opinion, a topic should be taught again next year or eliminated from the curriculum. These are questions related to historical significance; raising them allows students to become decision makers. Students decide what is valuable to know. In the process, they wrestle with criteria for making wise decisions. Instead of passive—even resentful—memorizers, they become active historical thinkers and evaluators of information.

This chapter shows you how to introduce and teach the concept of historical significance. It begins with an explanation of why the concept is important and what researchers have learned that can help us help students decide what is significant. Then it provides examples of historical nonfiction that support students' emerging understanding of historical significance. Finally, it details what fifth-grade teacher Debbi Aizenstain and I did to teach her students to think about and apply criteria for determining historical significance about the forced internment of Japanese Americans during World War II. The following questions, based on the three essential elements of history teaching described in Chapter 2—historical thinking, historical literature, and hands-on experience—guide the discussion:

* What do theory and research say about historical significance?

* How does nonfiction literature contribute to an understanding of historical significance?

* What activities help students understand the concept of historical significance?

What Do Theory and Research Say About Historical Significance?

Historical significance has been called "the valuing criterion" (Seixas, 1994, p. 281) because it is the standard historians use to decide what is most valuable to know. The words used to discuss historical significance—*importance, relevance, judgment,* and *selection*—all reflect value judgments. According to Tim Lomas, "History, to be meaningful, depends on selection and this, in turn, depends on establishing criteria of significance to select the more relevant and to dismiss the less relevant" (1990, p. 41).

Researchers tell us that the concept of historical significance is at the heart of the understanding of history (Barton, 2005; Cercadillo, 2001; Lee, Ashby, & Dickinson, 2001). It explains the role historians play in selecting and emphasizing some facts and information, and deemphasizing others. The sources historians value the most provide the basis of their historical accounts. As a result, historians write substantially different books based on what they believe to be the most valuable information.

Two ideas derived from the work of educational researchers are particularly useful in guiding our thinking about historical significance:

* Historical significance is a variable concept, not a fixed one. Ideas about significance change across time, across nations, and even within the same classroom. As a result, students will have different ideas about what is significant and why (Epstein, 1998, 2001).

* Criteria for determining historical significance have been identified (Hunt, 2000, 2003; Lomas, 1990; Partington, 1980). They can be introduced, discussed, debated, and put to use by students. I present these criteria later in the chapter.

These ideas help us deal with the question, What historical events, people, themes, and issues are important to remember? They also help us plan instruction and understand our students' responses to information about the past.

HISTORICAL SIGNIFICANCE IS A VARIABLE CONCEPT, NOT A FIXED ONE

As we all know, students do not all view the same information in precisely the same way. Whether they're discussing a popular song, a movie, or a presidential candidate, they have their own ideas about what is significant and why. The same is true for history. This is because historical significance varies according to (1) the impact of historical themes, time scales, and questions being considered, and (2) the impact of official and unofficial history on students' thinking. Let's look more closely at these factors.

"Conceptions of significance are at the heart of all history—and history education—and research on the development of students' ideas about this topic may provide insight into their overall frameworks for historical understanding. Comparative studies are particularly valuable, because they can call attention to the relationship between students' ideas and the social contexts of which they are a part."

Barton, 2005, p. 9

The Impact of Historical Themes, Time Scales, and Questions

The significance of the same event varies from person to person as a result of the questions we ask about the event and the context in which we ask them. Peter Lee, Rosalyn Ashby, and Alaric Dickinson (2001) point out that "the same action, event or process may have different significance in different *themes and timescales*" [italics added] (2001, p. 202). A theme such as the events leading up to the American Revolution is narrower and takes place over less time than a theme such as political decision making during the Colonial period. Ask yourself, Is the Battle of Lexington equally important if we are thinking about the events leading up to the American Revolution, compared to political decision making during the Colonial period? Is the Battle of Lexington as important in explaining leadership among American Patriots as it is in explaining 18th-century battle tactics? Is it as important in explaining the liberties and rights of colonists as it is in explaining their economic goals? The answers are, of course, a resounding "No!" As we vary the themes and time scales we are considering, our views of historical significance of an event will also vary. Lee, Ashby, and Dickinson suggest that when thinking about significance we consider the following questions: For what theme? For what time scale? For what question? These questions help us explain why historical significance is a variable concept.

The Impact of Official and Unofficial History on Student Thinking

In addition to the theme, time scale, and questions asked, historical significance depends on what students see as valuable to themselves. To repeat an idea I often hear from teachers, "Students need to be able to *relate to* the content." Researcher Peter Seixas has confirmed this idea: "A historical phenomenon becomes significant if and only if members of a contemporary community can draw relationships between it and other historical phenomena and *ultimately to themselves*" [italics added] (Seixas, 1994, p. 295).

But, how do students make these history-to-self connections? What frameworks do they draw on to relate to the content of history? It would be naïve to think that students only have at their disposal the official history that is taught in school. Keith Barton and Linda Levstik characterize this official history as a grand narrative of "progressive expansion of rights, opportunities, and freedom" (1998, p. 485). In other words, the grand narrative suggests that our society is getting better and better, and that life is improving for everyone.

Yet, in addition to this official history, students also have an unofficial history, also called a vernacular (or everyday) history that guides their thinking. Students learn this history from family members, films, books, and television. Because of the existence of official and unofficial histories, researchers have found divergent thinking about significance among students in the same classroom. Terri Epstein (1998), for example, found that African-American and European-American adolescents had different beliefs about the significance of people, events, and themes in U.S. history. When asked about significant people in U.S. history, African-American students most frequently selected Malcolm X and Harriet Tubman, while European-American students most frequently selected George Washington and John F. Kennedy. Although there was some overlap (interestingly, both groups chose Martin Luther King, Jr.), African-American students chose African-American people 75 percent of the time and European-American students chose European-American people 82 percent of the time. Similarly, Epstein (2001) reported that black and white elementary school students had different understandings of such topics in U.S. history as racial diversity and democracy.

Other researchers have found similar results among students outside the United States. Keith Barton (2005) examined Catholic and Protestant students in Northern Ireland and their judgments of historical significance. He not only found different judgments between those students, but also between students in the U.S. and Northern Ireland. For example, for both Catholic and Protestant students in Northern Ireland, "the most common reason for selecting an event as historically significant was the extent of death or hardship involved" (p. 19). Irish students often referred to the importance of remembering suffering and hardship, a point, Barton claims, that was not made by American students. He states, "In the United States, remembrance plays only a minor role in attitudes toward the past . . ." (p. 21).

As a result of his investigation, Barton arrived at two useful suggestions for teaching about historical significance:

* We need to connect topics of study to students' prior knowledge, especially topics students already see as significant.
* We need to extend students' understanding of significance by teaching them the many reasons we find people, events, and themes significant.

"'Significance' is at the heart of the subject matter of both academic and school history. It is fundamental to understand a distinctive feature of the discipline: discrete events are not understandable without their link to a frame of reference and a sense of authorship behind them. Academic and school history are not the same thing, but reducing the gap between both 'histories' becomes necessary in order to reach a more sophisticated historical understanding."

Cercadillo, 2001, p. 116

Specifically, Barton suggests introducing the idea of remembrance as a criterion for significance. That is, people should be remembered because of the hardships they endured and the sacrifices they made. I will return to this suggestion later in this chapter.

CRITERIA FOR DETERMINING HISTORICAL SIGNIFICANCE

Even though ideas about historical significance will vary, a sturdy set of criteria exists that explains how historians decide what is significant. This set is derived from the work of British educators who recognize the need to teach students about the concept of significance (Hunt, 2000, 2003; Lomas, 1990; Partington, 1980). Figure 4.1, which is based on that work, lists reasons that historians consider people, events, changes, and issues significant along with questions that students can use to guide their own thinking.

These questions can guide students as they are reading about the past and later as they discuss with classmates their ideas about what's worth knowing. Reading

What Criteria Should We Use
to Determine Historical Significance?

Criteria	Questions
1. Contemporary Significance	How important was it to people at the time?
2. Profundity	How deeply were people affected?
3. Quantity	How many people were affected?
4. Durability	How long lasting were the effects?
5. Relevance	How does it help us understand current issues and events?

Adapted from Hunt, 2000, 2003; Lomas, 1990; Partington, 1980

Figure 4.1: *Criteria for determining historical significance*

and discussing for this purpose is much more motivating than reading and discussing simply to remember. After all, what elementary and middle school students don't jump at the chance to tell us what they think?

Using quality historical nonfiction, you can show students how authors decide on significance and share their ideas with readers. Like students, many authors begin with what is personally relevant to them. Once they become involved in a topic, other factors beyond themselves—factors important to the larger social community—become relevant as well. The next section provides examples of how authors indicate both personal and social relevance in their writing.

How Does Nonfiction Literature Contribute to an Understanding of Historical Significance?

Most authors of historical nonfiction are not shy about telling us what they think is significant. Sometimes they tell us why a topic is important to them for personal, subjective reasons (Seixas, 1997). Other times they take a more objective stance, determining historical significance based on the criteria in Figure 4.1. They judge significance by the impact a person, event, or issue makes on them and others. These "others" could be people living during the time being studied or people living today. This section explains how nonfiction authors convey these two types of historical significance in their writing:

- ★ Historical Significance as Personal Relevance: "*I Can Relate to It*"
- ★ Historical Significance as Social Relevance: "*We Can Relate to It*"

My goal, once again, is to show that history cannot escape the perspective of the author. It is always about more than just the facts.

HISTORICAL SIGNIFICANCE AS PERSONAL RELEVANCE: "*I CAN RELATE TO IT*"

Researchers tell us how important it is for students to connect new information with known information, but authors actually show us how to do it. Usually, authors begin with a topic they know something about but are curious to know more about. In that way, they illustrate what M. Suzanne Donovan and John Bransford (2005) suggest is a major principle of learning in all subject areas: "New understandings are constructed on a foundation of existing understandings and experiences" (p. 4).

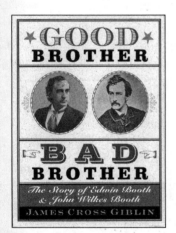

James Cross Giblin, author of *Good Brother, Bad Brother: The Story of Edwin Booth and John Wilkes Booth* (2005), explains the personal relevance of the topic this way:

Readers often wonder where the author got the idea for the book. In the case of Good Brother, Bad Brother, *the idea came to me one morning in the shower, complete with title. But it has its roots in almost a lifetime of personal interests and experience.*

From teenage on, I've had a serious interest in the theater. I acted in numerous plays in high school, college, and summer stock, and eventually branched out into directing and playwriting....

At the same time, I've had a serious interest with the American Civil War—the monumental struggle that brought an end to slavery in the United States, but only after a horrendous loss of life on both sides of the conflict. I longed to write about it, too, but couldn't think of a focus.

Then came that fateful morning in the shower when my two interests suddenly merged. The result was this joint biography of the Booth brothers, played out against the backdrop of the Civil War. (p. 223)

Notice how Giblin provides us with evidence of his prior knowledge. The topic he selected "had its roots in a lifetime of personal interests and experience." It stems from "serious interest" and "longstanding fascination." At the same time,

Giblin sees the topic as personally interesting and well worth investigating further. He states that he "longed to write about it."

Similarly, Andrea Davis Pinkney, author of *Let It Shine: Stories of Black Women Freedom Fighters* (2000), tells readers how her involvement in the Civil Rights movement motivated her to write. She describes the process as follows:

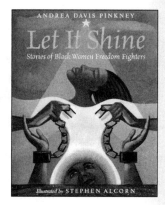

> *"Black empowerment" was more than a slogan in our home. It was a deeply held belief that my parents, through their example, instilled in their three children. To brand myself a product of the civil rights movement is no overstatement. So when in her brilliance, my editor Liz Van Doren approached me to write a collection of stories about black women freedom fighters, I said yes immediately. I had to write this book.*
>
> *But then came a million questions. What direction would the collection take? Which women would we include? How would the stories be told?*
>
> *After many long discussions with Liz, hours of reading and researching, and, of course, talks with Mom and Dad, I decided to focus the collection on ten women whose individual lives wove together one incredible story—a story of the challenges and triumphs of civil rights that spanned American history from the eighteenth century to the present day. (pp. x–xi)*

Like James Cross Giblin, Andrea Davis Pinkney had prior knowledge of her topic. The Civil Rights movement was "more than a slogan" in her home. Because of her parents' involvement, she witnessed important events and became convinced of the movement's importance. This personal relevance made the topic so appealing that she "had to write this book." Yet despite her extensive firsthand knowledge, she still engaged in "hours of reading and researching" to find new information. As these authors show us, personal relevance is and should be a starting point that leads to further investigation.

HISTORICAL SIGNIFICANCE AS SOCIAL RELEVANCE: "WE CAN RELATE TO IT"

In addition to stressing the personal significance of events, people, changes, and issues in their work, authors of historical nonfiction show how these things have significance for the larger community, both in the past and present. They make use of the criteria listed in Figure 4.1: contemporary significance, profundity,

TEACHING IDEA

Seek Evidence of Personal Relevance to the Author

As students read authors' comments about how they select topics, challenge them to find the words and phrases that signal personal relevance. What evidence of prior knowledge can they find? What evidence of the author's deepening interest in the topic can they find? What research did the author need to conduct to learn new information? You might want to use this example with students to get them started:

Here is how Pam Muñoz Ryan explains the personal relevance of the life of the celebrated singer Marian Anderson, the subject of her picture book *When Marian Sang* (2002):

> *I love spirituals, gospel music, musicals, and opera (when I was in junior high, I sang in an all-city honor chorus). Like many people, I knew a little about Marian Anderson—most specifically about her Lincoln Memorial concert. . . . I began researching and became fascinated by the depth of her talent. I felt as if I'd been introduced to someone who was a kindred spirit to the other characters about whom I'd written. . . . I wanted more people to know her inspiring story. It was with that conviction that I set out to write this book. (unpaged)*

Clearly, Ryan feels a personal connection to Marian Anderson, which comes through in a few ways. First, she loves music—especially the kind of music Marian Anderson sang. Second, although she knew a little about Anderson prior to starting the project, she comes to think of Anderson as a "kindred spirit" to characters she has previously written about, based on her research. Third, she becomes "fascinated by the depth of her talent" and wants other people to know about her.

quantity, durability, and relevance. In this section, I draw examples from literature to demonstrate how authors do that.

Highlighting Contemporary Significance:
How Important Was It to People at the Time of the Event?

In the author's note to *Bound for the North Star: True Stories of Fugitive Slaves* (2000), Dennis Brindell Fradin claims that the stories of men and women who escaped from slavery were important to contemporary 19th-century readers. He writes:

> *Books about such fugitive slaves as Harriet Tubman, Henry "Box" Brown, and Ellen and William Craft were popular among nineteenth-century readers. Then, as now, they provided inspiring examples of how human beings, in their desire for liberty, can overcome incredible difficulties. But the stories of the escaped slaves did more than that. They awakened thousands of readers to the evils of slavery, helping to bring on the struggle that freed more than four million people who hadn't been fortunate enough to escape. (p. xvii)*

Notice that the author highlights the significance of fugitive-slave stories at the time they were happening, emphasizing how those stories inspired many people of the time—even people who were not enslaved. The author goes on to suggest that the stories continue to be significant today in preventing intolerance and injustice.

Highlighting Profundity: How Deeply Were People Affected?

Authors often convey the significance of events by highlighting the profound effects they have had on people. In the moving book, *A Dream of Freedom: The Civil Rights Movement from 1954 to 1968*, author Diane McWhorter highlights the terrible impact of segregation on black Americans:

> *To appreciate the transforming achievement of the civil rights movement, you need to understand the vast social evil it overcame. Segregation was a surreal conspiracy of law, politics, economics, and tradition that trapped black Americans in a lowly corner of society. Segregation deprived African Americans of the freedom that, as Martin Luther King, Jr., put it, should have been theirs at birth. (p. 13)*

McWhorter continues to explain how black Americans had "their personhood . . . most systematically violated in the South" (p. 13). These were not petty grievances; they were deeply felt humiliations resulting from a "vast social evil."

Highlighting Quantity: How Many People Were Affected?

Sometimes authors present statistics—sheer numbers—to express historical significance. In *Children of the Dust Bowl: The True Story of the School at Weedpatch Camp* (1992), author Jerry Stanley informs readers of the numbers of people who abandoned the Oklahoma Panhandle and its surroundings for California during the 1930s:

> *The advertisements for workers led to what is called the Dust Bowl migration. It was the largest migration of people in U.S. history. Between 1935 and 1940 over one million people left their homes in Oklahoma, Texas, Arkansas, and Missouri and moved to California. (p. 12)*

This event was not minor. It bears repeating, "It was the largest migration of people in U.S. history." Why, we might wonder, did it happen? Why would all those people leave their homes? How does it help us understand modern-day natural disasters, such as Hurricane Katrina, that force people from their communities?

Highlighting Durability: How Long Lasting Were the Effects?

Authors can indicate historical significance by highlighting long-lasting effects. In *Black Potatoes: The Story of the Great Irish Famine, 1845–1850* (2001), for example, author Susan Campbell Bartoletti concludes with a section entitled

"The Legacy of the Famine" in which she reports, "One effect of the Famine was the bitterness and resentment it left behind" (p. 171). Generations of Irish never forgave the British government for its harsh treatment. Emigrants passed this bitterness along to their children and grandchildren. One granddaughter of an Irish immigrant reported hearing about the hatred of British rule all through her childhood.

Bartoletti discusses a second significant outcome of the Famine: emigration. She says:

> Another lasting effect was the scattering of the Irish people. For the next sixty years, emigration continued at a high rate, accounting for half of each rising generation. The Famine emigrants helped cities develop and grow as they fulfilled the need for immigrant labor in the United States, Australia, Canada, and Britain. By 1910, five million people had left Ireland for good. Today, Ireland's population numbers about four million, less than half the amount in 1845. (p. 171)

Although the Irish Famine ended in 1850, its impact is still felt today. One effect is that it left behind a legacy of bitterness and resentment against the British government. A second effect is more than forty million people in the U.S. who today claim Irish ancestry. Irish immigrants and their descendants have influenced American life in areas such as government, labor, and entertainment. Clearly, the effects of the Famine have been long lasting.

Highlighting Relevance: How Does It Help Us Understand Current Issues and Events?

Authors sometimes show us how the past helps us to understand the present. In *I Am an American: A True Story of Japanese Internment* (1994), author Jerry Stanley chronicles what happened to one young Japanese-American man, Shiro Nomura. In spite of his experiences in an internment camp where he was denied his rights as a citizen, he later used what happened to him and others to teach about tolerance. The author reports what Shiro Nomura told him:

> Referring to internment, he said, "It's easy to think that this is just a part of Japanese history. But it's really a part of American history, because this is what America is all about: tolerating different cultures, accepting people who look different. America is a nation of immigrants from all over the world, and they

have made America the greatest country in the world. When anyone sees a person of Japanese ancestry living in the United States, they should first think 'American' and only afterward 'Japanese.' This is the American way." (p. 90)

Today, in the aftermath of 9/11, this story has continuing significance as we question our treatment of and attitudes toward Muslims living in the U.S. Are we becoming increasingly suspicious of people because of the way they look and dress and what they believe? If so, is this appropriate for security's sake? How do we balance individual rights and national security? Educators can seize the

---

TEACHING IDEA

Explore What Authors Tell Interviewers About Historical Significance

Journals for teachers and librarians frequently feature interviews with authors. Many of those interviews provide insight into authors' views on historical significance. For example, in the March 2004 issue of *Book Links: Connecting Books, Libraries, and Classrooms*, Russell Freedman shared his view of the significance of the Bill or Rights, the subject of his book *In Defense of Liberty*, with interviewers Cyndi Giorgis and Nancy J. Johnson:

> If I didn't believe that the Bill of Rights is the bedrock of American culture and is what differentiates us from other countries—and if I didn't believe that it's endangered—then I don't think I could have written this book (Giorgis & Johnson, 2004, p.44).

Sharing this short but powerful quote with students—or better still, the entire interview—sends a strong message about what is important to Freedman.

Two other *Book Links* interviews that you might find useful are Gillian Engberg's with Ken Mochizuki, the author of *Passage to Freedom: The Sugihara Story* (Book Links, December 2002/January 2003, pp. 7–10), and with Phillip Hoose, the author of *We Were There, Too! Young People in U.S. History* (Book Links, June/July 2002, pp. 11-13). In each of these interviews, the author addresses issues related to writing history. Philip Hoose, for example, shares a realization he had when a young girl told him, "You know, it's like we're not even real in my history book. People don't even count until they're 20" (p. 12). Upon hearing that statement, Hoose identified an important gap in what was available to young readers—a gap that he was eager to fill.

opportunity to teach an important lesson in historical significance by making connections between those two events. As Karen Miksch and David Ghere (2004) observe,

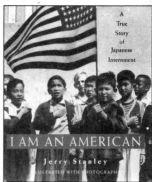

> . . . *The terrorist attacks of September 11, 2001 have generated a new interest in Japanese-American incarceration and in the lessons to be learned from this national experience. This World War II event has been in the news, as columnists and politicians debate the proper balance between civil liberties and security (p. 213).*

By reading quality historical nonfiction, you and your students will encounter examples similar to the ones shown here. When you do, consider whether the author's suggestion of what is historically significant seems valid. That is, do you agree with it? Do your students? Do other authors?

The next section describes how Debbi Aizenstain and I encouraged students in her fifth-grade class to try their hands at determining historical significance. As we did for the activities at the end of Chapter 3, we combined the essential elements of history teaching—historical thinking, historical nonfiction literature, and hands-on experience—to create a memorable experience for students. And once again, we tapped theory and research and put them into practice.

What Activities Help Students Understand the Concept of Historical Significance?

In order to help students put the concept of historical significance to work, Debbi and I carried out the following six-week plan, focusing on Japanese internment, the forced imprisonment of Japanese Americans following the attack on Pearl Harbor during World War II:

* **Weeks 1–3:** Teaching students to read with a focus on historical significance—both personal and social.

* **Week 4:** Guiding students as they shaped their conclusions about historical significance.

* **Weeks 5 and 6:** Introducing the R.A.F.T. strategy to encourage a variety of written responses.

WEEKS 1–3: READING WITH A FOCUS ON HISTORICAL SIGNIFICANCE

Drawing on the research in historical significance, Debbi and I kept in mind that views about significance vary from student to student. When reading history, we expected her fifth-grade students to have different ideas about what is important enough to remember and why. Their thinking would be influenced by what they had learned inside and outside of school, and they would bring these different ideas into the classroom.

We also anticipated some developmental hurdles—that is, students might not have progressed far enough in their thinking to consider all the criteria for determining historical significance. Researcher Lis Cercadillo (2001) has, in fact, made the case for a progression in students' thinking. Results of her study show that younger students tend to see significance in terms of how an event affected people living at the time of the event—contemporary significance. She suggests that contemporary significance might be how students begin to learn to distinguish what is important, and that other ideas develop later. If this is the case, our students might not have been thinking about other criteria, such as how an event from the past could have significance in the present.

Finally, we also knew that personal relevance—the I-can-relate-to-it factor—would vary among students. We would have to help students establish personal connections to the past.

Keeping these ideas in mind, we began by telling students that they would be reading about an event in the past and deciding for themselves what was important to remember about it—if anything—and why. We acknowledged that they might have different ideas about this event and that it would be interesting for us to discuss these ideas.

"The central matter . . . is that students understand how and why things can be important in the past. This means not just learning that certain events or processes were important, but also how notions like significance and importance work in the discipline of history.

Lee, Ashby, and Dickinson, 2001, pp. 202–203

To provide a way for students to record their ideas, we introduced the "fact pyramid" and the "because box" (Figure 4.2). The fact pyramid (Buehl, 2001) enables students to separate essential information from nonessential information, and to prioritize the essential information. The because box provides space for students to write reasons for their ideas about significance. It requires them to think beyond "It's just my opinion" to find evidence to support their ideas. (See page 188 for a reproducible version of this chart.)

To help students determine what is important to remember about history, we led a class discussion about establishing criteria.

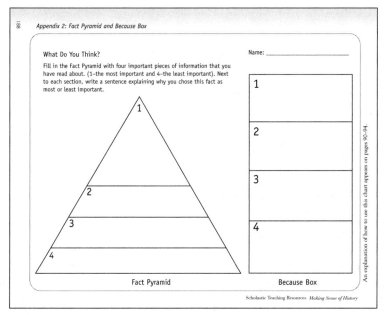

Appendix 2: Fact Pyramid and Because Box

What Do You Think?

Fill in the Fact Pyramid with four important pieces of information that you have read about. (1–the most important and 4–the least important). Next to each section, write a sentence explaining why you chose this fact as most or least important.

Name: _____

1

2

3

4

Fact Pyramid

Because Box

An explanation of how to use this chart appears on pages 90–94.

Scholastic Teaching Resources *Making Sense of History*

Figure 4.2: *Fact pyramid and because box*

We felt that this would be more effective than simply asking students what they thought was important to remember and hoping that they might stumble on some criteria—and it was. We asked the class questions such as "What makes something important enough to remember? How do you decide?" and listed their responses on a chart. Students summarized their ideas by suggesting that events are important to remember if:

* Many people were affected, not just one or two.
* Events lasted for a long time, not just a day or two.

Notice that both of these ideas relate to contemporary significance—how events affected the people who experienced them. This supports Cercadillo's claim that students begin to understand significance this way. Not one student suggested that past events might be significant because they help us understand the present, although this idea did come up in our later conversations.

After listening to the students' ideas about significance, Debbi and I then shared a chart we made based on criteria we found from researching the topic (Figure 4.3). We were surprised to see that students were already considering (1) the number of people affected (quantity), and (2) the long-lasting effects (durability). We thought that input from the chart would help students think historically, but we were also aware of the possibility that they might choose to ignore it altogether. It was interesting for us to watch and learn.

What Is Valuable and Important in History?

When people consider whether something is historically significant, they think about the following ideas:

- How important it was to people at the time
- How deeply people were affected
- The number of people affected
- How long lasting the effects were
- Whether it helps us understand current events and issues

Figure 4.3: *Determining historical significance: factors to consider*

After discussing our list of criteria with the students, Debbi and I turned to Jerry Stanley's *I Am an American* as a basis for our teaching. This book deals with the Japanese internment, the forced imprisonment of Japanese Americans during World War II solely on the basis of their ancestry. As Stanley explains,

> *The bombing of Pearl Harbor was a great tragedy in American history, but it resulted in a second tragedy that was no less important: the forced imprisonment in the United States of 120,000 people, two-thirds of whom were United States citizens. These citizens had committed no crime, broken no law, and when their rights were taken away, they were charged with no offense. Their only crime was that they were of Japanese ancestry. (p. 2)*

On February 19, 1942, President Franklin Roosevelt issued Executive Order 9066, authorizing the U.S. Army to relocate and incarcerate Japanese Americans. Even though there was no evidence that they had committed acts of sabotage or espionage, Japanese Americans were relocated to remote camps far away from U.S. military operations. These camps were enclosed by barbed-wire fences and guarded by military personnel. War hysteria, combined with racial prejudice and long-term discrimination of Japanese Americans, dominated the thinking of many Americans. The immediate appeal of the book is that it focuses on the experiences of a young man, Shiro Nomura, who is about to graduate from high school and propose marriage to his high school sweetheart when he and his family are forced to live in an internment camp. Shiro's story has emotional *I*-can-relate-to-it appeal, since we all have experienced unfairness.

Beyond its personal appeal, the book also has a broader social relevance, a *we*-can-relate-to-it appeal. It reminds us of the importance of guarding our civil rights. Although we have a Constitution with a Bill of Rights, which guarantees those rights on paper, we still need to protect them. This story is not, as Shiro Nomura tells us, only about Japanese Americans. It is about all of us as a society. All of these ideas about personal and social relevance were in my mind as Debbi and I introduced her fifth-grade students to *I Am an American*. Let's examine how the children responded.

Using the Fact Pyramid and the Because Box
to Support Discussions of Historical Significance

Debbi read aloud the introduction to *I Am an American* and briefly discussed the content with the students. Then she asked them to reread it, gave them copies of the fact pyramid and because box sheet, and asked the students to fill them in. She explained that they should write the information they felt was most important to remember on the top of the pyramid, the second most important piece of information below it, and so forth. She also instructed them to use the because box for explaining each of their decisions. In the top box, they should explain the information at the top of the pyramid, in the next box down they should explain the information on the second level of the pyramid, and so forth. If you try this, you may want to model it by reading a short selection and then writing your own fact pyramid and because box in front of your students. You might also ask your students if they agree with your choices or have other ideas about significance.

The introduction to *I Am an American*, "A Date Which Will Live in Infamy," describes the death and destruction that resulted from the bombing of Pearl Harbor and makes it clear that this was the event that caused the U.S. to enter World War II. The author goes on to explain the impact of imprisonment on 120,000 Japanese—those who were U.S. citizens and those who were not. He mentions Japanese people's attempt to prove their loyalty to the government by forming the Japanese American Citizens League. Only at the very end of the introduction, in the last paragraph, is Shiro Nomura mentioned. There are two photographs in the introduction. One photograph, on the first page, shows the bombing of Pearl Harbor. (See Figure 4.4.) On the next-to-last page is a second photograph, not of Shiro Nomura, but of typical Japanese-American high school students dressed in American clothing. Overall, Jerry Stanley's introduction emphasizes the impact of the larger event, the bombing of Pearl Harbor, and then situates within it the smaller story of what happened to Shiro Nomura.

When the class met to discuss their ideas about the introduction, I began by asking, "What did you find important enough to remember? Why?" Even though I expected a variety of responses, it was still exciting to witness. Students shared the ideas from their fact pyramids and because boxes. Some students, like Areeba, selected broad social issues (Figure 4.5). She referred to the number of people affected by the bombing of Pearl Harbor ("2,335 servicemen were killed") and the number of people imprisoned in relocation camps ("120,000 people—two-thirds were United States citizens . . ."). She also referred to the importance of these events for people living at the time. She mentioned, for example, that Asians were considered nonwhite and suggested that they were treated "the way they treated African Americans."

Figure 4.4: *First page of* I Am an American

In contrast, Simran focused on "fairness" issues, explaining how unfairly the Japanese Americans were treated (Figure 4.6). Simran suggested that ". . . the Japanese people had done nothing," "that they thought that they were Americans," and even so ". . . the Americans didn't want them living with them." This I-can-relate-to-it response stems from a common theme in elementary and middle-school thinking—the need for fair treatment of everyone. Even though Areeba and Simran selected some of the same events, they did so for different reasons.

When all the students shared ideas about what was historically significant and why, the variety of viewpoints came through loud and clear. We got similar results as we read and discussed the rest of the book, and I welcomed them. Our discussions provided an opportunity to hear a variety of responses and to respectfully acknowledge them. These discussions were interesting for all of us. Instead of the single correct answers that are often associated with learning history, we had a variety of original, related ideas to exchange, ponder, and debate.

For each chapter, students completed a fact pyramid and because box, which prepared them for discussions. Personal and social responses dominated these discussions as we continued reading the book. When discussing a chapter about the evacuation of Japanese from their homes, for example, Simran was still pointing out that the evacuation "wasn't fair," and Areeba was pointing out the social impact of trying to act "un-Japanese" on "family traditions and Asian heritage."

In addition, several students pointed out the need to learn from our mistakes—the relevance for today. In discussions of how the U.S. government finally admitted that the internment was unjust, many students noted that it was important to recognize mistakes and learn from them. One student wrote that "the camps were a mistake and Americans should know," while another stated that the internment "was a disgrace to freedom and human rights."

What Do You Think?

Fill in the Fact Pyramid with four important pieces of information that you have read about (1—the most important—to 4—the least important). Next to each section, write a sentence explaining why you chose this fact as most or least important.

Name: Areeba

Fact Pyramid

1 On December 7,1941 Japanese warplanes bombed the United States Naval Base at Pearl Harbor, Hawaii. United States then declared war on Japan, and it's allies.

2 During World War II, on February 19, 1942 Japanese were removed from the west and were imprisoned in relocation camps.

3 In 1930, the Nisei formed the Japanese American Citizens League to fight discrimination against the Japanese and demonstrate Nisei loyalty to America.

4 The Naturalization Act of 1790 limited citizenship to "any alien, being a free white person." African Americans had been granted citizenship in 1870.

Because Box

1 Because nineteen ships were destroyed and 2,335 service-man were killed. It is just like what happened on 9/11. A honored landmark was destroyed and lives were lost.

2 Because 120,000 people - two thirds were United States citizens, were imprisoned. They had committed no crime, had broken no law and their rights were taken away.

3 Because, it was influential on Washington, Oregon and California, were 9.5 percent of the Japanese lived. They also recited their own pledge to show loyalty for America.

4 Because Asians were considered non-white. They should be treated like whites. It is just like the way they treated African-Americans.

What Do You Think?

Fill in the Fact Pyramid with four important pieces of information that you have read about (1—the most important—to 4—the least important). Next to each section, write a sentence explaining why you chose this fact as most or least important.

Name: Simran

Fact Pyramid

1 Japanese people were imprisoned because they were Japanese.

2 The war which killed many people and destroyed ships.

3 The Nisei wanted to show people that they were loyal to America.

4 The Japanese people were taken to the location camps.

Because Box

1 Because the Japanese people had done nothing and they were imprisoned.

2 Because this is why the Japanese people were imprisoned.

3 Because they thought they were Americans.

4 Because the Americans didn't want them living with them.

Figures 4.5 and 4.6: *Areeba and Simran's fact pyramids and because boxes*

Chapter 4: Historical Significance

The issue of remembrance, which Keith Barton (2005) cited as a historically significant factor for students in Northern Ireland, also surfaced here. One student concluded that "having a special occasion or site to remember such an injustice is important so that we don't make the same mistakes again." What he is saying is that a monument and/or a special day recognizing what happened to Japanese Americans during World War II might prevent us from denying other citizens their rights and freedoms without cause. It would keep this event alive in our collective memory.

All of these divergent responses provided Debbi and me with weeks of interesting conversation. Students not only drew from their knowledge of *I Am an American*, but had the option of consulting other books as well.

Week 4: Shaping Conclusions About Historical Significance

While students were willing—even eager—to read with a focus on historical significance at the start of the six-week study, their understandings were limited by their background knowledge. As they were reading about the Japanese internment, they were learning how it all turned out. They didn't know it from the beginning. As Hunt (2000) and Lee, Ashby, and Dickinson (2001) pointed out, ideas of significance are reshaped over time and according to different time scales. So Debbi and I wondered, Would our students think differently after learning about the entire event? Would knowing how it turned out affect their ideas about historical significance?

To find out, we gave students a final, enlarged version of the fact pyramid and because box for them to use when considering everything they knew about the Japanese internment. This enlarged version provided plenty of space for students to explain their thinking. We asked them, once again, to consider, What is worth knowing and remembering? Why?

Areeba, who originally responded to broader social aspects of the internment, was now including issues of fairness. She wrote about Japanese Americans being forced to "sell their belongings and leave their homes because they were being punished for crimes that they didn't commit!" She mentioned the impact of rumors and phony stories. Simran, who originally responded to issues of fairness, now included broader social aspects of the internment. She wrote about the impact of the internment, noting that "the number of people affected were all the Japanese people in the west coast." She also introduced the concept of perspective when she wrote "I think that the whites should have put themselves in the shoes of the Japanese and thought more carefully." Perhaps this mix of personal and social factors was the result of the classroom discussions. Areeba and Simran heard a range of ideas expressed by their classmates and may have incorporated some of what they heard into their own thinking.

In these enlarged pyramids and because boxes, students listed ideas that captured the full range of criteria for determining historical significance from Figure 4.1. Debbi and I shared these ideas during class discussions, providing an opportunity for students to hear what their classmates thought about the Japanese internment now that they had a more complete picture of it. Here are just a few of their ideas:

* **Contemporary Significance: How Important Was It to People at the Time?** "The attack on Pearl Harbor killed many people and destroyed a historical landmark, the Pearl Harbor Naval Base. This event changed people's opinion toward the Japanese."

* **Profundity: How Deeply Were People Affected?** "The government found out the total cost of property and income lost by Japanese Americans was $6.2 billion in today's dollars. This is very significant because a lot of people were affected deeply, and the effect lasted almost for the rest of their lives."

* **Quantity: How Many People Were Affected?** "On December 7, 1941, the Japanese warplanes bombed the United States Naval Base at Pearl Harbor, Hawaii. This is important because it affected a lot of Japanese. They destroyed nineteen ships and 2,335 servicemen were killed. The Americans don't trust the Japanese anymore. They think that Japanese are dangerous because they're part of [sic] the Japanese ancestry."

* **Durability: How Long Lasting Were the Effects?** "After America won the war, white people still treated the Japanese cruelly. The Japanese fought for them and many white folks still refused to accept the Japanese. Some white people even refused to cut Japanese hair."

* **Relevance: How Does It Help Us Understand Current Issues and Events?** "President Franklin D. Roosevelt said that Pearl Harbor was 'a date which will live in infamy.' This is important because it is showing the long-lasting feeling of Pearl Harbor and that it will never be forgotten. It shouldn't be forgotten because America will not make that mistake again, and it will remind us that everybody that lives in America is an American."

Students can apply the concept of historical significance in their reading, writing, and thinking, so address significance no matter what curriculum topic you are exploring. Students want to believe that what they are learning is valuable and relevant to their lives. They need to "relate" to it, plain and simple. Using the fact pyramid and the because box helps you make these connections visible.

WEEKS 5 AND 6: INTRODUCING THE R.A.F.T. WRITING STRATEGY TO ENCOURAGE A VARIETY OF WRITTEN RESPONSES

Because students spent so much time reading about and discussing the Japanese internment, they knew a great deal of information that they could further explore through writing. The strategy we used—R.A.F.T.—encouraged them to examine the Japanese internment from a variety of perspectives. The R.A.F.T. strategy is a way to jump-start student writing by isolating four key elements:

* **R**ole: Who is writing?

* **A**udience: Who is being addressed?

* **F**ormat: What is the genre or type of writing?

* **T**opic: What is being written about?

R.A.F.T. (Buehl, 2001; Gallavan & Kottler, 2002) broadens the scope of student writing. According to Buehl, using R.A.F.T. "involves writing from a viewpoint other than that of a student, to an audience other than the teacher, and in a form other than a standard theme or written answers to a question" (Buehl, p. 114). But the strategy accomplishes even more: it requires that students reread the text (or texts) to select information to include in their writing. Gallavan and Kottler report that "the repetition serves as a reinforcement to increase retention and provides a structure for students to personalize the information . . ." (p. 267).

We tapped into both of these benefits when our students used R.A.F.T. to write about the Japanese internment. First, they wrote in forms that included the protest letter, poetry, persuasive argument, journal, and friendly letter. In that way, we bypassed the standard question-and-answer formats. Second, students quite naturally began to reread as a way of refreshing their memories and searching for useful details.

To begin, Debbi constructed a grid based on the four key elements—Role, Audience, Format, and Topic. In the R, A, and T columns she filled in people and events in *I Am an American*. In the F column, she filled in appropriate writing genres. (See Figure 4.7.)

Her completed grid gave students a range of interesting choices. It was far better than reporting back information. The individual R.A.F.T. prompts—which were created using the elements across each row—challenged students to think about the perspectives of a variety of people and to use formats that they may not have considered for writing about the past. Based on Figure 4.7, these are the prompts we used:

* **Prompt #1:** You are Shi and you are very angry about the Japanese internment. So you decide to write a letter of protest to President Roosevelt, making it clear how much you object to the government's policy.

* **Prompt #2:** You are Amy and you miss Shi very much. It is his birthday, so you have written a special poem to him to share your feelings and to wish him a happy birthday. Along with the poem, you are sending him a sweater you made.

* **Prompt #3:** You are General DeWitt and you are convinced that the Japanese pose a serious threat to U.S. security. They must be rounded up and placed in internment camps. You decide to write a letter to Congress, persuading them to do this immediately.

* **Prompt #4:** You are A. T. Tjaden, a farmer in northern Montana, and you have never seen a Japanese person before. Write a journal entry, recording your impressions of them. Describe how surprised you were that they could speak English.

* **Prompt #5:** You are Mrs. Ruby McFarland, the sympathetic and caring neighbor of the Nomura family. Write a friendly letter to the family, explaining how you are taking care of their property while they are in the internment camp.

R.A.F.T.

Role	Audience	Format	Topic
Shi	President Roosevelt	Protest Letter	Japanese Internment
Amy	Shi	Poem	Birthday
General DeWitt	Congress	Persuasive Argument	Why the Japanese should be interned
Tjaden	Himself	Journal	About the Japanese workers on furlough
Mrs. Ruby McFarland	Mr. & Mrs. Nomura	Friendly Letter	About the internment and their property

Figure 4.7: *R.A.F.T. grid*

Examples of student writing show how successful the R.A.F.T. strategy was in prompting students to present facts with feeling:

Ichien   *Manzanar Internment Camp*
                             Block 21
                            April 25, 1942

Dear President Roosevelt,

*   The Japanese need freedom!*

*   I can't believe we have to be interned, just because we're of Japanese ancestry. We are citizens of this country, America, and we deserve to be free. Why should we be interned?*

*   The internment camps are horrible! We don't even have any privacy. We can't even use the bathroom alone. We have to sit back to back with others when we use the bathroom. Do you think that's appropriate? The only thing that separates us from strangers are sheets. It's not fair! The sections where we live in the camps have no closets, cupboards or furniture. The food doesn't even taste good. Everything in the camp is terrible!*

*   There was also an incident where an old man was too close to the barbed wire fence, and got shot by a soldier. The man wasn't even going to escape! Do you even know how the man's family felt? I'll bet they feel very depressed, and they can't take this anymore!*

*   Please just think about how we feel. Do you think that even kids are a danger to National Security? It is difficult for me to imagine that you think all Japanese are perilous.*

*   How would you feel if you were imprisoned?*

*   We just need liberty! We have been loyal to this country, and this what we get back?*

*   Sincerely,*
*   Shiro Nomura*

In a letter from Shiro Nomura to President Roosevelt, the student writer implores President Roosevelt to think about how the Japanese feel:

Please just think about how we feel. Do you think that even kids are a danger to National Security? It is difficult for me to imagine that you think all Japanese are perilous.

A birthday poem to Shi that accompanies a gift from his girlfriend Amy, who is interned in another camp, requests:

Each time you wear this sweater
Remember me please.

Happy Birthday Poem to Shi

Oh, Shi, the birthday boy,
Wishing you all my love!
Happy Birthday!
Here is a sweet gift I made.

I couldn't find any others.
I hope it is your favorite color,
Each time you wear this sweater
Remember me please.

I can't believe
That even though we all showed our loyalty
It didn't pay off
And we still got interned.

I wanted to tell you something
But I know that
Someone will read this letter
before you.

After internment,
Let's see if we get married.
Happy Birthday!

Paarth

Persuasive Argument to Congress

Dear Congress,

    I'm writing to inform you that all Japanese are enemies! First, they attacked Pearl Harbor and now the Japanese living in America are saboteurs! I don't care if they are citizens or not! They are still aiding Japan.

    The Japanese are aiding Japan by planting crops in the shape of an arrow, so it will show the Japanese bombers where to attack next. The Japanese are also trying to invade the West coast. For example, the Issei fishermen have Japanese naval uniforms hidden in their boats waiting for the invasion.

    The Japanese who are trying to prove they are loyal, are disloyal to America in every way! They are saboteurs! They hid all the evidence that proved they were loyal to Japan from us when we were searching, to make it seem like they weren't saboteurs!

    The Japanese don't deserve any rights as citizens of this wonderful and great country. To stop the Japanese from aiding Japan, I have a plan! Executive Order No. 9066, is an order that will give the military the power to remove the Japanese from the West Coast.

    If you want the Japanese moved into relocation camps, sign the Executive Order No. 9066.

                   Sincerely,

Niveditha   General John.L.Dewitt

A letter from General John Dewitt to members of Congress argues that the Japanese are disloyal:

The Japanese who are trying to prove they are loyal, are disloyal to America in every way! They are saboteurs! They hid all the evidence that proved they were loyal to Japan from us when we were searching, to make it seem like they weren't saboteurs!

Making Sense of History

Tjaden's Journal

May 24, 1942

Dear Journal,

Today was the crew's first day out on the field harvesting beets. The Japanese really weren't what I had expected. When they arrived I was expecting to see a bunch of men with horn-rimmed glasses, narrow slitted eyes and buckteeth. What I saw was very different. Even though their skin color was a little different and they did have slitted eyes, they seemed like regular people.

They also spoke perfect English. Who would have thought that a Japanese person could speak perfect English.

They looked surprised when my wife served them a hearty breakfast of bacon, eggs and milk.

I really believe that the government was wrong about the Japanese being saboteurs, because while the crew has been here, they haven't tried to do anything wrong. They have only tried to help me harvest my beets and I am also very grateful. I really wish I could pay them more than $2.00 a week.

The crew did fairly well on their first day. They seemed to get the quick lesson on harvesting beets. The man named Shi cut open the back of his left hand with the barb and cut open a vein. Boy, I tell ya that was one bloody mess!

I wonder what the crew will do on Saturday in the town while I drive down to Conrad.

Caitlin

A diary entry from a farmer named Tjaden records his surprise that the Japanese workers "seemed like regular people":

When they arrived I was expecting to see a bunch of men with horn-rimmed glasses, narrow slitted eyes and buckteeth. What I saw was very different. Even though their skin color was a little different and they did have slitted eyes, they seemed like regular people.

Sol   *Berkeley, California*

May 21, 1942

Dear Hachizo and Tsuru Nomura,

I am sorry about your family's internment. I am taking care of your property like I promised to.

Your vegetables and fruits are growing splendidly. I give water to them everyday and cultivate the soil. I'm not an expert on farming like you, but I try my best.

People come to me daily and offer low prices for your property, but I say, "NO"! Whites try to steal the crops at night. I am ashamed of my kind.

I stored all of your furniture in my basement, so nobody can take it. I go to your house all the time to check on it, and I also clean your furniture to keep it nice and clean. Until you come back, I will take care of your property at my best!

Best Wishes,
Ruby McFarland

A letter from a sympathetic neighbor emphasizes that she will care for the Nomura family's property:

I stored all of your furniture in my basement, so nobody can take it. I go to your house all the time to check on it, and I also clean your furniture to keep it nice and clean. Until you come back, I will take care of your property at my best!

Chapter 4: Historical Significance

The R.A.F.T. strategy was useful in helping the class capture the variety of viewpoints that coexisted at the time of the Japanese internment. The writing that it inspired showed quite clearly that some people were sympathetic to the Japanese and some weren't. And some, like the farmer in the Midwest, had no knowledge of the Japanese at all except for the propaganda he had heard.

> ### TEACHING IDEA
>
> ....
>
> **Use R.A.F.T. in Social Studies and Beyond**
>
> After you have demonstrated how to use the R.A.F.T. strategy, encourage students to try it on their own. Not only is the strategy useful for writing about history, it can also be applied to writing about science and mathematics.

Concluding Thoughts

Nobody wants to learn things considered irrelevant, useless, and boring. Yet, I am sorry to say, these terms are often applied to history. One way to turn matters around is to focus learning on things considered relevant, useful, and intriguing. When students are allowed to decide what is historically significant, the content they value becomes the focus of discussion. In an age-appropriate way, they learn to do what historians do—emphasize what they consider valuable and deemphasize the rest. That's reading, writing, and thinking according to the historian's "rules of the game." It is an authentic experience.

Acknowledging multiple perspectives is another important part of historical thinking. The next chapter explains how this might become the focus of reading, writing, and thinking about the past. It deals with the question "How can I help students understand that people in the past did not all see things the same way?"

Chapter 5

Multiple Perspectives

How Can I Help Students Understand That People in the Past Did Not All See Things the Same Way?

* In the 1770s, before the American Revolution, did *all* American colonists support a revolt against the British?
* In the early 1900s, during the Industrial Revolution, did *all* Americans believe child labor was good for children?
* Before 1920, when women were denied the right to vote, did *all* men in the U.S. oppose women's suffrage?

The answer to all of these questions is an emphatic "No!" First, some American colonists had no problem with British rule. According to historian Christopher Collier, "Large numbers of people were neither Whig [Patriot] nor Tory [Loyalist] and just wished to get on with their lives" (Collier, 1999, p. 4). Second, not all Americans in the 1900s believed that child labor benefited young people, but some did. An investor in a southern textile mill commented, "The most beautiful sight that we can see is the child at labor" (Meltzer, 1994, p. 64). Third, there were many male supporters of women's suffrage. In 1870, when Victoria Woodhull was nominated for president of the United States at the convention of the Equal Rights Party, "Men shouted themselves hoarse, standing on their seats, throwing hats in the air" (Krull, 2004b).

Our challenge as teachers is to show students that no single voice explains what happened in the past. Instead, as illustrated by the questions and answers above, there are multiple voices and multiple perspectives. Researcher Linda Levstik suggests that we teach "a perspectival history" so that students encounter what historians refer to as "an ever growing chorus of voices" (Levstik 1997, p. 48). In that way, students learn about the complexity of history and do not see it as a simple narrative told from a single point of view.

In this chapter, I explain why it is important to teach the concept of multiple perspectives and how to teach it. To begin, I explain the theory and research that have implications for everyday practice. Then I discuss historical nonfiction literature that you can use to introduce the concept to students. Finally, I explain how I have taught multiple perspectives, first with one fourth grader and then with teacher Debbi Aizenstain and her entire fifth-grade class.

As in earlier chapters, the following questions based on three essential elements of history teaching—historical thinking, historical nonfiction literature, and hands-on experience—guide the discussion:

* What do theory and research tell us about multiple perspectives?

* How does nonfiction literature contribute to an understanding of multiple perspectives?

* What activities help students understand the concept of multiple perspectives?

What Do Theory and Research Tell Us About Multiple Perspectives?

Current scholarship focuses on two types of thinking required for understanding multiple perspectives—*imaginative* thinking and *analytic* thinking. Imaginative thinking is based on wondering, supposing, and empathizing, while analytic thinking is based on evidence, context, and chronology. Both types of thinking work together: imaginative thinking leads us to creative ideas and analytic thinking helps us hold these ideas in check by keeping them rooted in evidence (Davis, 2001). These notions have implications for classroom practice:

* ✱ Students must be able to think *imaginatively* and *analytically* to understand multiple perspectives.

* ✱ Although students cannot feel the actual feelings of people from the past, they can understand that people held different perspectives. They can understand what caused people to think and act the way they did.

STUDENTS MUST BE ABLE TO THINK *IMAGINATIVELY* AND *ANALYTICALLY* TO UNDERSTAND MULTIPLE PERSPECTIVES

Understanding how people thought and acted in the past means learning to balance imaginative and analytic thinking. If imaginative thinking dominates, students leap into the realm of fantasy, beyond the bounds of credible history. If analytic thinking dominates, students become buried in emotionless facts—and, most likely, bored. When the two types of thinking work together, though, true historical thinking emerges. Researcher O. L. Davis, Jr., explains this balance as "thinking about particular people, events, and situations in their *context*, and from *wonderment* about reasonable and possible meanings within . . ." (2001, p. 3 [italics added]).

Because imaginative thinking can take students beyond the bounds of evidence, many theorists and researchers oppose classroom practices that require students to identify with historical characters and claim to feel what they felt. Stuart Foster, for example, emphasizes that students should not try to "get behind the eyeballs of people in the past or 'identify' with them" (1999, p. 19). Instead, he suggests that they should develop an "appreciation of historical context and chronology," "thorough analysis and evaluation of historical evidence," and "appreciation of the consequences of actions perpetrated in the past" (1999, p. 19).

Matthew Downey, too, takes a similar stand for intellectual, evidence-based practices. He defines perspective taking as an "attempt to understand an historical character's frame of reference, without assuming that one can or need identify with his or her feelings" (1996, p. 115). Instead, it is "constructed on the basis of historical information and evidence" (p. 115).

Deborah Cunningham (2004) identified a number of dilemmas that arose when teachers tried to balance imaginative and analytic thinking. She found that teachers struggled to help students understand the perspectives of people from the past and keep their work securely connected to historical evidence. While using imagination enhanced some students' perspective taking, it didn't for others. Cunningham found that flights of fancy clearly don't work. Students need to ground their work in evidence. She also found that teachers worried about whether students would be able to connect emotionally with figures from the past. They might, instead, be overwhelmed by facts and fail to identify with those figures. These dilemmas have been reported by other researchers as well (Foster, 2001; Yeager & Foster, 2001).

In spite of these cautions and criticisms, I believe it is unwise to drop imaginative thinking from the history curriculum. Instead, it is important to help students maintain a balance between imaginative and analytic thinking. When studying multiple perspectives on the past, we can encourage students to use imaginative thinking to see the world as others did, while at the same time emphasizing the need to support this thinking with evidence. This is not an impossible task. Elizabeth Ann Yeager and Stuart Foster sum up this approach by suggesting, "historical empathy combines the adductive and logical thinking associated with the use of evidence and the inferential and appropriately creative skills that seek to bridge the gap between what is known and what may be inferred from history" (2001, p. 15). In short, perspective taking involves imagination and analysis.

STUDENTS CAN UNDERSTAND WHAT CAUSED PEOPLE TO THINK AND ACT THE WAY THEY DID

Sherry Field, editor of the journal *Social Studies and the Young Learner*, notes that "to teachers of young children, teaching for empathy typically is understood as helping children to gain historical perspective and to understand others" (Field, 2001, p. 115). In a study of twelve volumes of the journal, Field found a wide-ranging collection of articles dealing with understanding multiple perspectives. After reviewing these articles, she concluded that "elementary social studies teachers understand that children can and do learn to take perspectives at a young age" (p. 130). We do our students a disservice when we don't teach multiple perspectives because we think they can't handle it. Research shows that they can.

Journal articles and books continue to feature reports of successful perspective-taking activities in elementary and middle school. For example, Theresa McCormick (2004) writes about how fifth graders studying the American Revolution wrote letters as if they were eyewitness to the Battle of Trenton. Tarry Lindquist (2002) reports that as part of their study of the Civil

War, students in her class wrote "newspapers" from three different perspectives—Southern whites, Northern whites, and free blacks. Eula Fresch, in her book *Connecting Children with Children, Past and Present* (2004), shows how students used historical photographs of children who worked in factories approximately one hundred years ago to raise questions about these children's lives and then try to answer the questions the way the factory children might have. These books and articles provide evidence that students can successfully engage in perspective taking.

Following the leads of teachers Theresa McCormick, Tarry Lindquist, and Eula Fresch, we can provide students with exercises for examining perspectives that coexisted in the past. We should do this not because students can do it, though, but because it promotes historical understanding. As British researchers Peter Lee and Rosalyn Ashby (2001) note, ". . . historical understanding comes from knowing how people saw things, knowing what they tried to do, and knowing *that* they felt the appropriate feelings . . ." (p. 25).

How Does Nonfiction Literature Contribute to an Understanding of Multiple Perspectives?

Authors of historical nonfiction literature often present the past from multiple perspectives because it is an effective way to capture the complexity of history without overwhelming young learners. While always basing those perspectives on factual information, authors sometimes tell them through imagined voices and sometimes through real voices. Imagined voices—for example, of an Egyptian scribe discussing his work—reflect a more imaginative slant toward multiple perspectives. Real voices—for example, of an actual immigrant describing her experiences—reflect a more analytic slant toward multiple perspectives. This section explains these two types of literature:

* Factual information, imagined voices
* Factual information, real voices

FACTUAL INFORMATION, IMAGINED VOICES

When authors use imagined voices, they put words into the mouths of people of the past, words that are based on fact. These authors make it clear that their presentation is firmly rooted in fact by presenting their sources of information in bibliographies, historical notes, and authors' notes. They often acknowledge fact checkers, experts in the field who have reviewed their manuscript for accuracy of text and illustration.

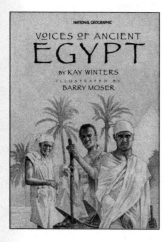

The book *Voices of Ancient Egypt* (2003), written by Kay Winters and illustrated by Barry Moser, presents the imagined voices of thirteen types of workers from the time of the pharaohs: scribe, farmer, pyramid builder, herdsman, bird netter, washer of clothes, weaver, goldsmith, embalmer, dancer, carpenter, sailor, and marshman. These workers speak for themselves, giving readers an understanding of their different roles and experiences. Winters presents some jobs as more prestigious and privileged than others. The scribe sees his job this way:

While others bear lashes to build tombs,
dodge crocodiles to fish the Nile,
weave cloth in airless rooms,
I unlock secrets in ancient scrolls,
weave wisdom from times gone by.
In a kilt of white, I measure the Nile,
count the cattle, register the harvest. (p. 5)

In a historical note about ancient Egypt, Winters tells readers, "…I have tried to re-create the voices of people who might have lived, worked, played, and died during this time" (p. 30). She was able to do this because she thoroughly researched her topic. Based on this research, Winters also includes a paragraph of additional information about each type of worker. A bibliography follows. In addition, the author, illustrator, and publisher thank a museum curator for reviewing the text and illustrations. All of these features provide the factual support for this imaginative text.

Voices of the Alamo (2000), written by Sherry Garland and illustrated by Ronald Himler, provides a series of imagined voices from the 1500s to today, discussing the history of the Alamo. Garland presents a chronological sequence of short free-verse poems in the voices of an Indian woman, a Spanish *conquistador*, a missionary, a Spanish soldier, a rancher, a farmer, a young tourist visiting the Alamo today, and others. What emerges is a complex array of perspectives. The Indian girl tells us:

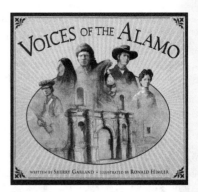

I am a Payaya maiden,
gathering pecans beside the river.
When flowers blanket these hills in spring
and buffalo thunder across the plains,
my heart sings with joy.
But this earth does not belong to me,
for who can own the wind or rain? (unpaged)

This perspective is fascinating in and of itself, but when we compare it to the perspectives of others, it becomes even richer. For example, the *conquistador* states, "I search for cities of gold and take what I please" (unpaged). We can then contrast those views with those of the farmer from the United States, who states "this land is mine" (unpaged) and with those of General Santa Anna who saw the Texans as "illegally taking Mexican lands" (unpaged).

Like *Voices of Ancient Egypt*, this book contains a number of features that provide factual support for the imagined voices. An acknowledgment tells us that a historian and curator of the Alamo reviewed both text and illustrations for historical accuracy. The author includes an extensive, research-based note explaining the history of the Alamo from the 1500s to the present. A glossary of Spanish words and phrases, a selected bibliography, and suggestions for further reading are also included. These features help readers appreciate the factual basis of the book.

FACTUAL INFORMATION, REAL VOICES

Some authors choose to use the real voices of people from the past and present by capturing their words in interviews and historical documents such as newspapers, letters, and diaries. Two types of real voices—the voices of young people and the voices of ordinary people—are particularly important to introduce to students because they show that history isn't only about high-profile and/or high-ranking adults. It is about everyone.

Voices of Young People

In his compelling introduction to *We Were There, Too! Young People in U.S. History* (2001), Phillip Hoose explains the importance of presenting multiple perspectives on history to students. He states that ". . . no single person's story, even that of a president, tells enough about a historical event or time. There are

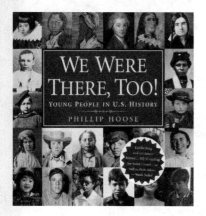

always other perspectives worth understanding" (p. vii). The particular focus of this book is on the "stories of young people who were a part of U.S. history between 1492 and the present" (p. vi).

This extensive collection is extremely useful if you want to include children's experiences in your history curriculum. A section entitled "Hard Times: Wars, Depression, and Dust," for example, tells the stories of real children from the beginning of World War I through the end of World War II. The author profiles children who lived during the dust storms and the Great Depression of the 1930s, such as 13-year-old Harley Holladay. Here is Harley's description of what happened when the storms of Black Sunday hit Kansas in 1935, as reported by Hoose:

> *For a long time it was total blackness inside, except for one thing. When I looked out the window I could see our radio antenna outlined in static electricity. There were little balls of fire all over it caused by dirt particles rubbing together. It was*

TEACHING IDEA

Use Factual Information to Create Imagined Voices

After reading aloud *Voices of Ancient Egypt* or *Voices of the Alamo*, challenge students to create imagined voices from a time period or event they are currently studying, by writing free-verse poems, stories, journal entries, or letters. If your class is studying the Civil War, for example, students can write in these voices:

- a Confederate soldier
- a Union soldier
- a Northern boy or girl
- a Southern boy or girl
- a woman whose husband or son is fighting
- a free African American person
- an enslaved African American person
- a newspaper reporter

Students can assemble their pieces in a class book and include a bibliography, historical note, authors' note, and acknowledgment to prove the factual basis of their work.

Making Sense of History

spooky. Finally the sun began to shine as a faint glow of orange light coming through the windows. As it got lighter, I could see baskets and brush sailing past us. It felt like we were flying through space. (pp. 196–197)

By describing the dust storms as "spooky" and explaining how they caused people to feel like they "were flying through space," Harley enables young readers to see the event as he saw it.

Similarly, 15-year-old Peggy Eaton gives us her perspective on the Great Depression by describing her experiences "ridin' the rails." Peggy and her friend Irene left Wyoming and headed for Washington in search of opportunity. During their journey, they joined a group of indigent travelers and hopped on board a freight train. Here is her description of that experience:

When the engine started up a wave of bums rose up like one person and rushed for that open door. I was the first one there. Someone behind me picked me up by the nape of the neck and the seat of the pants and pitched me into the car. Irene was right behind me. It was dark inside, and scary. We were the only girls. (pp. 199–200)

Peggy gives us a sense of the fear and excitement she felt. It was "dark" and "scary." She and Irene "were the only girls." And yet, during this time of desperation, she was cared for by men she typically referred to as "bums." Were they really just desperate young men facing the same problems she was? Peggy's experiences make us realize that all girls and young women didn't just sit back passively, waiting for the Depression to end.

In the foreword to S. Beth Atkin's *Voices from the Fields: Children of Migrant Farmworkers Tell Their Stories* (1993), Francisco Jiménez of Santa Clara University explains that "this book gives a voice to the children of migrant farmworkers, our country's most exploited and deprived group of people" (p. 5). Atkin, who interviewed migrant workers in the Salinas Valley, tells readers that "workers were friendly when I approached them in the fields, and always willing to talk to me" (p. 6). As a result, she was able to collect poetry written by migrant children and conduct extensive interviews with them. The voices of these children are strong and clear, as proven in a passage in which 12-year-old Julisa Velarde describes the confusion of moving from place to place:

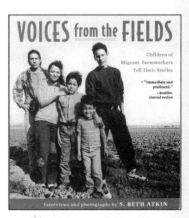

VOICES from the FIELDS

Children of
Migrant Farmworkers
Tell Their Stories

"Immediate and profound."
—*Booklist,*
starred review

Interviews and photographs by S. BETH ATKIN

When we move, sometimes I don't remember where I am. Once in Yuma, I woke up in the middle of the night, and I saw my aunt and I didn't know where I was. I was scared because I thought I was still in Salinas and I didn't know what she was doing there. To remember better where I am, I bring special things with me. (p. 23)

Nine-year-old José Luis Ríos tells about working the fields instead of going to school:

My parents work in la fresa *[the strawberries] and* la mora *[the raspberries], and my mom sometimes packs mushrooms. During the week, they leave in the morning around six o'clock. I go and help them, mostly on weekends. I help pick*

TEACHING IDEA

Write Poetry About Real Experiences

In addition to interviews, *Voices from the Fields* includes poems by children of migrant workers. In a poem about picking strawberries, Silvino M. Murillo hints at his aspirations for the future. The poem ends this way:

> The strawberry worker says good-bye again
> to go and cut more berries
> even though his back is twisted,
> in spite of his headaches.
>
> I say good-bye now
> because I'm not a strawberry worker.
> My back won't get twisted
> because I'm a writer.

After sharing this poem and others in *Voices from the Fields,* have students write poems about their experiences as young people and their aspirations for the future. Remind them that, since they are part of history, their experiences and aspirations count. Here are some topics for students to write about:

- Work
- Play
- School
- Travel
- Important People in Their Lives
- Memories
- Difficulties and Obstacles
- Goals
- What or Whom They Admire

Making Sense of History

the strawberries and put them in boxes. Last year my father took me to the fields a lot during the week, too, instead of bringing me to school. (p. 12)

Although José reports that he likes helping his parents, he is under the legal age to work. His experiences, along with Julisa's, raise questions about the obstacles migrant children face in getting an education and realizing their hopes and dreams. The labor system requires that families move from place to place, following the harvest—and nobody feels the impact more intensely than the children. By using their real voices, Atkin reveals how they cope.

Voices of Ordinary People

History includes the common, everyday experiences of ordinary people—and, therefore, the best nonfiction for children includes them also. Two books by Milton Meltzer provide a collage of voices of ordinary people caught up in wartime experiences: *The American Revolutionaries: A History in Their Own Words, 1750–1800* (1987/1993) and *Voices from the Civil War: A Documentary History of the Great American Conflict* (1989/1992).

In *The American Revolutionaries: A History in Their Own Words, 1750–1800*, Meltzer states that "the focus here is not so much on official papers as on the experiences and observations of ordinary Americans, men or women, young and old. They speak in their own words" (pp. xi–xii). As such, when discussing the Battle of Lexington, Meltzer includes the written words of a shoemaker living in Woburn, Massachusetts, who states, "I immediately arose, took my gun, and with Robert Douglass went in haste to Lexington" (p. 53). The shoemaker then describes the arrival of the British troops in Lexington, claiming that "there was not a gun fired by any of Captain Parker's company [Patriots], within my knowledge" (p. 54). In contrast, British Lieutenant Frederick Mackenzie wrote in his diary that "during the whole of the march from Lexington the rebels kept an incessant irregular fire from all points at the column . . ."(p. 56). Historical evidence, as these quotes show, isn't so neatly packaged into an agreed-upon narrative. It's the job of historians to use eyewitness reports like these to make the best case for what happened.

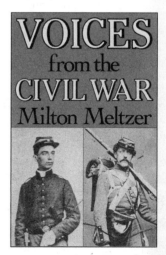

In *Voices from the Civil War: A Documentary History of the Great American Conflict*, Meltzer presents the views of contemporary people and reminds us that "their words carry the passions and prejudices of their time" (p. xi). For example, in describing the two presidents serving in 1861—Jefferson Davis, president of the Confederate States of America, and Abraham Lincoln, president of the United States—we see these passions and prejudices at work. In his diary, William Russell of the *London Times* described Jefferson Davis this way:

> *The expression of his face is anxious, he has a very haggard, careworn, and pain-drawn look, though no trace of anything but the utmost confidence and the greatest decision could be detected in his conversation. (p. 27)*

Author Nathaniel Hawthorne, in turn, described Lincoln as "a tall, loose-jointed figure, of an exaggerated Yankee port and demeanor, whom (as being about the homeliest man I ever saw, yet by no means repulsive or disagreeable) it was impossible not to recognize as Uncle Abe" (p. 27). This honest, uncensored writing brings the subject of the Civil War alive.

As you and your students read about the past, take time to consider the perspectives of the people you are studying. What voices can you identify? How are they different? What information helps you understand what they are saying?

In the next section, I show how students' answers to these questions produces writing that is alive with information and imagination. First, I describe how a fourth grader wrote a biography of the champion swimmer Gertrude Ederle from the perspectives of nine different people. Then I describe how teacher Debbi Aizenstain and I encouraged her fifth graders to work in pairs to consider the divergent perspectives on Cleopatra, the Queen of the Nile, by those who surrounded her. In designing these activities, we combined the essential elements of history teaching—historical thinking, historical nonfiction literature, and hands-on experience—as we did in designing the activities described in earlier chapters. Once again, theory and research shaped our practice.

What Activities Help Students Understand the Concept of Multiple Perspectives?

Perspectives on people and how they behave can be a source of consensus or conflict. Do we see the actions of the current president, for example, as moral or immoral? Constructive or destructive? Appropriate or inappropriate? Progressive or out-of-date? Looking at a range of perspectives associated with just one person is a good way to introduce the concept of multiple perspectives. Using biographies, we can help students identify how different people saw another person, and what they thought of that person's actions.

INVESTIGATING A RANGE OF PERSPECTIVES: ONE STUDENT'S EXPERIENCE

Maeghan, a fourth grader, researched, planned, and wrote a book about Gertrude Ederle—the first woman to swim the English Channel—from the perspectives of nine people: Ederle's mother, father, sister, first trainer, second trainer, a newspaper editorial writer, New York City Mayor Jimmy Walker, President Calvin Coolidge, and Gertrude herself. This may seem like a daunting task for a fourth grader, but I supported Maeghan's efforts by giving her several planning sheets for capturing her ideas so that she could refine them later. Maeghan also had access to literature that served as a model of what she was striving to write on her own. In addition, she had time to read primary and secondary sources, search the Internet, and talk about Gertrude Ederle to build her background knowledge and become an expert on the swimmer.

First, here is a little background on Gertrude Ederle. As a child, Gertrude did not set out to be a swimmer. However, after she fell into a pond and nearly drowned, her father decided she must learn to swim. When she did, she discovered that she loved it, and that was the start of her career. She began to enter races and ultimately made the U.S. Olympic swim team.

When Ederle completed her historic swim across the English Channel in 1926, it was her second attempt. During her first attempt, her trainer touched her while trying to convince her she was too tired to continue, an act which disqualified her. Some people speculated that he touched her intentionally, since he had tried unsuccessfully to swim the English Channel many times and couldn't bear the thought of a woman outperforming him. To make matters worse, in 1926, newspapers characterized women as "the weaker sex" and predicted that Gertrude Ederle would fail. When she didn't, supporters everywhere rejoiced and critics were forced to reexamine their ideas about women in sports.

Maeghan and I followed these steps to investigate multiple perspectives on Gertrude Ederle:

* Reading, researching, and talking
* Using literature as a model for writing
* Using a "frame" to prepare an introduction

* Using a planning sheet to focus on multiple perspectives
* Preparing a biography from multiple perspectives

Reading, Researching, and Talking

We began by reading *America's Champion Swimmer: Gertrude Ederle* (2000),

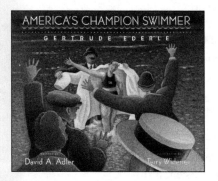

written by David Adler and illustrated by Terry Widener. This picture-book biography, with its colorful, informative illustrations and clearly written text, gave Maeghan a sense of historical context. It begins with a full-page picture of a woman (Gertrude's mother?) bathing a child (Gertrude?) in a sink in a sparsely furnished New York City apartment. The opposite page shows a woman walking down the street and passing a building with a sign saying "MEN ONLY." The text reads, "In 1906 women were kept out of many clubs and restaurants." It goes on to say, "many people felt a woman's place was in the home. But Gertrude Ederle's place was in the water" (Adler, 2000, unpaged).

It was immediately apparent to Maeghan that times were different. As Gertrude learned to swim and attempted more difficult races, some people responded with disbelief and scorn. But she persisted and, with the help of her sister and her trainer, she swam the English Channel, beating the men's record at that time. She did it with the support of her father and her sister, but not necessarily her mother, who referred to Gertrude as a "plain home girl." President Coolidge, in contrast, called her "America's Best Girl" and women everywhere applauded her achievement. The fact that these different perspectives coexisted is clearly presented in this book.

The story appealed to Maeghan for a number of reasons, including the fact that she, like Gertrude, loves to swim and lives in Flushing, New York, where Ederle lived. Maeghan talked to family members about Ederle. To her surprise, her grandmother and uncle had recollections to share. Maeghan's mother helped her search the Web and gather material to read and think about. (See Zarnowski, 2004, for a list of related Web sites.) Maeghan and I located a local newspaper's report of Gertrude's death which not only provided information about her achievements, but also discussed her connection to the borough of Queens in New York City, where Maeghan lives.

After this promising start, Maeghan and I read *America's Champion Swimmer* several times and examined material from the Internet. We discussed this material, sharing what we thought about Gertrude, her friends, and her critics. These discussions were important. As literacy specialist Dixie Lee Spiegel reports, discussion "is a tool that leads to deeper understanding, active participation, and higher-level thinking" (2005, p. 20). This was certainly true for Maeghan.

Using Literature as a Model for Writing

We used Nikki Grimes's *Talkin' About Bessie: The Story of Aviator Elizabeth Coleman* (2002), which won the Coretta Scott King Award, as a model for Maeghan to follow for her book about Gertrude Ederle. The book explains what different people knew and thought about the life of the famous aviator Bessie Coleman. It begins with an introduction that describes what it was like to grow up in the South in the late 1800s, when Bessie was born. The author explains what was happening in the field of aviation and how Bessie was caught up in the events of her time. This was a time of Jim Crow laws and racial segregation, but also a time when the Wright brothers were making aviation history. In other words, the introduction presents the historical context in which Bessie lived.

The balance of the book is made up of memories of people who attended Bessie's funeral after she was killed in a plane crash at the age of 34. We hear from her father, mother, sister, brother, teacher, classmate, flight instructor, news reporters, Bessie herself, and others. The author provides a blend of imagination and analysis. To do this, she analyzed information drawn from sources about Bessie Coleman and the field of aviation, but also used her imagination to describe what people would say about Bessie and how they would say it. At the end of the book Grimes writes that although the characters in the book are real, ". . . the voices, styles of speech, and characterizations are all imaginary devices used to bring Bessie's true story to life" (unpaged). As you will see in the following sections, Maeghan used the format of *Talkin' About Bessie* as a way of telling about Gertrude Ederle. She, too, was able to combine imagination and analysis.

Using a "Frame" to Prepare an Introduction

Nikki Grimes's introduction consists of three paragraphs:

* Paragraph 1 describes the social climate of Bessie's world.
* Paragraph 2 describes her growing interest in aviation.
* Paragraph 3 describes her accomplishments as an aviator.

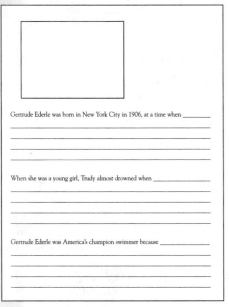

Gertrude Ederle was born in New York City in 1906, at a time when _____
_____
_____
_____

When she was a young girl, Trudy almost drowned when _____
_____
_____
_____

Gertrude Ederle was America's champion swimmer because _____
_____
_____
_____

Figure 5.1:
Frame for writing the introduction

Using this structure, I created a frame for Maeghan to use to write her introduction to her piece on Gertrude Ederle. (See Figure 5.1.) Figure 5.2 shows Maeghan's initial attempt to fill in the frame. Notice that the frame enables her to work on the content of each paragraph, without getting bogged down in how to structure that content. In the second paragraph, for example, Maeghan replaces her second sentence with three other sentences (shown next to the illustration) that give much more detail.

Maeghan's final introduction, which is shown in Figure 5.3, follows Nikki Grimes's model perfectly. It gives readers the background they need to understand the various perspectives that will follow. Some—like

He tied one end of a rope to her and held the other end. He threw her into the water and told her to paddle like a dog. She mastered that and joined the other kids.

Gertrude Ederle was born in New York City in 1906, at a time when women were not allowed to go to some clubs and restaurants and were not allowed to vote in some states. At that time, people said when it came to sports, women were the weaker people.

When she was a young girl, Trudy almost drowned when she went to Germany visiting her grandma. After that her father taught her how to swim, then he was teaching her to paddle like a dog she mastered that and joined the rest of the kids.

Gertrude Ederle was America's champion swimmer because she swam the English Channel and women were not the weaker people any more. The President, Calvin Coolidge, called her, "America's Best Girl."

This way ole kids ←

Gertrude Ederle was born in New York City in 1906, at a time when women were not allowed to go to some clubs and restaurants and were not allowed to vote in some states. At that time people said when it came to sports, women were the weaker people.

When she was a young girl, Trudy almost drowned when she went to Germany visiting her grandma. After that her father taught her how to swim. He tied one end of a rope to her waist and held the other end. He threw her into the water and told her to paddle like a dog. She mastered that and joined the other kids.

Gertrude Ederle was America's champion swimmer because she swam the English Channel and women were not the weaker people anymore. The President, Calvin Coolidge, called her, "America's Best Girl."

Figures 5.2 and 5.3: *Maeghan's initial introduction and final introduction*

Making Sense of History

Gertrude's sister—will be supportive of Gertrude Ederle's attempts to become an outstanding swimmer; others—like her first trainer—won't.

Using a Planning Sheet to Focus on Multiple Perspectives

To help Maeghan gather multiple perspectives on Gertrude Ederle and her career, I created the planning sheet shown in Figure 5.4 for her to think about and write down how various people in Gertrude's life felt about and understood her. (See page 189 for a reproducible version of this sheet.)

The sheet also provided a space for Maeghan to illustrate her ideas. In *Talkin' About Bessie*, Grimes provides a small picture of each speaker and a large picture illustrating his or her comments. Maeghan also created these small and large pictures to illustrate her work.

I made multiple copies of the sheet so that Maeghan could create many drafts before arriving at the ones that satisfied her. Figure 5.5 shows her completed planning sheet for writing from the perspective of Gertrude's father. Figure 5.6 shows the draft Maeghan wrote based on the sheet, and Figure 5.7 shows the final perspective and illustrations.

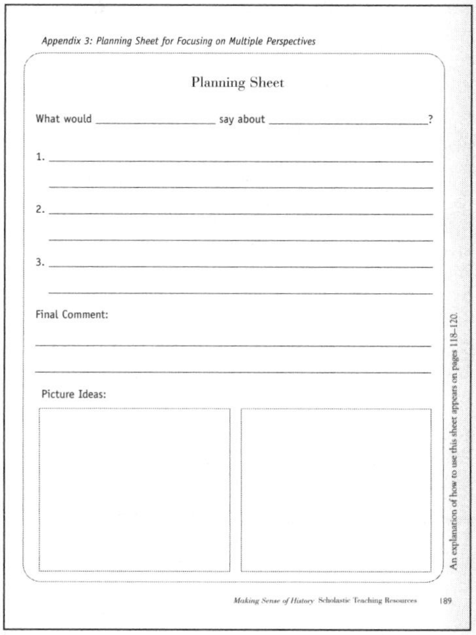

Appendix 3: Planning Sheet for Focusing on Multiple Perspectives

Planning Sheet

What would _____ say about _____?

1. _____
2. _____
3. _____

Final Comment:

Picture Ideas:

Making Sense of History: Scholastic Teaching Resources   189

An explanation of how to use this sheet appears on pages 118–120.

Figure 5.4: *Planning Sheet*

Preparing a Biography From Multiple Perspectives

Maeghan used the planning sheet to construct nine perspectives on Gertrude Ederle's career. To see the variation among the perspectives, compare the one Maeghan wrote for Gertrude's sister, Margaret (Figure 5.8), to the one she wrote for the editorial writer (Figure 5.9). Margaret is confident that Gertrude can swim the English Channel, but the editorial writer isn't. Differences like these provide us with the opportunity to discuss people's beliefs and how these beliefs influence their behavior. To quote Matthew Downey (1996), perspective taking is an "attempt to understand an historical character's frame of reference, without assuming that one can or need identify with his or her feelings" (p. 115). In her writing Maeghan shows that she understands the frame of reference of both Margaret and the editorial writer. Because the editorial writer believes that women are weaker, he assumes Gertrude will fail. Because Margaret believes in

Planning Sheet

What would ___Dad___ say about Trudy?

1. almost drowned

2. teaching how to swim-- rope

3. copied what the other kids did

Final Comment about Trudy:

the best swimmer
I am ~~proud~~ proud

Picture Ideas:

Small

Big

This trophy was awarded to Gertrude Ederle.

Dad

Trudy almost drowned when she slipped into a pond in Germany when she visited her Grandma.

I had to teach her how to swim so she wouldn't be afraid anymore. My first lesson was that I tied one end of a rope to her waist and held on to the other end. Then I told her to paddle like a dog and she mastered that. After that she copied all the other kids' strokes, and before you know it she was better then any of them.

I was so proud of her.

Trudy almost drowned when she ~~sliped~~ slipped into a pond in Germany ~~while~~ (when) she visited her Grandma.

I had to teach her how to swim so she wouldn't be afraid anymore. My first ~~leason~~ lesson was that I tied one end of the rope to her waist and held on to the other end. Then I told her to paddle like a dog and she mastered that. After that she copied all the other kids' strokes, and before you know it she was better then any of them.

I was so ~~protied~~ (proud) of her.

Figures 5.5 and 5.6:
Completed planning sheet and draft for writing from Dad's perspective

Figure 5.7: *Final copy*

Making Sense of History

her sister's ability, she assumes Gertrude will succeed. Maeghan's work proves that she understands these differences.

In addition to the introduction and nine perspectives, Maeghan included an "About the Author" page (Figure 5.10), in which she compares herself to Gertrude Ederle. Like Gertrude, Maeghan lives in Flushing, New York, and loves to swim. Like Gertrude, she feels "triumphant" because she has completed what she set out to do. The photograph of Maeghan as a swimmer reinforces the connection between her subject and herself. There are clearly shared perspectives here.

A project like this can easily be adapted for the whole class. To begin, you might read aloud a biography and work together to prepare an introduction and one or two perspectives. Use *Talkin' About Bessie* to provide a model for the format and structure. Show students how to write a text like *Talkin' About Bessie* by demonstrating Nikki Grimes's technique on a chart or overhead.

"Get going, lazybones!"

I thought it was going to be a near disaster when my father tied a rope around Trudy's waist and put her in the water. But it wasn't. It was actually great.

The next year Trudy said that she was going to swim from Manhattan to Sandy Hook, New Jersey and whenever she slowed down I would say, "Get going, lazybones!"

Before Trudy swam across the English Channel, I coated her with lanolin and heavy grease. I believed she could swim the English Channel.

Margaret

Figure 5.8: *Margaret's perspective*

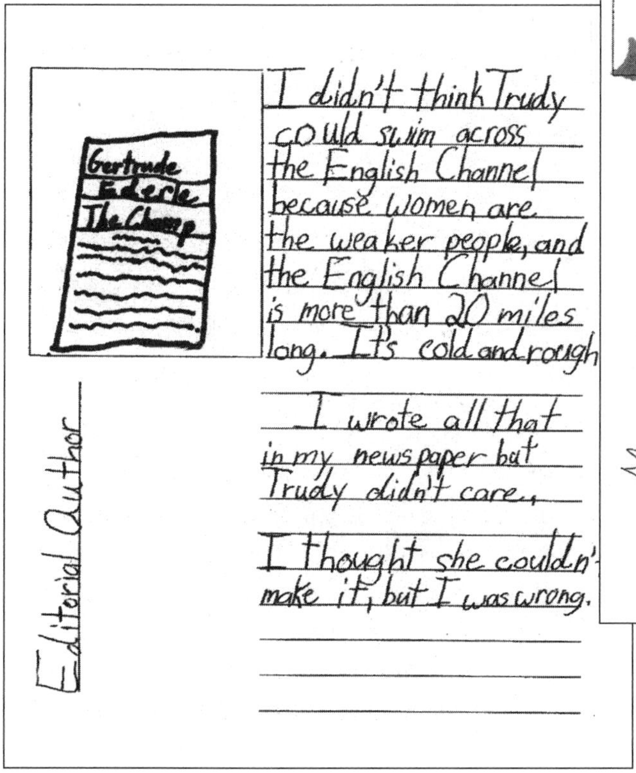

Gertrude Ederle The Champ

I didn't think Trudy could swim across the English Channel because women are the weaker people, and the English Channel is more than 20 miles long. It's cold and rough

I wrote all that in my newspaper but Trudy didn't care.

I thought she couldn't make it, but I was wrong.

Editorial Author

Figure 5.9: *Editorial author's perspective*

About the Author

Maeghan Terry lives in Flushing, New York, just like Gertrude Ederle. She loves to swim. In fact, she likes many sports: soccer, baseball, basketball, and tennis. You could even say she likes all sports.

I liked writing this book because it was fun and I actually put alot of effort into it. I was TRIUMPHANT!! I finishe it.

I hope you enjoyed the book. Call me and tell me if you liked it. (If you didn't, don't bother calling.)

21

Figures 5.10: *About the Author page*

Then, have groups of students work together to prepare biographies from multiple perspectives. Since this is a group effort, each student will only need to prepare one or two perspectives. As students work, you can conference with them and provide suggestions. Students can discuss and critique their work within their groups, and later share their work with the rest of the class.

INVESTIGATING ONE PERSPECTIVE IN DEPTH: A CLASSROOM EXPERIENCE

Debbi Aizenstain introduced the concept of multiple perspectives to her fifth-grade students by discussing the word *perspective*, which she defined as "a viewpoint—a way of looking at or considering something." She placed the idea in the familiar context of the playground and asked students to remember a past squabble. Students shared their memories and, by doing so, discovered that they had different versions of how and why the squabble took place.

Debbi told the students that they would be reading about the life of Cleopatra, and that they would see that people had different viewpoints about the decisions Cleopatra made as a young girl, as a woman, and as Queen of Egypt. She introduced the book *Cleopatra* by Diane Stanley (2002), which she used as a basis for the study.

Cleopatra was an excellent choice as a subject because she was and continues to be such a controversial figure. Some people see her as a wise, intelligent woman, while others see her as a power-driven plotter and schemer. Further, she is somewhat of an enigma because of gaps in the available evidence. In a "Note on Ancient Sources," Diane Stanley tells us, "Everything we know about Cleopatra was written by her enemies" (unpaged). In addition, the vivid accounts of her life written by the Greek historian Plutarch were written more than a hundred years after her death. As a result, knowing the "real" Cleopatra is complicated and challenging.

Before beginning to read the book, Debbi began a word wall so that the class could compile a list of words related to Cleopatra. As new words were encountered and discussed, they would be added to the wall. In that way, students would have the words available to use in their speaking and writing. Debbi began by introducing the words *Macedonia, Ptolemy, Caesar,* and *Plutarch.* She explained that Cleopatra was not Egyptian; she was a Macedonian Greek. Her younger brother Ptolemy was King of Egypt, but Cleopatra was eager to overthrow him and rule on her own. In this goal, she was helped by Julius Caesar, a Roman.

Debbi told students that much of our knowledge of Cleopatra's life comes from a historian named Plutarch, but that it was hard to know how much of what he wrote is accurate. Plutarch lived long after Cleopatra's time and might have been influenced by rumors and gossip about her. Even so, they should do their best to understand her life story.

Debbi then followed these steps to help her students consider multiple perspectives on the life of Cleopatra:

* **Weeks 1 and 2:** Reading with a focus on multiple perspectives
* **Week 3:** Modeling writing from a historical perspective
* **Weeks 4–6:** Partner writing to investigate one perspective in depth: drafts and conversation; rewriting and refining meaning

Weeks 1 and 2: Reading With a Focus on Multiple Perspectives

Debbi read much of Stanley's book aloud while students followed along. She asked questions such as these to help them recognize various perspectives:

* How did different people view Cleopatra?
* What were their thoughts and opinions?
* What comments might they have made about her?

In the beginning of the book, readers learn that Cleopatra, at the age of eighteen, was ruling Egypt with her ten-year-old brother Ptolemy XIII. She was even married to him, a customary practice among royalty, though they never really lived as husband and wife. Since he was so young, Ptolemy had three advisors who spoke for him. These advisors envisioned powerful roles for themselves. Because Cleopatra was also ambitious and wanted to be the sole ruler of Egypt, the advisors saw her as a threat and drove her out of Egypt.

After reading and discussing this information, Debbi paused to ask her three questions about perspective. How did Ptolemy and his advisors view Cleopatra? What were their thoughts and opinions? What comments might they have made about Cleopatra? She shared her answers and then encouraged students to share theirs.

As Debbi and the class continued to read the book, more characters and perspectives emerged. Students learned about Cleopatra's alliances with Julius Caesar and Mark Antony. They learned about the anger and outrage the Roman leader Octavian and many Roman citizens felt towards Cleopatra and her ambitions to extend her empire. As this information emerged, it was also questioned. How did each of these people view Cleopatra? What were their thoughts and opinions? What comments might they have made about her?

Books About Cleopatra

Cleopatra (Usborne Famous Lives) by Katie Daynes. Illustrated by Serena Riglietti. Usborne.

Cleopatra: Egypt's Last Pharoah by Don Nardo. Lucent.

Cleopatra: Goddess of Egypt, Enemy of Rome by Polly Schoyer Brooks. HarperCollins.

Cleopatra: The Life of an Egyptian Queen (Graphic Nonfiction) by Gary Jeffrey and Ross Watton. Rosen.

Cleopatra: Queen of Ancient Egypt by Richard Worth. Enslow.

Cleopatra: Queen of Kings by Fiona MacDonald. DK.

The Life and Times of Cleopatra by Michelle Medlock Adams. Mitchell Lane.

Collective Biographies That Include Cleopatra

Extraordinary Women in Politics by Charles Gulotta. Children's Press.

Lives of Extraordinary Women: Rulers, Rebels (and What the Neighbors Thought) by Kathleen Krull. Illustrated by Kathryn Hewitt. Harcourt.

Ten Queens: Portraits of Women in Power by Milton Meltzer. Illustrated by Bethanne Andersen. Dutton.

Making Sense of History

Debbi made other books about Cleopatra available to students for their independent reading. These books contained additional information which supplemented and extended the information from Stanley's book. See list on the previous page.

Week 3: Modeling Writing From a Historical Perspective

Once the reading was completed, Debbi modeled the process of writing from a historical perspective. This was the process students would use when they worked in pairs to investigate and write about one perspective on Cleopatra. Debbi told the class that their writing would be collected in a book made up of the perspectives of various people on Cleopatra's life.

Debbi chose to write from the perspective of Apollodorus, one of Cleopatra's closest allies. As I mentioned earlier, Ptolemy's advisors banished Cleopatra from the palace to prevent her from trying to take power and rule by herself. Despite those advisors' attempts to close the palace off, Cleopatra and Apollodorus hatched a clever scheme. Apollodorus tucked Cleopatra inside a roll of bedding and had the bedding delivered to Caesar as a gift. Here is what Debbi wrote:

Apollodorus

I have been Cleopatra's loyal servant for many years. She is a very generous and beautiful lady who knows how to take care of her servants.

Cleopatra can outsmart any man when it comes to military planning. Many other rulers wouldn't trust servants with their lives, but she trusts me. I think she really deserves to be queen.

This simple exercise was enough to give Debbi's students a solid understanding of writing from a particular perspective. Your students may need more examples. If so, continue modeling by writing from other perspectives. Encourage your students to contribute ideas, and incorporate them into your writing.

Weeks 4–6: Partner Writing to Investigate One Perspective in Depth

Together, Debbi and the class listed the people that that might be interesting to investigate:

* Cleopatra
* Ptolemy XIII
* Julius Caesar
* Roman Citizen
* Octavian
* Mark Antony

She divided the students into pairs and assigned a person to each pair. Allowing pairs to choose was impossible because all people had to be addressed in order for the final product to show the multiple perspectives.

Over the following two weeks, the students wrote drafts, revised them, and conferred with each other, Debbi, and me. Some of the issues that cropped up during this time prompted us to conduct conferences and mini-lessons on the following topics:

Identifying Your Perspective

We showed students how to indicate, from the beginning of their pieces, that they were writing from a particular historical perspective. We advised them to do this by telling the reader directly who they are. Here are a few examples students completed after this lesson:

> "I, Julius Caesar came to find my enemy in Egypt and defeat him, but he was already dead."
>
> "After Julius Caesar was assassinated, I, Mark Antony, wanted to take the place of the most important man in Rome.
>
> "I, Cleopatra, had gotten married to my ten-year-old brother, Ptolemy, when I was 18 years old!"

Voicing Strong Opinions and Feelings

Sometimes students would write about actions, but not opinions and feelings. Through mini-lessons and conferencing, Debbi and I suggested ways students might use their imaginations as well as factual information. This is important because, as theorists have pointed out, to truly understand historical perspective, students must tap into their imaginations. They must wonder, imagine, and speculate.

Two students writing from Cleopatra's perspective addressed her plan to get into the palace and meet Caesar. First they wrote: "I wanted to meet this man, but Ptolemy and his guards probably had the whole palace surrounded! Because of that I had a plan." After conferencing with Debbi, they added, "Surely Caesar would take my side because he would be captivated by my beauty and intelligence, I had thought."

Another pair writing from Caesar's perspective told how he had Cleopatra's statue placed in the Temple of Venus. After our mini-lesson, they added, "I wanted everyone to love her as I do."

Two students wrote from Cleopatra's perspective about how she became Queen when she was eighteen years old, in 51 B.C. After our mini-lesson, they added, "I felt proud, excited and important because I ruled Egypt and I was able to make choices that would help the country."

Debbi and I emphasized using the imagination to present perspectives in a strong, convincing way. The combination of information and imagination made students' writing more powerful.

Giving Detailed Information

Sometimes students described an event in their writing without giving enough detail to understand that event or its implications fully. When that happened, with student permission, we isolated a specific sentence that needed further explanation and asked the students to provide it. We then shared examples during the mini-lesson, such as this one from two students writing as Mark Antony: "I have already sent Cleopatra three letters, but she has not responded." After some discussion with Debbi and me, they added, "While I was on a military campaign in Tarsus, I sent three letters to Cleopatra, ordering her to come to Tarsus, in Cilicia. I had some matters I wished to discuss with her. With all our combined power it will [sic] enable me to control all Rome."

This revision helps readers understand Mark Antony's motivation for wanting to meet with Cleopatra. In addition, Cleopatra's refusal to come when ordered indicates that she will not respond to his commands. Clearly, these two students understand Mark Antony's situation, based on the reading and research they have done.

Providing examples of the process is helpful. This can be done using students' work, as we did, or by creating a sentence that requires further detail and providing the additional information yourself. The important thing is to give students just the amount of help they need.

Incorporating Imagination and Analysis Into Writing From Multiple Perspectives: Examining the Results

The student writing about Cleopatra incorporated both aspects of historical empathy—imagination and analysis of information. To illustrate, Figure 5.11 provides excerpts of student writing from each of the identified perspectives. In the first excerpt, for example, Cleopatra tells us that Ptolemy's three advisers have driven her out of Egypt and that she is furious. In contrast, in the second excerpt, the advisers' move to banish Cleopatra from Egypt makes her younger brother feel safe. These excerpts are a mix of facts and imagined feelings. In each case, though, historical accuracy holds the imagination in check.

Perspective	Excerpt of Student Writing
Cleopatra	I, Cleopatra, had gotten married to my ten-year-old brother, Ptolemy, when I was 18 years old! Ptolemy's three advisers thought that they could rule the country in his name. However, I was queen and I wanted Egypt to be like it was under the rule of Pharaoh Thutmose III, fourteen hundred years ago. I had to accomplish this myself, but Ptolemy's advisers drove me out of Egypt—out of my own country!
Ptolemy XIII	I had three advisers who helped me rule Egypt because I was only ten years old. It made me feel safe that these people made the most important decisions for me. They did all the ruling in my name, but Cleopatra wanted to be the ruler of Egypt instead of me. Before she could take over, my three advisers ran her out of Egypt. I was glad that they made her leave because the kingdom now belonged to me. I really didn't like her very much because she was selfish and all she wanted to do was get rid of me and rule alone. Cleopatra thought she was so brilliant, but if she was so smart, how did she let the advisers run her out of Egypt?
Julius Caesar	Although I have a wife, I love Cleopatra more because she is sweet, beautiful, intelligent, and powerful. She is so great that I built a statue of her in the Temple of Venus and declared her to be a goddess. Also, I put a statue of myself next to the Seven Kings of Ancient Rome. The people got mad, but who cares? They're not as powerful as I am. Next, I found out that I would be King of all the Roman provinces. I can't wait! I am going to the Roman Senate, even though my wife says not to go, because I WANT TO BE KING!
Roman Citizen	Cleopatra . . . stole one of our favorite men who we all admired, Mark Antony. I believe he was spellbound by her beauty and intelligence. He was in Tarsus when he met Cleopatra, and followed her back to Egypt. Even though Mark Antony had a wife, Octavia, he lived with Cleopatra and had three children with her. I was shocked when Cleopatra and Antony gave land to their four children, when the land wasn't even theirs to give.

Figure 5.11: *Multiple perspectives on the life of Cleopatra: Excerpts from student writing*

Roman Citizen *(continued)*	A few years later, Mark Antony deserted his troops during the Battle of Actium and fled to Egypt with Cleopatra. I felt angry and betrayed. How dare he? How could he do this to his own countrymen? We all looked up to him, and he abandoned us for that Egyptian. When the news got back to Rome that Mark Antony was dead, we were both happy and sad. We were happy because he got what he deserved, but sad because he really was a good leader before he met that woman!
Octavian	After Julius Caesar, my adoptive father, died, I wanted to be ruler of the Roman Empire. At this time, there was also a general and statesman, Mark Antony, who seemed to be in my way of ruling Rome as well as a third statesman, Marcus Aemilius Lepidus. We compromised and agreed to share the ruling of Rome with each other. We broke the Roman Empire into three different sections. Antony took the eastern area, I took the west, and Lepidus took Africa. Then I forced Lepidus out of the triumvirate and took Africa. So, the battle for control of the Empire was between Antony and me. But soon after, Antony left Rome and headed east on a military campaign. He stopped at Tarsus and sent a message to Cleopatra, the ruler of Egypt, a stubborn, power-hungry woman, ordering her to meet him. From what I heard, she did not reply to his message, but eventually, they met. That weakling Antony was charmed by Cleopatra's beauty. In my opinion, they fell in love with each other because they wanted each other's power.
Mark Antony	I, Mark Antony, was a great general and statesman who had the loyalty of the soldiers and admiration of the Roman people. I, along with Octavian and Marcus Aemilius Lepidus, ruled the Roman territories, after Julius Caesar was assassinated. Octavian had taken over Lepidus' land and wanted to take over my part of Rome. I knew a war was coming. I commanded Cleopatra to come to Tarsus to discuss important matters. She was a little stubborn and didn't come right away. During Cleopatra's visit at Tarsus, I fell deeply in love with her because of her dazzling beauty. . . .

Cleopatra

I, Cleopatra, had gotten married to my ten-year-old brother, Ptolemy, when I was 18 years old! Ptolemy's three advisers thought that they could rule the country in his name. However, I was queen and I wanted Egypt to be like it was under the rule of Pharaoh Thutmose III, fourteen hundred years ago. I had to accomplish this myself, but Ptolemy's advisers drove me out of Egypt--out of my own country!

I prepared an army in Syria to go to war against my brother. This battle was just about to begin, when Julius Caesar, the most powerful man in Rome, arrived in Alexandria. Why did Caesar come here? Did he want to make peace between the two sides? Didn't he know that Ptolemy and his advisers would never agree? I wanted to meet this man, but Ptolemy and his guards had the whole palace surrounded! Because of that, I had a plan. Surely Caesar would take my side because he would be captivated by my beauty and intelligence, I had thought.

First I sailed to Alexandria with my trusty servant, Apollodorus. There he wrapped me in a blanket, and carried me into the palace, where he told the guards that he had a special delivery. Apollodorus took me to Caesar, and unwrapped the blanket to reveal me! What a loyal servant Apollodorus had been, for I had entrusted him with my life!

The final pieces were compiled into a class book entitled *A View of Cleopatra Through Different Eyes* and proudly shared with the principal, Lori Golan, who commended the students on their writing and their enthusiasm for learning history. Figure 5.12 shows the cover and sample pages from the book.

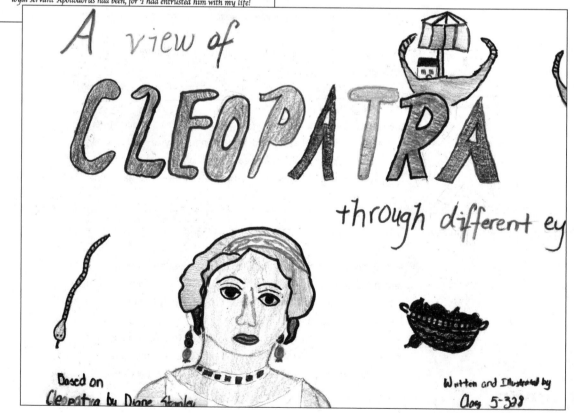

Figure 5.12: *Cover and sample pages from the class book*

Making Sense of History

Julius Caesar

I, Julius Caesar was trying to settle a fight between Cleopatra and her brother Ptolemy XIII. While I was in the palace, guarded by soldiers, a servant delivered a rug to me. I thought the rug was an ordinary rug, until the servant unwrapped the woman of my dreams...Cleopatra! Her intelligence got her into the palace and that amazed me.

The next thing I was amazed by was her beauty; those eyes sparked like the sky when I looked in them. I was so captured by her beauty that I forgot to go back to Rome.

Later, I asked her to follow me back to Rome and she did, with our son Ptolemy Caesar, who we called Caesarion.

Although I have a wife, I love Cleopatra more because she is sweet, beautiful, intelligent, and powerful. She is so great that I built a statue of her in the Temple of Venus and declared her to be a goddess. Also, I put a statue of myself next to the Seven Kings of Ancient Rome.

The people got mad, but who cares. They're not as powerful as I am. Next, I found out that I would be King of all the Roman provinces. I can't wait!! I am going to the Roman Senate, even though my wife says not to go, because I WANT TO BE KING!

Kumar & Shadai

Concluding Thoughts

When students grapple with the concept of multiple perspectives, they come face to face with the idea that there is no single story about the past. They encounter a variety of voices—voices of people who have traditionally been heard and voices of those who have previously been overlooked. The newer voices include those of children, migrant workers, immigrants, and ordinary people. Students learn that evidence is the basis for understanding these voices, but there is also room for imagination to fill in some of the gaps.

In the next chapter we move on to a related question: When studying history, what boundaries should be placed on the imagination? Does historical fiction help students learn history or does it confuse them? Debbi and I tackled these questions in her classroom as we incorporated historical fiction into our teaching. I'll share with you what we saw as the benefits and the drawbacks of this material.

Chapter 6

Historical Truth

How Can I Encourage Students to Use Historical Fiction to Build Their Understanding of History?

When I taught seventh grade, I thought I was doing the right thing by introducing my students to historical fiction. Surely it was better than the oversized textbook my students were supposedly reading—a book they referred to disdainfully as "the T." Historical fiction would put human feeling into history; it would be that spoonful of sugar to help the medicine go down.

Or so I thought, until something happened as my class and I were working our way through *Johnny Tremain* (Forbes, 1943/1998)—a fictionalized account that takes place during the American Revolution. As I mentioned in an earlier chapter, a student asked me, "Johnny Tremain was real, wasn't he?" When I said he was not, that same student asked me about Sam Adams, John Adams, Paul Revere, and John Hancock. Were they real? How was the student to know? How would anyone who was given both informational books and fiction distinguish between them unless they were given tools to do so? So began my mistrust of historical fiction. How, I wondered, could a literary work that was part fact and part fiction be helpful in learning history, a discipline rooted entirely in fact? How would students know if they were reading fact or fiction? There was something not quite right about this approach.

After that incident, I became a confirmed user of nonfiction to teach history. I selected books from the yearly lists of outstanding nonfiction for children such as the Notable Trade Books in the Field of Social Studies and the National Council of Teachers of English's Orbis Pictus award winners. It seemed logical to me that students should learn history from history books. I was convinced that outstanding nonfiction is just as absorbing as outstanding fiction.

Still, historical fiction was becoming increasingly popular with series like Dear America, My America, and Orphan Train Children. Students were reading it by choice, and teachers like Tarry Lindquist (n.d.) were writing articles praising its usefulness in the classroom. A trusted colleague of mine in the history department at Queens College, Barbara Troetel, assured me that historical fiction was good for children because it introduced them to so much accurate history and was so well researched. I thought it was time to reconsider.

This chapter describes my reexamination of historical fiction in the classroom. First, I discuss the theory and research related to historical truth—especially as it relates to historical fiction. Second, I examine current historical fiction as a means of learning historical truth. Finally, I describe what fifth-grade teacher Debbi Aizenstain and I did to introduce her students to historical fiction in a way that allowed them to feel the emotional impact of a story while never losing sight of historical truth.

As in the previous chapters, the three essential elements of history teaching—historical thinking, historical literature, and hands-on experience—guide the discussion:

* What do theory and research tell us about historical truth?
* How does historical fiction contribute to an understanding of historical truth?
* What activities promote students' understanding of historical truth? What part can historical fiction play in these activities?

What Do Theory and Research Tell Us About Historical Truth?

Students know the difference between telling the truth and telling lies. They even know something about stretching the truth. Yet, in my experience, their knowledge about truth telling doesn't quite work when it comes to understanding history. Because historical truth is about more than telling the truth and avoiding lies, we need to give our students a broader, more discipline-based understanding. Here are some ideas drawn from existing theory and research that you can use when teaching about historical truth:

* Historical truth is a broader concept than our everyday, common-sense notion of what is true or false.
* Historical fiction written for children and young adults reflects only a narrow range of historical interpretations and perspectives, limiting students' access to historical truth. Therefore, we need to introduce a broader range of voices—especially those that have been silenced in the past.
* Teachers report that historical fiction is appealing to students and sparks interest in learning.

Knowledge about historical truth does not develop automatically. We have to intervene actively, applying what we learn from theory and research.

Historical Truth Is a Broader Concept Than Our Everyday, Common-Sense Notion of What Is True or False

For historians, truth is a complex concept. According to historian Matt Oja (1988), when determining truth, "the common-sense reaction, that the difference lies in the fact that history deals with true events and fiction with invented ones, is unfortunately of little help" (p. 115). Instead, Oja claims there are different kinds of truth:

Literal Truth: An account that can be verified, such as an event that actually occurred at a certain time. Example: A textbook author states, "On July 4, 1776, the Declaration was officially approved by the delegates" (Hakim, 1993, p. 103).

Artistic Truth: An account that can't be verified, but seems true based on what we know about human nature—a well-crafted account that "rings true." Example: An eight-year-old boy describes how happy he felt during the celebration of the first Independence Day. He watched people ringing bells, hoisting a liberty pole, firing guns, and marching in a parade.

Historical Trueness: An account that cannot be verified, but is likely to have happened based on what we know about historical context. It might have happened based on the evidence that we have, in other words. It's plausible. Example: A soldier overhears George Washington say that the Declaration of Independence is one of the greatest documents ever written.

Literal truth—the verifiable kind—is almost always emphasized in nonfiction, while artistic truth and historical trueness—the non-verifiable kinds—are almost always emphasized in historical fiction. Later in the chapter I'll show you how to use children's literature to introduce students to all three types of truth.

While some historians like Oja want to broaden our understanding of historical truth, others emphasize the unique contribution of fiction in helping us understand historical truth. They claim that fictionalized history concentrates on the human interest aspects of history—values, responsibilities, and personal predicaments (Adhikari, 2002). Historian Cushing Strout (1992) refers to the responsible fictionalizing of history as exercising veracious imagination and the irresponsible fictionalizing as exercising voracious imagination. Veracious (truthful) imagination focuses on social and cultural settings, not on changing historical events. It places actual people in minor roles rather than setting imagination out "on a collision course with the historian's enterprise" (p.155). Voracious (untruthful, out-of-bounds, overreaching) imagination, in contrast, is imagination gone wild and headed directly for that collision with history.

A book like *My Brother Sam Is Dead* (Collier & Collier, 1974) is an example of veracious history because the main characters—Sam and his family members—are fictional. The authors concentrate on their predicaments during the American Revolution without distorting major historical events. There are characters in the book who really existed—General Israel Putnam, Colonel Read, William Heron—but they play minor roles. When teaching about historical truth, it's important to select books such as *My Brother Sam Is Dead* that don't make huge changes to history.

For teachers, the implications of these ideas about historical truth are worth considering. If we are willing to use sources beyond those that emphasize literal truth, we can introduce a wider range of material. We can consider books that present artistic truth and others that present historical trueness. In each case we will be emphasizing the more personal, social, and cultural side of history—the side that too often gets deemphasized in the more factual histories. At the same time, we will need to make sure that students understand the type of material that they are reading and what they can expect to learn from it.

HISTORICAL FICTION WRITTEN FOR CHILDREN AND YOUNG ADULTS REFLECTS ONLY A NARROW RANGE OF HISTORICAL INTERPRETATIONS AND PERSPECTIVES

While many historians claim that historical fiction is an effective means of learning historical truth, scholars of children's literature are not entirely persuaded. They caution us against using historical fiction uncritically. Chandra Power (2003) found that historical fiction provides young readers with only limited access to the broad range of historical interpretations. She claims that most historical fiction represents only the dominant interpretation of history—the traditional version of history most likely to be found in textbooks. This narrow range of historical interpretation—referred to as the *selective tradition* in children's literature—often excludes the voices of minorities and, therefore, limits students' access to the truth.

Power studied several examples of historical fiction that were criticized as being *presentist*. That is, the writers were accused of giving present-day thoughts, beliefs, and concerns to characters from the past and, as such, presenting an inaccurate view of the past. Karen Cushman, the author of *Catherine, Called Birdy* (1994), for example, has been criticized for giving her heroine, young Catherine, current feminist ideas that would never have entered her "medieval" mind. In the novel, thirteen-year-old Catherine actively resists her father's plans to marry her off, shows distaste for domestic chores such as sewing and embroidery, and acts with unusual independence and self-assurance. However, by investigating histories of medieval times, Power was able to show that Catherine's behavior and attitude was a possible choice, even in her time.

Power also investigated the charge of presentism on the part of critics. That is, a number of critics were charged with imposing their present-day thoughts, values, and understandings when evaluating historical fiction. She suggests that a book like *Sounder* (Armstrong, 1969), which presents a black family as hopelessly passive in the face of prejudice and unfair treatment, should not be seen—as it has been by a number of critics—as representative of all black families in the 1890s. Unlike many activist black women of the time, the mother in *Sounder* teaches her son to abandon his goals and embrace hopelessness. The difficulty such material presents for teachers and young readers is that this one response—that of hopelessness—is seen as the only response that could have occurred at that time. This belief is not supported by historians. According to Power,

> While Sounder (Armstrong, 1969) *may depict one possible response to oppression and the stringent Jim Crow world, the critics who argue that the characters would have had no other possible response to oppression in the South in the 1890s are imposing their own ahistorical understanding of African American history. (p. 454)*

What does this mean for teachers? First, we need to be aware that one piece of historical fiction cannot provide a broad range of possible historical interpretations. We need to use a variety of materials to capture multiple perspectives and experiences, especially the perspectives and experiences of those who have been silenced. As you will see later in this chapter, there are books available to help you do that.

Second, taking a critical stance toward reading historical fiction is essential. Just because a book has been published does not mean it is accurate. In a very eye-opening study, Laura Apol and her colleagues (Apol, Sakuma, Reynolds, & Rop, 2003) found that their undergraduate students were reluctant to evaluate historical fiction critically and make accuracy a priority. When they were presented with information showing that the book *Sadako* (Coerr, 1993) contained inaccurate information about Japanese customs and history, the students still claimed that as teachers, they would use it with children. They valued the "uplifting moral lesson," the "evocative illustrations," and the "cross-curricular possibilities" offered by the book (p. 448). Apol and her colleagues describe their students' preferences for personal connection over historical accuracy as follows:

In their eagerness to make direct connections between child readers and texts, the undergraduate students in our classes forget that readers' responses to historical fiction need also to take into account the historical context, the author's purpose, and the author's and readers' ideological predispositions. (p. 449)

As teachers, if we disregard the historical context, the author's purpose, and ideological predispositions, we run the risk of selecting inappropriate and inaccurate material. If we still choose to use material that is questionable in terms of its historical accuracy, we should be aware of its limitations and share those limitations with our students.

TEACHERS REPORT THAT HISTORICAL FICTION IS APPEALING TO STUDENTS AND SPARKS INTEREST IN LEARNING

While scholars of children's literature present us with a sobering view of historical fiction, classroom-based researchers are much more positive about its impact. They tend to focus on how fiction can be used to engage students in history-related activities. For example, Wanda Brooks and Gregory Hampton (2005) found that historical fiction provided a safe context for examining and discussing racism. Middle school students who read Mildred Taylor's *Roll of Thunder, Hear My Cry* (1976) found a "safe space for critical thought" (p. 92), gaining historical information about racism through story, not direct experience. Dave Martin and Beth Brook (2002) report that when students read and then write original historical fiction, it focuses their historical research in an appealing way. They claim that writing historical fiction gives students "a purpose to their historical research" (p. 30) because "they are finding out about the past in order to make their settings, characters and plots authentic" (p. 30). Similarly, Linda Levstik and Keith Barton (2001) report that students who read a variety of genres, including historical fiction, are able to create original historical-fiction narratives.

Despite these encouraging reports, classroom-based researchers caution us about students' unquestioning acceptance of fiction as truth. Even though historical fiction presents a point of view, students didn't question its perspective or authenticity. Brooks and Hampton (2005) report that the middle school students who read Mildred Taylor's *Roll of Thunder, Hear My Cry* "did not respond to Taylor's narrative by questioning the plausibility of the events in the novel. . . . In other words, the questions of 'is this real?' or 'could that really have happened?' may never emerge as problems . . ." (p. 93). Levstik and Barton (2001) similarly report that children are not naturally critical readers of narrative. They suggest that it is important for teachers to raise questions and introduce activities that help students question what they read.

All of this suggests that while historical fiction is appealing, it requires teacher intervention to help students think about it critically instead of swallowing its perspective whole. One way to do this is to use historical fiction as a springboard for inquiry, a technique frequently advocated by classroom-based researchers. Tarry Lindquist (n.d.) reports that after reading a historical novel aloud, she asks each student to raise a question related to it. These questions then provide the basis for a class inquiry. In my work with Debbi Aizenstain, which I describe later in this chapter, we also used this technique.

How Does Historical Fiction Contribute to an Understanding of Historical Truth?

When using historical fiction to teach about historical truth, naturally, the content of the literature you select matters. You can select titles that capture previously silenced voices, thereby doing your part to end the selective tradition of teaching with children's literature. As students read historical fiction, you can encourage them to raise questions as they search for truth. Later, you can introduce nonfiction literature to help them answer those questions. By using both fiction and nonfiction, you give students access to all three types of historical truth—literal truth, artistic truth, and historical trueness. This section explores types of literature that you will find useful when encouraging students to seek historical truth:

* Historical fiction that contains previously unheard voices
* Historical fiction and nonfiction on the same topic

HISTORICAL FICTION THAT CONTAINS PREVIOUSLY UNHEARD VOICES

Several recent works of historical fiction offer students access to voices previously unheard in children's literature. Reading these books allows students to see that history is not one story, but many stories. When used in addition to—not instead of—traditional historical novels, students gain a more accurate, more complete understanding of what happened in the past.

In *The Birchbark House* (1999), Louise Erdrich shows how the Native-American population was affected by westward expansion during the 1840s, providing a perspective that has long been missing in children's literature. This is precisely the same period of time described by Laura Ingalls Wilder in the Little House books. One reviewer of *The Birchbark House* commented, "Why has no one written this story before? Why are there so few good children's books about the people displaced by the little house in the big woods?" (Rochman, 1999).

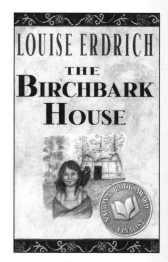

This beautifully written book, which details the daily life of the members of an Ojibwa community, focuses on the experiences of seven-year-old Omakayas and her family. We learn about her life in good times and bad. Omakayas has one chore she particularly dislikes—scraping an animal skin to make it soft enough for moccasins:

> *Omakayas sat near the cooking fire and slowly, with deep inner fury, ate a bowl of cold stew. She dragged out time waiting for her hateful job to start. Mama was wrestling that hide out of the stream now, where it had been soaking for days and nights, gathering up its scummy, wooly slime. Mama had already set up the dreaded frame of branches and there were strings of hide nearby that she would use to tie the skin up tight so that it could be worked. Omakayas knew how important it was to tan the skin, how her mother would cut up the soft smoked hide and sew on the winter's makazins all summer . . . Yes, it was an important task, but Omakayas still didn't want it. (pp. 16–17)*

Omakayas also experiences tragedy. When a visitor comes and infects the community with smallpox, he leaves behind more than illness. He leaves behind a legacy of fear and despair:

> *Although the visitor's body was taken to the farthest end of the island, although everything he'd touched was burned, including the lodge he'd stayed in and the blankets he wore, although the generous family who let him in purified themselves in the sweat lodge, burned all of their belongings, and threw themselves upon the mercy of the mission, fear abounded in the settlement. Had the visitor left another, more horrible visitor behind? Sickness? Death? (p. 142–143)*

Omakayas has good times, too. As her family is feasting one evening after a long stretch without food, Omakayas' brother Pinch entertains everyone when he gets too close to the hearth, catches his pants on fire, and races to a water bucket to extinguish the flames:

"Mama!" He jumped away, a little flame shooting from his rear. In sudden inspiration, he sat down directly in the water bucket. Everyone looked at him, at first in shock, and then once he was seen to have suffered no harm it was Mama, first of all, who started to laugh. And Pinch laughed, too. Laughed so hard that he wedged his behind farther into the bucket, and could not get out. Laughed and laughed. Harder and harder! Ever after that terrible winter, as though he understood from then on how important it was to be funny, Pinch gave laughter to them all. (p. 185)

In *The Game of Silence* (2005), the sequel to *The Birchbark House*, Omakayas, now nine years old, continues to develop the skills she will need to survive—drying fish, sewing, sugaring, learning to heal—and skills she will need to get along with others—patience, kindness, loyalty. So when the government forces the Ojibwa to leave their homes and move westward, Omakayas is capable of bravely facing the future. "Here, after all, was not only danger but possibility" (p. 248).

Erdrich's books are extraordinary resources for teachers who want to provide their students with a Native-American perspective on the settlement of the West. As children's literature critic Carol Hurst (1999, p. 1) noted, "*The Birchbark House* is what many of us have been seeking for many years: a good story through which the Native-American culture during westward expansion of the United States is realistically and sympathetically portrayed." When used with other books about westward expansion, students gain a truer, broader, more inclusive perspective on the past.

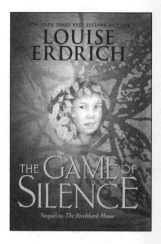

Worth (LaFaye, 2004) is another historical novel that provides a perspective that has been missing in children's literature. The story takes place sometime between 1854 and 1930, when "orphan trains" carried children from the streets of New York City to homes in the West. This program, run by the Children's Aid Society, was responsible for placing more than 200,000 homeless children. Although there are several excellent books—fiction and nonfiction—about the orphan trains and the children who rode them, *Worth* is the only one that gives voice to a child's feelings of anger and resentment when his parents take in an orphan. Because eleven-year-old Nate has been permanently injured, his parents take in orphan John Worth to help work their Nebraska farm.

By choosing Nate as the narrator, author Alexandria LaFaye lets readers examine events from his perspective. She gives voice to a child who feels displaced by an orphan. According to LaFaye, "I'm always looking for the untold story, the point of view we haven't seen yet" (Rochman, 2005, p. 1673).

Nate's attitude toward John changes over time. At the beginning of the novel, both Nate and his mother resent John and do not consider him part of the family. He is not allowed to sleep in the house or eat meals with the family. Nate says, "I wasn't going to let that no account city boy bury me alive" (p. 20).

Later, Nate is shocked to learn that John has lost his entire family in a tenement fire in New York City. A fire escape, which would have been his family's route to safety, collapsed as terrified occupants rushed down it, leaving John's family trapped. Nate pictures this horrible scene:

In my mind, I could see those folks on the fire escape tumbling to the ground in a rush of screams and cracking metal. I held my breath against the horror of it all. The people on the top floors had no way out. The fire would eat them or they could jump to their deaths. (p. 123)

As Nate begins to understand John's terrible loss, he reports, "I felt like such a fool" (p. 124).

In the end, they all grow closer and become a family as they learn to help one another. This spare but intense novel won the 2005 Scott O'Dell Award for

Compare Historical Novels About the Orphan Trains

To see how including historical novels that feature previously silenced voices gives readers a broader, truer sense of history, compare *Worth*, which gives voice to a boy whose family is taking in an orphan, to *Rodzina* (Cushman, 2003), which gives voice to a stubborn and mistrustful orphan girl who is traveling west. How are their experiences with the orphan train program different? What truth about the program can you learn by seeing the events from each character's perspective? Ask students to consider these questions:

- What are the main characters' problems and worries?

- How are these problems resolved?

- How do these books help you understand how children were affected by the orphan train program?

Consider also reading and discussing Joan Lowery Nixon's Orphan Train Children series, consisting of *Lucy's Wish, Will's Choice, Aggie's Home,* and *David's Search*. These books provide additional information about the feelings and personal predicaments of orphans (artistic truth) as well as information about the historical context (historical trueness).

Historical Fiction. One reason for this, I suspect, is the powerful way Alexandria LaFaye brought a previously untold story to life.

When you use this book in combination with other books on the experiences of orphans—books such as *Orphan Train Rider: One Boy's True Story* (Warren, 1996), *We Rode the Orphan Trains* (Warren, 2001), and *Alone in the World:*

Orphans and Orphanages in America (Reef, 2005)—students gain a fuller understanding of the past. The historical truth is better revealed because multiple perspectives are represented—those of the orphans, the parents who took them in, and the children who were already part of the family.

Day of Tears: A Novel in Dialogue (2005) by Julius Lester gives voice to some of the 900 slaves on Pierce Butler's plantation in Georgia. On March 2 and 3, 1859, over 400 of them were sold in what we now know is the largest sale of slaves in American history. Using a mix of dialogue and monologue, Lester creates what he calls an "emotional biography" (p. 176). In an author's note, he tells readers, "This book is another in my attempts to make real those who did not have the opportunity to tell their stories for themselves" (p. 176). To do this, he explores the innermost thoughts of everyone involved. For example, he contrasts the master's belief that the slaves "probably weren't feeling anything" (p. 19) about the sale with a slave's observation that it was "like watching people die" (p. 8). He uses his imagination to explore why slaves seemed to retreat within themselves, as illustrated in the words of twelve-year-old Emma, a young slave on the plantation:

> It's not going to be hard to remember anybody's face because everybody is wearing the same one. Their mouths are set in a straight line. Their eyes look straight ahead and over the crowd. It's not like there's something they're looking at, but more like they've closed their eyes while keeping them open. (p. 67)

When Emma is unexpectedly sold, she says,

> I don't know what to feel. I want to scream. I want to cry. And at the same time I feel like my heart has stopped beating and I will never feel anything again. (pp. 89–90)

TEACHING IDEA

Use *Day of Tears* for Readers Theater

Since *Day of Tears* is written as a series of powerful monologues and dialogues, it is excellent material for Readers Theater. This material is appropriate for middle school students—grade 6 and up.

- "The Kitchen" (pp. 3–14). In this section, two slaves, Mattie and her husband, Will, discuss the upcoming sale of slaves with their daughter Emma.

- Interlude 1: "Emma as an Old Woman" (pp. 15–17). In this monologue, Emma recalls the horror of that day and claims that no picture can capture what it felt like.

- "The Dining Room" (p. 18–29). This dialogue is largely a conversation between the Master and the Slave-Seller on the morning of the sale.

Karen Coats (2005), reviewer for *The Bulletin of the Center for Children's Books*, wrote that the book makes "stunning readers theater or dramatic reading in classes or book groups, and it will occasion equally stunning discussion afterward" (p. 497).

Emma's story and those of other slaves make an emotional impact.

This story, like *The Birchbark House* and *Worth*, contributes to readers' understanding of historical truth by introducing voices that have previously been unheard. Readers get a fuller, more complete picture of the past—and a truer one.

HISTORICAL FICTION AND NONFICTION ON THE SAME TOPIC

When students read historical fiction, they may not understand what is historically accurate and what isn't. Like my students when they read *Johnny Tremain*, your students may not know whether characters and events are real or imaginary. And, more seriously, as researchers such as Brooks and Hampton (2005) and Levstik and Barton (2001) have pointed out, they may not even think of raising questions about those matters.

Therefore, we must intervene by helping students question what they read. One way to do that is by pairing fiction and nonfiction books on the same topic, and comparing their similarities and differences with students. This section focuses on what such an intervention looks like. Using historical fiction/nonfiction pairs, you can intervene by:

* Providing students with examples of different kinds of historical truths.
* Showing how questions raised while reading historical fiction can often be answered by reading nonfiction.

Your instruction might be very structured or very unstructured. Sometimes, you might teach directly, explaining the differences between the two genres, using good examples. Other times, you might observe students at work and support their efforts as needed. I talk about this kind of intervention in greater detail in the final section of this chapter.

Providing Examples of Different Kinds of Historical Truths

As discussed earlier, historian Matt Oja (1988) points out three kinds of historical truths—literal truth, artistic truth, and historical trueness. By pairing fiction and nonfiction for children and young adults, we can illustrate these truths and make the distinctions between them clear.

An outstanding historical fiction/nonfiction pair dealing with the 1793 yellow fever epidemic in Philadelphia is *An American Plague* (Murphy, 2003) and *Fever 1793* (Anderson, 2000). Both books explain the extraordinary role of the Free African Society in helping white citizens deal with yellow fever.

Fever 1793, like most works of historical fiction, revolves around the lives of imaginary characters. Mattie's family runs a coffeehouse that employs Eliza, a free black woman, as a cook. During the epidemic, Eliza works for the Free African Society, a group originally created to promote the welfare of black citizens. As the epidemic worsens, this group works tirelessly for the welfare of the general population. Readers learn about the work of the Free African Society only as it impacts these characters. When Mattie is searching for Eliza, she is directed to an unfamiliar house where she hears about the work of the Free African Society:

"I'm looking for Eliza. I was told she was here."
"We have no Eliza here," he answered.
I looked at the children again.
"Did two women just come to deliver those rolls?"
The man nodded. "Saints. Angels. They're from the Free African Society, God Bless them. If one is the Eliza you seek, you might yet find her. They had several other homes to visit." (p. 167)

Readers continue to learn about the work of the Free African Society by following Eliza on her daily rounds caring for white citizens. They also get an evaluation of the work of the Society through her eyes:

The Society has done a remarkable job, and I don't mind saying that with pride. The Africans of Philadelphia have cared for thousands of people without taking notice of color. (p. 176)

Compare the description of the Free African Society in *Fever* with Jim Murphy's description in *An American Plague*. Murphy explains the purpose of the Free African Society without referring to any single individual:

The Free African Society was founded in 1787, the first organization in America created by blacks for blacks. Its purpose was to help members who were destitute and to provide care for widows and fatherless children. On that Thursday [September 5, 1793] the elders of the society assembled to consider something extraordinary: Would they use their association members and their skills to help their struggling white neighbors? (p. 47)

Later, Murphy explains how volunteers of the Free African Society assisted fever victims:

Whenever anyone requested help, the society sent a volunteer as quickly as possible. No set fee was charged for their services, which might include nursing the individual, cleaning up the sickroom, washing clothes and linens, going out to buy food and medicine, and caring for other family members. If an individual could afford to pay a dollar or two for a full day's care, the money was accepted. But since the people they helped were usually poor, the black nurses often stayed and helped a person for no money at all. (p. 51)

These books provide two very different examples of historical truth. *Fever 1793* gives us artistic truth by showing us that Mattie and Eliza acted the way many people in similar circumstances would—by helping others in need. Their deeds are consistent with what we know about human behavior. Those deeds also embody historical trueness. That is, they are plausible because historical records show that many people did, in fact, help their neighbors—especially people who were members of the Free African Society. *An American Plague*, in contrast, is based heavily on fact, or literal truth. The facts presented by Jim Murphy are documented in an extensive bibliography, making it possible for readers to check the sources and verify the information. Sharing books like these lets you show students how historical fiction and nonfiction present historical truth in different ways.

Showing How to Answer Questions Raised While Reading Historical Fiction

One of the most troubling research findings is that students are often reluctant to question what they read (Brooks & Hampton, 2005; Levstik & Barton, 2001). One way to help them is to model how to raise questions while reading and then look for answers. Here is one example of modeling based on the novel *Worth* by Alexandria LaFaye and the nonfiction book *Orphan Train Rider* by Andrea Warren.

To begin, read aloud the following excerpt from *Worth* (LaFaye, 2004), in which Nate's mother tells him that his father is bringing home an orphan boy:

I didn't understand. She'd already said he wasn't bringing home a farmhand. "What boy?"

   "An orphan boy."

   Could've been neck deep in snow for how cold I felt right then. I'd heard tell of those orphan trains that brought in city kids to be picked out of a herd on a church stage and brought home like a new steer. The Campbells got a new son that way after their boy was taken by the measles, but I wasn't dead.

   "He adopted a son?"

   Ma rushed into the room, her face shiny with tears. "No. Not a son. Just a boy to help around here." (pp. 17–18)

After reading this passage to your students, raise questions like these:

1. How many children were brought to the country on the orphan trains?

2. Could any family just pick out an orphan and take that child home?

3. Were orphans usually adopted by the families that took them in, or were they just considered family helpers?

Raise questions that arise from reading fiction, but are not answered by it. You can also encourage students to come up with their own questions.

Since students won't be able to find the answers to these questions in *Worth*, introduce *Orphan Train Rider* (1996) by Andrea Warren. Find the passages in which answers can be found and read them aloud to students. For example: "By 1930, when they stopped running, the trains had carried about 200,000 homeless children from the city streets and orphanages of the East to new homes and families in the West, Midwest, and South" (p. 21) [question #1]. "Most families could just pick out an orphan and take that child home, but in some cases local committees had to approve the families" (p. 34) [question #2]. "Most orphans were not adopted, but some were" (p. 35) [question #3].

Not all questions raised by reading historical fiction can be so easily answered by reading nonfiction. Sometimes, despite our best efforts, we can't find an answer. Take heart, though. The point is not to "find answers," but to question as we read, finding the answers as the text reveals them.

One book will not provide the answers to all student questions. But using a historical fiction/nonfiction pair initially is a good way to jump-start an inquiry.

TEACHING IDEA

Ask These Questions When Reading Historical Fiction

Usually when reading historical fiction, students only raise questions about the details of what happened in the story. But, to understand the historical context fully and tease out facts from fiction, students need to ask deeper questions. Here are a few to get them started:

- How does the book help me understand daily life in the past?
- Could the events described have happened? What evidence do I have?
- Which events really happened? How do I know?
- Which characters really existed? How do I know?

Questions like these should lead to further inquiry.

Historical Fiction/Nonfiction Pairs for Students to Investigate

The following list of historical fiction/nonfiction pairs provides a starting point for student inquiries into historical truth. Start by reading the historical fiction to students to engage them in the topic, or have them read it on their own. After reading it, have students raise questions about historical truth: What actually happened? What might have happened? Then have students attempt to answer their questions by reading the nonfiction.

Topic	Historical Fiction	Nonfiction
American Revolution	*My Brother Sam Is Dead* by James Lincoln Collier and Christopher Collier	*Give Me Liberty!* by Russell Freedman
Child Labor	*January 1905* by Katharine Boling	*Kids at Work* by Russell Freedman
California Gold Rush	*The Ballad of Lucy Whipple* by Karen Cushman	*The Great American Gold Rush* by Rhoda Blumberg
Coal Mining	*Coal Miner's Bride* by Susan Campbell Bartoletti	*Growing Up in Coal Country* by Susan Campbell Bartoletti
Dust Bowl	*Out of the Dust* by Karen Hesse	*Children of the Dust Bowl* by Jerry Stanley
Irish Potato Famine	*Nory Ryan's Song* by Patricia Reilly Giff	*Black Potatoes* by Susan Campbell Bartoletti
Orphan Trains	*Rodzina* by Karen Cushman	*Orphan Train Rider* by Andrea Warren
Slavery	*Day of Tears* by Julius Lester	*Slavery Time When I Was Chillun* by Belinda Hurmence
Teddy Roosevelt	*The President's Daughter* by Kimberly Brubaker Bradley	*Theodore Roosevelt* by Betsy Harvey Kraft
Yellow Fever Epidemic, 1793	*Fever 1793* by Laurie Halse Anderson	*An American Plague* by Jim Murphy

When you encourage students to raise questions about what they read, you motivate and enable them to continue doing that in future independent reading. You give them a skill they need in order to learn the things they really want to know. I think you will be surprised at the difference in attitude you will see when students answer their own questions, not the questions posed at the end of a textbook chapter.

What Activities Promote Students' Understanding of Historical Truth? What Part Can Historical Fiction Play in These Activities?

In this section, I describe how Debbi Aizenstain and I used a historical fiction/nonfiction pair about life in the Dust Bowl to encourage students to ask questions and then to answer their questions for themselves. We had several goals when we began teaching students about the Dust Bowl era of the 1930s, those trying times when farmers in the Oklahoma panhandle lost their farms because of the terrible dust storms, and were often forced to migrate west with their families in search of a better life.

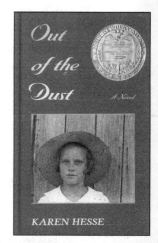

* We wanted students to encounter different kinds of historical truths—literal, artistic, and contextual—by reading historical fiction and nonfiction. This would give them a rich, complex understanding about the time.

* After reading historical fiction, we wanted students to raise questions of fact that would be the basis of further inquiry.

* Using these questions, we wanted students to read related nonfiction in order to write a class question-and-answer book.

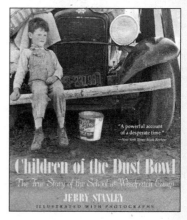

Our historical fiction/nonfiction pair was Karen Hesse's *Out of the Dust* (1997) and Jerry Stanley's *Children of the Dust Bowl* (1992). Both books contain vivid descriptions of life in the 1930s, and both explain the terrible impact of the dust storms, especially on children. The major difference is that the authors rely on different kinds of historical truth to accomplish this.

Out of the Dust focuses on a fictional character named Billie Jo. She experiences personal hardship (a horrible accident is responsible for the deaths of her mother and newly born baby brother) and shared hardship (poverty, despair, and concern for the future) due to the times. Through short, descriptive free-verse poems written from Billy Jo's point of view, we follow her life from 1934 through 1935. We learn about the oppressive circumstances of the time, but we also learn about her small but meaningful joys, such as winning a prize for playing the piano and having good friends. This book has artistic truth because Billy Jo's experiences "ring true." Her life is believable because she thinks in the way a sensitive young girl would think. The book is also true to its historical context because it describes life as it was for midwesterners in the 1930s, people who were growing poorer and more desperate.

Children of the Dust Bowl, in contrast, is an informational narrative. Instead of focusing on a single child, Stanley focuses on an actual group of "Okies"— children from the Oklahoma panhandle—who left their homes and traveled with their parents to Bakersfield, California, to find work. He tells about the difficult journey and the discrimination they faced because they were poor, dirty, and homeless. Although Stanley also tells about the extraordinary contribution of one man, Leo Hart, who helped the Okie children, the book emphasizes what happened to the children. Stanley also suggests some larger moral questions: What was the right thing for the citizens of Bakersfield, California, to do when the Okies arrived? What, if anything, was their responsibility to these poor people? Because the characters and events are not fictional, this book offers readers the literal truth of the times.

Debbi and I followed several steps to make use of this historical-fiction/nonfiction literature pair:

* **Weeks 1 and 2:** Reading historical fiction: savoring the story and sorting fact and fiction

* **Weeks 3 and 4:** Reading nonfiction: clarifying "Not Sure" items

* **Weeks 5 and 6:** Writing a class question-and-answer book: documenting the facts. Students produce an informative and attractive book about the Dust Bowl, based on their reading of historical fiction and nonfiction.

Weeks 1 and 2: Reading Historical Fiction: Savoring the Story and Sorting Fact and Fiction

Debbi began by asking her students what they knew about historical fiction and writing down their ideas on a chart:

Historical Fiction

1. Tells about something that happened in history, but not to the exact person it happened to.
2. The dates are real, and some people might be real.
3. The events might be real, but the author might change them a little.
4. The places might be real.

Impressed by their knowledge of some of the characteristics of historical fiction, she moved on. Debbi handed out copies of *Out of the Dust*, explaining that it was a piece of historical fiction, written in verse, about life in the 1930s. Assigning sections of the book was quite easy, since it is divided into seasons— winter, spring, summer, autumn—for the years 1934 and 1935. We had students read two sections (for example, winter and spring) at a time.

Debbi told the students that they would be reading this book for two purposes— (1) to savor the story and (2) to sort fact and fiction. While reading a book, readers can shift between reading for enjoyment and reading for information. This kind of reading activity has been called "dances between stances" because the reader's stance, or purpose, continually shifts (Holland & Shaw, 1993). Yet, in spite of these shifts, one purpose needs to be emphasized more than the other so that students have a clear purpose for reading. We emphasized sorting fact and fiction.

Savoring the Story: A Subordinate Stance

Though it was not our main objective, Debbi and I encouraged students to savor the story—to read it for enjoyment and pleasure. They read for descriptive and figurative language, for example, where Hesse describes the allure of California as a place "where rain comes, / and the color green doesn't seem like such a miracle, / and hope rises daily, like sap in a stem" (p. 59). This contrasts sharply with descriptions of Oklahoma such as this: "On Sunday, / winds came, / bringing a red dust / like prairie fire / hot and peppery, searing the inside of my nose . . ." (p. 46).

Students also read to find out what happens. Even though the story is told as a series of free-verse poems, it has a riveting plot with building action, conflicts, and resolutions. Debbi's students wanted to find out what happens to the main character, Billy Jo. Does she run away? Does she move in with her aunt in Texas? Does she patch up her relationship with her father? Does she develop a relationship with the boy she likes? Searching for answers to questions like these was a source of great enjoyment.

Debbi structured each class discussion by having students briefly share what they were enjoying about the book; she asked questions such as these: *How did the story make you feel? What are you picturing in your mind as you read? Have you ever felt the same way as Billy Jo? Are there particular parts of the novel you want to share?* She then had students switch stances to sort fact and fiction, and in the process gain a broader understanding of historical truth.

Sorting Fact and Fiction: A Predominant Stance

As classroom researcher and writer Stephanie Harvey notes, confusion about what happened and what didn't is a "roadblock to comprehending historical fiction" (1998, p. 185). She refers to this as the "hazard of historical fiction" (1988, p. 185). Debbi and I wanted to clear this roadblock for students so that they could distinguish between literal truth and artistic truth.

Although *Out of the Dust* contains a number of references to actual people and events that are critical to understanding the story, Debbi and I were not sure our students would recognize them. Would they, for example, know about FDR, government loans to farmers, the Dionne quintuplets, hopping freight trains, or dust pneumonia? Would they care enough to ask? To find out, after reading each assigned section of *Out of the Dust*, we asked students to sort information from the book into three categories: Fact, Fiction, and Not Sure.

As they read each section of the book, students filled out a chart. Figure 6.1 shows one student's first effort to sort fact and fiction. (See page 190 for a reproducible version of this chart.) Donna is familiar with many facts embedded in the novel (people heading from Oklahoma to California, FDR as president, the prevalence of dust everywhere, and the practice of clubbing jackrabbits who attacked the crops). She is aware of fictional characters (Billy Jo, Livie Killian, Mr. Hardly). Surprisingly, her Not Sure list is as long as her list of facts. She wonders if the weather (the number of days of the drought, the snow occurring after a dust storm), places (Amarillo, Texas; Joyce City), and the prices for food that Hesse mentions are real. Although the length of Donna's Not Sure list may

Out of the Dust — Donna

Fact	Fiction	Not Sure
1. Giving birth at home	1. Billie Jo	✗1. Pockets had holes
2. Cimarron County	2. Livie Killian	✗2. 170 days of the drought.
3. People stored food	3. Mr. Hardly's Store	3. Rained during 1934
4. Clubbed rabbits	4. Piano gleaming in dusty room.	✗4. FDR and his man.
5. People moved west to California	5. The characters in the town are not real	5. Snow after the dust storm.
6. School activities		6. weather.
7. FDR President		✗7. Joyce City
8. Warm Springs Foundation		✗8. Amarillo, Texas
9. President was sick		✗9. School was important.
10. People made donations even though they didn't have a lot		✗10. Mud goes in peoples mouths during storms.
11. Used feed sacks to make clothing		✗11. Mud tears
12. Dust was everywhere		✗12. If the wheat would grow.
13. Birthday celebrations for FDR		✗13. locomotive
14. Buys goods for less		✗14. Flannel
15. Just potatoes to eat		✗15. Wonder Bread door
		✗16. Prices of food

Figure 6.1: *One student sorts fact and fiction in* Out of the Dust.

seem like cause for concern, we were actually delighted that she was so willing to share her uncertainties because they gave us starting points for our teaching.

Students brought their filled-out Fact, Fiction, Not Sure sheets to class discussions. We asked them to share their ideas, but we were careful not to answer their Not Sure questions. Instead, we compiled them into a class list which we used as the basis of student research using nonfiction literature. (See Figure 6.2.) Notice that the class list is a mix of questions and topics. Debbi did not insist that students frame every Not Sure item into a question. Her priority, instead, was gathering the uncertainties in whatever shape the students provided them.

Class 5–325's "Not Sure" List for *Out of the Dust*

1. FDR—Government feeding people
2. dust storm—Dust 2 feet high?
3. burlap (flour sack) for babies' clothing
4. government lending money for farms
5. Did people really give away their babies?
6. Could there be snow after a dust storm? Rain? The other way around?
7. Was there night school?
8. Was Madame Butterfly a real play?
9. Did people travel through towns exchanging work for food and clothing?
10. dust pneumonia
11. Franklin Roosevelt's advice
12. Farmers didn't have to pay the loans until the crops grow.
13. Did people really leave their homes and the dust to go to California?
14. Is there a Route 66 or Crystal Hotel?
15. What is the CCC?
16. How dry was the Oklahoma Panhandle?
17. Were there government agents standing at train stations looking for runaways?
18. grasshoppers eating everything
19. Can wheat grow at all when the dust blows?
20. Did kids have to go to school?
21. How did people get money if they didn't find work?
22. cooking up moonshine, apple pandowdy, sorghum

Figure 6.2: *Class's "Not Sure" list*

Making Sense of History

WEEKS 3 AND 4: READING NONFICTION: CLARIFYING "NOT SURE" ITEMS

Once the students finished reading and discussing *Out of the Dust* and compiling the Not Sure list, Debbi gave them copies of *Children of the Dust Bowl*. She told them that it covered exactly the same time period as *Out of the Dust*, but, being a work of nonfiction, it focused on the experiences of actual people. She read aloud the book's introduction and part of Chapter 1 to orient students to the narrative voice and then asked them to read the remainder of the chapter on their own.

She provided the students with copies of the Not Sure list and challenged them to find relevant information about each item. If they found information, she told them to write the page number next to the item. From there, she told them that they would discuss their findings as a class. She assigned one or two chapters each day, which enabled students to finish the book in two weeks.

Finding the answers was exciting. Students who had been puzzled by the references to "feed-sack nighties" (pp. 16, 21) in *Out of the Dust* learned that children did, in fact, wear clothing made from feed sacks. In *Children of the Dust Bowl* they read about girls who "wore dresses made out of chicken-feed sacks" (p. 39) and they saw a picture of a girl with a feed sack wrapped around her (p. 38). None of the students were familiar with the burlap material sometimes used to make feed sacks. So when one girl brought a small piece of burlap to class, everyone wanted to examine it as if it were some rare

---

Books About the Dust Bowl

Children of the Dust Days by Karen Mueller Coombs. Carolrhoda.

Children of the Great Depression by Russell Freedman, Clarion.

Driven from the Land: The Story of the Dust Bowl by Milton Meltzer. Benchmark.

The Dust Bowl and the Depression in American History by Debra McArthur. Enslow.

The Dust Bowl: Disaster on the Plains by Tricia Andryszewski. Turtleback.

Dust to Eat: Drought and Depression in the 1930s by Michael L. Cooper. Clarion.

Life During the Dust Bowl by Diane Yancey. Lucent.

This Land Was Made for You and Me: The Life and Songs of Woody Guthrie by Elizabeth Partridge. Viking.

---

commodity. There were many similar discoveries. Several students found out that the dust pneumonia mentioned in *Out of the Dust* (p. 149) was explained in depth in *Children of the Dust Bowl*. Other students learned that many of the places they had read about in *Out of the Dust* were real—places such as Route 66 and the town of Guymon. In addition to *Children of the Dust Bowl*, students consulted other nonfiction books on the Dust Bowl to shed light on their Not Sure items. The box below provides a list of nonfiction books you can use when researching the Dust Bowl.

Weeks 5 and 6: Writing a Class Question-and-Answer Book: Documenting the Facts

Debbi told the students that they were going to make a class book with the information they found during weeks 3 and 4. She divided the class into small groups and assigned each group an item from the Not Sure list. Students who got statements were asked to rephrase them into researchable questions. Students with the item "dust pneumonia," for example, changed it to the question "What is dust pneumonia?" Here is a complete list of questions the class researched for the book:

* How dry was the Oklahoma Panhandle?
* Could wheat grow at all when the dust blew?
* What is dust pneumonia?
* Were there dust storms [drifts] two feet high?
* Did Okie children really have to wear clothing made from feed sacks?
* Did people really leave their homes to go to California?
* Are the places in *Out of the Dust*, like Route 66, real?
* Did people travel through towns exchanging work for food and clothing?
* How did Okie families get money if they didn't find work?
* Were there government agents standing at train stations looking for runaways?
* Could there be snow or rain after a dust storm?
* Did kids have to go to school?
* Was there a night school?

Students went back to *Children of the Dust Bowl* for information and consulted other sources. They spent several days researching their questions and writing drafts of their answers. When they completed their drafts, students shared them with classmates for peer editing. Finally, Debbi and I proofread the drafts, and the students typed and illustrated them. The final book, entitled *Historical Fiction/Nonfiction*, consisted of the following parts:

* An introduction explaining the project
* The Not Sure List
* Questions, Answers, and Illustrations

The introduction explains the book's question-and-answer format, identifies the historical fiction and nonfiction books we used, and admits that only some of the questions have been answered. Placing the Not Sure list in the front of the book gives readers a sense of the importance of questioning as a way of initiating learning.

As you can see by the samples here, the final pieces have the unmistakable voice of young writers. At the same time, they contain a lot of important information. Clearly, Debbi's students learned quite a bit about the Dust Bowl, but they still

---

Are The Places in *Out of the Dust,* Like Route 66, Real?

by Ashini and Daniel

Route 66 was a real route. It was called the Mother Road for the Okies because they used this route from Oklahoma to go to California. This route started from Oklahoma City and went through Northern Texas (Shamrock and Amarillo), New Mexico (Tucumcari and Albuquerque), to parts of Arizona (Holbrook, Flagstaff, and Kingman), and finally into California (Needles, Barstow, and Bakersfield). The Okies who used Route 66 to get to California had a hard time passing the Tehachapi Mountains and the Mojave Desert. Many of the jalopies got flat tries and ran out of gas. Many Okies had to push their cars.

Another place that is real is Guymon in the Oklahoma Panhandle. This was mentioned as one of the big towns in *Out of the Dust.*

What is Dust Pneumonia?

by Fara and Edward

Dust pneumonia is a horrible disease that killed many Dust Bowlers. The people died when the dust caused severe damage to their lungs. There was so much dust that people breathed it in even if they were inside their homes. People would wake up from sleep with dust in their noses and mouths.

A dust storm was a nightmare experience. Bessie Zent said, "It was as dark as the middle of the night and stayed that way all day long. The dust storm scared us to pieces."

Quote from *Children of the Dust Bowl* (p.8) by Jerry Stanley.

Pages from the class question-and-answer book.

Could Wheat Grow at All When the Dust Blew?

by Arabi Moorthy, Annie Qiu
Class 5-325

When the dust blew, wheat couldn't grow because the wind blew away the seeds from the furrows. If there had been enough rain, the Okies could have revived their crops and grown wheat. But after 1931, there wasn't enough rain and the Okies had to sell their livestock, farm machinery, and borrow money from the bank.

The Okies had no irrigation system, no reservoirs to store water, and had no canals to bring water to revive their crops. Also, the crops shriveled from the sizzling heat coming from the sun. When the crops shriveled, there was no wheat or other plants growing on the farm. Farming was impossible when the dust blew, and the sun burnt the wheat and other crops.

sound like kids! One group of writers confirms that some of the places mentioned in *Out of the Dust* are real. Another group explains the cause and effects of dust pneumonia. A third group discusses why wheat couldn't grow when the dust blew. All of these pieces are focused and informative. The book as a whole provides background information that confirms students' understanding of the facts surrounding the Dust Bowl. No wonder the students valued it enough to include it in their school's yearly literacy fair, an annual celebration of student writing at all grade levels.

Concluding Thoughts

If we accept the idea that historical truth is more than just the facts, then we can use historical fiction as well as nonfiction to teach history. I have come to accept this idea and have modified my earlier views. Using historical fiction, though, requires that teachers explain the difference between artistic truth and literal truth. This is why Debbi and I explicitly taught students to read historical fiction for two purposes—to savor the story and to sort fact and fiction, emphasizing the latter. Adding historical fiction to our programs introduces students to voices that have previously been silenced or missing from historical accounts for elementary and middle school students. Another benefit is that students can read it for enjoyment and to raise questions for further inquiry. History, of course, is more than knowing the facts. It's also knowing that, no matter what historical account we read, some facts are always missing. In the next chapter, I explore this issue.

Chapter 7

Historical Accounts

How Can

I Show

Students That

Accounts Are

Incomplete

and Require

Additional

Facts to Tell the

Whole Story?

Have you noticed that books about Thomas Jefferson, John Adams, and Benjamin Franklin keep appearing? You might think there is nothing left to say about these men, but no!—the books keep coming. This phenomenon is what historian Joseph J. Ellis has referred to as "the Founders' Surge [that] keeps rolling along" (2005, p.15).

Although the number of subjects may be limited, the authors' approaches to them are vastly different. Historical accounts differ based on each author's interests, interpretations, and expertise. For example, there are several recent best-selling books about George Washington, who has been called "the Foundingest Father of them all" (Ellis, 2004, xiv): Joseph J. Ellis's *His Excellency: George Washington* (2004), David McCullough's *1776* (2005), David Hackett Fischer's

Washington's Crossing (2004), and Paul Johnson's *George Washington: The Founding Father* (2005). These books differ largely because of the fact that the authors ask different questions about Washington and, as a result, rely on different evidence to answer those questions. *His Excellency: George Washington* (2004) is, in Ellis's words, "a fresh portrait focused tightly on Washington's character" (p. xiii); the author concentrates on Washington's ambition, resentments, kindness, compassion, and self-control. *Washington's Crossing* (2004), in contrast, focuses on Christmas 1776, when Washington and his poorly equipped army crossed the Delaware River, surprising and defeating the Hessian soldiers, and turning the tide of the American Revolution. Fischer sees this event as part of a larger web of choices and decision making. He concludes, "This book is mainly about contingency, in the sense of people making choices, and choices making a difference in the world" (p. 364).

Ellis is asking, What kind of person was Washington? How can I understand his character? Fischer is asking, How did Washington's decision to cross the Delaware change the course of American history? To answer their questions, Ellis and Fischer selected different evidence and wrote different accounts.

Similarly, there are many accounts of George Washington written for children and young adults, which also raise different questions and contain different evidence to answer those questions. Thomas Allen's *George Washington, Spymaster: How the Americans Outspied the British and Won the Revolutionary War* (2004) deals with Washington's involvement in espionage during the American Revolution. From this book we learn that "he built and ran an intelligence operation that helped him outwit his foe and win the war" (p. 146). Rosalyn Schanzer's *George vs. George: The American Revolution as Seen from Both Sides* (2004) contrasts the life and times of George Washington and King George III during the American Revolution. The book begins by introducing contrasting careers of the two men: "There were once two enemies who were both named George. George Washington was the man who freed the American colonies from the British, and George III was the British king who lost them" (p. 7). Again, as in the books for adults, what makes these accounts unique are the questions the authors raise and the evidence they use to construct their explanations. Allen is asking, What was George Washington's involvement in a spy network? Schanzer is asking, How were the careers of George Washington and King George III different?

Although it may be clear—even obvious—to you that historical accounts differ, it is not clear and obvious to students. Nor is it clear to them that historical accounts are based on evidence rather than on firsthand experience and are,

Examine Accounts of the Life of George Washington

To show that accounts of the same person differ, have students read two or more of the books below about George Washington. As a class or in small groups, consider the following questions:

- What question about Washington is each author answering? (Questions may be directly stated or implied. If they are implied, you may have to figure them out for yourself.)
- How do these accounts differ?
- Why do you think it's important to have multiple accounts of one person?

Picture Books:

George vs. George: The American Revolution as Seen from Both Sides by Rosalyn Schanzer. National Geographic.

George Washington by Cheryl Harness. National Geographic.

George Washington: First President by Mike Venezia. Children's Press.

George Washington: A Picture Book Biography by James Cross Giblin. Illustrated by Michael Dooling. Scholastic.

Take the Lead, George Washington! by Judith St. George. Illustrated by Daniel Powers. Philomel.

Where Washington Walked by Raymond Bial. Walker.

Chapter Books:

George Washington: An Illustrated Biography by David Adler. Holiday House.

George Washington and the Birth of Our Nation by Milton Meltzer (out-of-print, but worth searching for in the library or buying used). Watts.

George Washington, Spymaster: How the Americans Outspied the British and Won the Revolutionary War by Thomas B. Allen. National Geographic.

George Washington and the Founding of a Nation by Albert Marrin. Dutton.

therefore, incomplete. Many students are convinced that there is only one true version of history. They think that most authors of history books dealing with the same topic provide exactly the same information, but use different words. And if they do spot differences in information between books, one book must be wrong and the other right. They believe that if you want the best, most complete account of what happened in the past, you should choose the biggest book. Often, these are the naïve ideas that drive students' thinking.

This chapter explains how to challenge and broaden students' ideas about historical accounts. First, I discuss what theory and research tell us about accounts. Second, I provide examples of books for young people that explicitly address the topic of historical accounts—books that prompt students to think deeply about this concept. Finally, I describe the hands-on activities that fifth-grade teacher Debbi Aizenstain and I carried out to help her students learn about historical accounts.

In other words, once again, the three essential elements of history teaching—historical thinking, historical literature, and hands-on experience—guide the discussion. In this chapter, I consider the following questions:

* What do theory and research tell us about historical accounts?
* How does historical nonfiction literature contribute to an understanding of historical accounts?
* What activities help students understand the concept of historical accounts?

What Do Theory and Research Tell Us About Historical Accounts?

Research about students' understanding of historical accounts has, until recently, come largely from the British research project CHATA (Concepts of History and Teaching Approaches) which has been studying children's understanding of history for over a decade. From the CHATA studies of children between the ages of 7 and 14, two powerful understandings have emerged that have tremendous implications for practice:

* Over time, students develop sophisticated ideas about how historical accounts are written and judged.
* Students need to understand that history is based on evidence left behind, not on direct observation.

Understanding these ideas helps us plan classroom instruction that challenges students' naïve ideas and moves them toward more sophisticated ones. It also helps us answer the question, How can I help my students understand that historical accounts differ?

OVER TIME, STUDENTS DEVELOP SOPHISTICATED IDEAS ABOUT HOW HISTORICAL ACCOUNTS ARE WRITTEN AND JUDGED

As students develop, their ideas about how historical accounts are written and judged change. (See Figure 7.1.) The results of the CHATA studies (Lee, 1998; Lee & Ashby, 2000; Lee & Shemilt, 2004) show that young students initially think there is only one correct account of past events and that differences between accounts are due merely to differences in wording. As they mature, students begin to consider problems associated with not being able to witness past events; they question whether we can know the past because we haven't seen it for ourselves. They worry about gaps in information and fabrications by authors. Later, students come to terms with our inability to witness past events, but they explain the differences between accounts simply as opinion, each account having its own spin; in their estimation, one account is as good as another. It is only in the later stages of the progression that students come to understand that accounts vary because authors select different questions to research and write about and that accounts can be judged on the basis of

Student Thinking	What It Means
1. All accounts are about the same thing.	The only differences between two accounts are the differences in the words used.
2. We can't know the past.	Because we never saw what happened in the past, we can't know what happened.
3. We can know the past, but not all of it.	Gaps in information and errors cause differences in accounts.
4. Authors can distort accounts.	Authors can actively contribute to distorting the past by exaggerating, giving in to bias, and telling lies.
5. Accounts reflect the author's viewpoint.	Authors may select different questions to answer.
6. Accounts will, of necessity, differ.	No account will be complete. Accounts will be judged by history-specific criteria.

Figure 7.1: *The six-stage progression in student thinking about historical accounts. Adapted from Lee, 1998; Lee & Ashby, 2000; Lee & Shemilt, 2004*

history-specific criteria. So, in our teaching, it is important to aim for this final "criterial" stage.

Researchers in other countries have arrived at similar results. In the U.S., Bruce VanSledright and Peter Afflerbach (2005) found that fourth graders believed that we can examine and come to know the past but did not know the history-specific criteria for doing so. The youngsters they studied were in the middle stages of the CHATA progression. Other researchers have found that the CHATA model applies to Portuguese students in fifth through seventh grades (Gago, 2005) and to Taiwanese students in junior high school (Hsiao, 2005). This is convincing evidence that learning about historical accounts develops in a clearly identified way over time.

What does this mean for teachers? First, we are likely to see a range of understanding as students consider historical accounts. Some ideas will be quite naïve, while others will be more sophisticated. It helps to know that this range is typical and predictable. It represents how students think. Second, we can aim for specific goals in instruction. The progression helps us understand what our students already know and what they will find challenging. Finally, in showing students how to understand historical accounts, we build skills that are useful to students well beyond the subject of history—skills that are useful in becoming thoughtful citizens who can assess evidence and evaluate ideas before reaching conclusions and making decisions (VanSledright & Afflerbach, 2005).

STUDENTS NEED TO UNDERSTAND THAT HISTORY IS BASED ON EVIDENCE LEFT BEHIND, NOT DIRECT OBSERVATION

Students sometimes assume that if no one was there to directly observe an event in the past, then we can't know about it. However, history is not based on direct observation. Instead, it is based on the study of evidence left behind. This is quite different from thinking about the recent past—the everyday thinking that students do to recall, for example, the events of last week (Lee, 2005).

Students must learn that history relies on the use of evidence, and that there are two kinds of evidence. Firsthand evidence comes from eyewitness accounts, while secondhand evidence comes less directly—perhaps from people who spoke to witnesses or read accounts by them. Students can rely on both kinds of evidence to help them make sense of history.

Students need to know that historians rigorously question the available evidence; they do not accept it unconditionally. They question the motives and intentions of authors. They then try to corroborate evidence by finding additional examples that agree with the evidence at hand. At the same time, they try to understand evidence in its own context. This type of thinking is germane to the discipline of history and, therefore, is critical to learning.

To make sense of historical accounts in this way, students need what Robert Bain calls "history-specific cognitive tools" (2005, p. 202). Not to be confused with general reading strategies—such as locating the main idea, finding cause and effect, predicting and confirming, or using context clues—these are, according to Bain, history-specific strategies that help students "learn content, analyze sources, frame historical problems, corroborate evidence, determine significance, or build historical arguments" (p. 203). Other researchers concur. VanSledright and Afflerbach call for teaching students "about the criteria investigators use to assess sources' reliability" (2005, p. 16). Lee and Shemilt call for giving students the means for "grappling with the ways in which accounts may differ legitimately without being merely matters of 'opinion'" (2004, p. 31). Later in this chapter, I describe how Debbi Aizenstain and I taught her fifth-grade students how to isolate and understand the differences in historical accounts by using history-specific strategies.

How Does Historical Nonfiction Literature Contribute to an Understanding of Historical Accounts?

Some authors of historical nonfiction do more than tell what happened; they also comment on the process of writing historical accounts. Their approach is "metahistorical"—they focus on their method of doing history. As a result they provide more than a factual narrative. This section features books that explore the differences between historical accounts—books that challenge the naïve notion that all accounts are the same. Authors do this by:

* Providing multiple accounts
* Revealing gaps in available evidence
* Pointing out people and events that have been intentionally omitted from the historical record

PROVIDING MULTIPLE ACCOUNTS

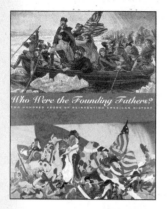

Who Were the Founding Fathers?: Two Hundred Years of Reinventing American History by Steven H. Jaffe (1996) presents multiple ways of describing the Founding Fathers:

On the morning of July 4, 1776, fifty-six traitors stride into the Pennsylvania colony's statehouse in Philadelphia. Some are fools, but most are shrewdly selfish and evil men. They are rebels against the king who has always protected them. For over a year, they have been in armed rebellion against the legal and just right of Parliament to tax them and to regulate their affairs. Their goal is to increase their personal power at the expense of the king's duly appointed officers. Today, they take their treachery even further. By the evening, they will, in a foul and daring act of treason, declare independence and thus announce to the world their intention of destroying the British Empire.

Or:

On the morning of July 4, 1776, fifty-six hypocrites straggle into the Pennsylvania statehouse. Most are wealthy men—landowners, lawyers, and businessmen—and all are white. The Declaration they will ratify this evening claims that "All men are created equal." But these statesmen will do little or nothing to challenge the great evil of slavery that curses their country. Indeed, most of the southerners in the hall—including the author of the Declaration, Thomas Jefferson of Virginia—are there because the labor of their human property allows them to be. By proclaiming an equality that applies to white men only, these so-called heroes fail miserably, for they lack the courage to create what the world cries out for: a nation that lives up to its high-toned pronouncements on liberty by freeing its slaves.

Or:

On the morning of July 4, 1776, fifty-six patriots enter the building that will soon be known to the world as Independence Hall. They risk their lives, for they dare to challenge the most powerful empire in the world. They have spent the hot days of this summer debating the wisdom and justice of declaring the independence of the thirteen colonies united in resistance to British tyranny. Some doubt whether an independent American nation can succeed. Yet their dedication to the principle of government by and for the people gives them courage. By evening, they will have created the greatest nation the world has ever known, a nation committed to liberty, equality, and the rights of man.

Which version is the correct one? Each has been advanced as a true account by different people at different times. (pp. 3–4)

This excerpt, which comes from the introduction to the book, is wonderful to share with students. Jaffe not only shows how accounts of the Founding Fathers vary, but also explains why. People reinterpret accounts in response to the questions and issues of their times, making history relevant to themselves. In later chapters of the book, Jaffe shows how accounts of the Founding Fathers have changed from 1776 though the 1990s.

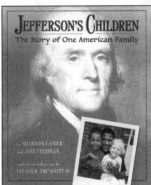

Jefferson's Children: The Story of One American Family (2000) by Shannon Lanier and Jane Feldman provides an account of Thomas Jefferson's family that stands in stark contrast to all the previous accounts that deny that Jefferson had children by Sally Hemings, his African-American slave.

Lanier tells what happened when the account he heard at home about being a black descendant of Thomas Jefferson bumped up against the traditional account presented at school:

> *I remember when I was in first grade, on Presidents' Day, I stood up and told the class I was the sixth great-grandson of Thomas Jefferson. The teacher told me to sit down and quit telling lies. I was so hurt I came home that afternoon and told my mom all about it. The next day, she marched in there and told the teacher that her son wasn't lying. "Where is your proof?" the teacher asked. "Where in the history books does it say that this is so?" And my mom told her that she had learned from her mama as her mama had learned from hers, and so on, from lips to ears, down through the generations.* (p. 11)

As the author describes how recent DNA findings have changed our understanding of the Jefferson family, he also draws on the reports of oral historians, scholars, and fellow members of his family. He learns from Annette Gordon-Reed, a law professor at New York University, that Jefferson's legacy lives on: "He was at the center of the birth of this nation. He continues to be at the center of its development as we ponder how we came to be the people we are today" (Gordon-Reed quoted in Lanier & Feldman, 2000, p. 31). In other words, the accounts of Jefferson are being reconsidered and rewritten.

REVEALING GAPS IN AVAILABLE EVIDENCE

Because they simply can't know all the details of what happened in the past, all authors of historical nonfiction deal with gaps in information. Sometimes the gaps are so small that they can just be acknowledged and not interfere with our understanding of whatever topic the author is addressing. But other times they are so large they limit our understanding. For example, in *George Washington and the Founding of a Nation* (2001), author Albert Marrin explains a significant shortage of evidence about George Washington because of an unfortunate event:

> *It is not always easy to learn about Washington. In a sense, we have both too much and not enough information. He wrote more than any other president in his own handwriting; he left at least 25,000 letters and several thousand diary pages. These writings deal with official business and everyday matters. Usually, they make for slow reading.*
>
> *Washington was a private person who did not like to talk about himself or share his inner self with others. His wife, Martha, protected his privacy and their relationship. We know that they exchanged hundreds of letters during the forty years of their marriage. After he died, she burned all but two. What did the burned letters say? Was it embarrassing? Did her husband ask her to burn the letters, or did she do it on her own? These are interesting questions, but we will never know the answers. Realizing this tells us something about history. However much we may know about the past, much of it remains unknown and unknowable. (p. 14)*

Pointing out the "unknown and the unknowable" provides important insight into the work of historians. No matter how hard they try to provide as much evidence as possible, there will always be information that is unavailable and beyond their reach.

The Power of One: Daisy Bates and the Little Rock Nine (2004) by Judith Bloom Fradin and Dennis Brindell Fradin is an account of the extraordinary efforts of Daisy Bates to promote school integration. By ensuring that a handful of African-American students, the Little Rock Nine, could attend a previously all-white high school in Arkansas, she "awakened the nation's conscience to the evils of segregation and hatred" (p. 145).

Daisy Bates's role as a civil rights activist is well known, but her early life is obscure. The authors comment on the lack of evidence about her birth:

> *Various sources list the year of her birth as 1912, 1914, 1920, and 1922. The problem is, no original birth certificate exists for Daisy Lee Gatson. Many southern towns kept scanty records for black people in the early 1900s. Black children frequently were born at home, and no one bothered to make or place on file official record of their birth. In a 1957 interview L. C. Bates told a newspaper reporter that his wife had been born thirty-five years earlier, "give or take a couple of years," which would make her birth year sometime between about 1920 and 1924. (p. 7)*

Pointing out the gap in evidence alerts readers to a couple of important points. First, in the South during the early part of the 20th century, officials didn't think it was important to record the births of black children. Second, it is impossible to determine the exact date of Daisy Bates's birth. To complicate matters further, Daisy Bates filed a "delayed birth certificate" for herself, claiming her date of birth as November 11, 1914. Her childhood friend, Beatrice Cowser Epps, disagrees. She told the authors that Daisy Bates was born the same year she was—1913—and that they had started school together and had always been in the same grade. Are you convinced? Would your students be convinced? You may not consider Daisy Bates's date-of-birth as significant as Washington's personal history, but both points make an equally compelling argument for the importance of revealing gaps in evidence. Sometimes history simply cannot be established with the evidence at hand.

Pointing Out People and Events that Have Been Intentionally Omitted from the Historical Record

Authors of historical nonfiction often alert readers to information that historians have consciously chosen to exclude from accounts. Why do these omissions happen? Sometimes because historians don't think the information is worth mentioning. It's simply not that important. Other times, it's because they are uncomfortable dealing with the information. It's a form of self-censorship.

In *With Courage and Cloth: Winning the Fight for a Woman's Right to Vote* (2004), Ann Bausum gives an account of the efforts of Alice Paul, who played a major role in the women's suffrage movement. The group of "silent sentinels" that Paul organized held cloth banners in front of the White House, asking President Woodrow Wilson to answer questions related to suffrage—questions that he had been avoiding. These "silent sentinels," members of Paul's National Woman's Party, were arrested for picketing and sent to jail. In an afterword, Bausum speculates about why Alice Paul has not been included in most historical accounts:

> It seems reasonable to expect the National Woman's Party [Alice Paul's organization] to be remembered. It was, after all, the group that promoted the same techniques of nonviolent resistance later popularized by Martin Luther King, Jr., during the Civil Rights Movement. "When all suffrage controversy has died away, it will be the little army of women with their purple, white, and gold banners, going to prison for their political freedom, that will be remembered," suffragist Doris Stevens predicted.
>
> However the silent sentinels and jailbirds were largely overlooked when historians recalled woman suffrage (if they did so at all). Sometimes historians simplified the suffrage story, telling about Elizabeth Cady Stanton and Susan B. Anthony but not Lucy Stone, or describing Catt's NAWSA but not Paul's National Woman's Party. Perhaps Paul's pickets seemed too radical, still too "unwomanly," to deserve mention. Perhaps omitting their role allowed historians to avoid the uncomfortable subject of the government's attempts to suppress these protesters. Perhaps, at least when most historians were men, presenting the whole story may not have seemed that important. Not until the 1970s did a growing number of women historians begin to uncover the subtleties of the history of woman suffrage. Their work has yet to be fully integrated into the nation's popular understanding of the past. (pp. 88–89)

This excerpt is not about Alice Paul's work, but about why she has not been part of conventional, mainstream historical accounts. Does she deserve to be included? By raising the concern, Bausum alerts us to the continuing struggle among historians to determine whose stories should be told.

Ida B. Wells: Mother of the Civil Rights Movement (2000) is an account of the life of the civil rights leader whom authors Dennis Brindell Fradin and Judith Bloom Fradin consider "one of the least known—yet one of the most important" (p. ix). Ida B. Wells was a founder of the NAACP, a women's suffrage advocate, and an unstoppable protestor of the lynchings of black citizens. So why is she relatively unknown? Here's what the authors suggest:

> *One reason Ida B. Wells is not better known is that she was militantly outspoken at a time when black people were expected to "know their place." . . . She made black people almost as uncomfortable as she made white people. Several times black leaders asked Ida to "soft-pedal" her criticisms. Wells refused and, by so doing, became the most militant voice of black protest of her time and the spiritual mother of our country's civil rights movement. (p. xii)*

Have historians been so uncomfortable with Ida B. Wells that they've failed to write her into historical accounts? This is a possibility to ponder. It is also one explanation for the differences among the few accounts we do have.

Books like the ones discussed in this section raise important questions about historical accounts. As you read historical nonfiction, see if you can spot comments about why accounts differ. Then discuss these comments with students to stimulate their thinking about the process of reading and writing history.

What Activities Help Students Understand the Concept of Historical Accounts?

Debbi Aizenstain and I selected the California gold rush of 1849 as the topic we would focus on when considering historical accounts with her fifth graders. Besides wanting them to learn the facts surrounding the gold rush, we wanted students to:

* see that not all accounts of the gold rush include the same evidence.
* discuss their thoughts and feelings as they read an account of one African-American man's experience during the gold rush.

* revise an account to include omitted information.
* extend the experience by writing and illustrating historical scrapbooks.

To begin, we selected *Hurry Freedom: African Americans in Gold Rush California* (2000) by Jerry Stanley as a book that the class would read and discuss. Debbi's class consisted of good readers who could, with our assistance, deal with the content of this interesting, well-written book. If that had not been the case, we could have chosen a less sophisticated book or made accommodations, such as providing taped readings of the Stanley book.

Like other books by Jerry Stanley (for example, *Children of the Dust Bowl, Big Annie of Calumet, Frontier Merchants*), *Hurry Freedom* focuses on a historical event through the experience of one or two people—in this case, an African-American man named Mifflin Gibbs who is discouraged with his life in Philadelphia and decides, against the advice of his family and friends, to head to California during the gold rush. He is desperate to move ahead in the world.

This engrossing story follows Gibbs as he travels to Panama, crosses the jungle, and finally takes a steamship to San Francisco. He arrives broke but hopeful. In time, Gibbs becomes a financial success. With his partner, Peter Lester, he opens a shoe store, and the two men become involved in politics in the black community. They are outraged by the fact that blacks in California do not have the right to testify in court. If they are wronged, they have no legal recourse. So Gibbs, along with fellow black citizens and white supporters, sends a petition to the state legislature six times and, heartbreakingly, six times it is defeated.

With this final defeat, Gibbs abandons California for Canada, and does not return to the U.S. until 1869. In 1870, he is admitted to the Arkansas bar association, becomes a judge, and is later appointed U.S. Ambassador to Madagascar. Stanley draws this conclusion about the life of Mifflin Gibbs: "It was a long road traveled to a fitting end and a lesson well learned: history has a knack for justice" (p. 80).

Debbi and I thought that this book would grab the students' attention, and it did. The mix of adventure, hardship, courage, and well-deserved victory is gripping. Through this unique account, students learned about Mifflin Gibbs and the California gold rush at the same time. They also learned, through the activities we provided, that historical accounts can be altered.

To introduce and develop an understanding of historical accounts, we followed these steps:

* **Weeks 1 and 2:** Reading and responding to an account of the gold rush: *Hurry Freedom: African Americans in Gold Rush California* by Jerry Stanley
* **Weeks 3 and 4:** Inserting information into an excerpt from a more general account: *The Gold Rush* by Bobbie Kalman
* **Weeks 5 and 6:** Extending the experience by creating scrapbooks detailing Mifflin Gibbs's experiences

WEEKS 1 AND 2: READING AND RESPONDING TO AN ACCOUNT OF THE GOLD RUSH

Debbi began by reading aloud the introduction to *Hurry Freedom* and stopping to discuss some of the points that Stanley makes. She spent time with the class discussing general information about the California gold rush, the free and enslaved black population that worked in the gold fields, and the unique case of Mifflin Gibbs—a free black man who recorded his experiences during the gold rush. This was important background information the class would need to understand the book.

Debbi created a word wall of words from the book, including *California, gold rush, forty-niners, African Americans,* and *prospectors.* As she added words, she discussed them with the class, encouraging students to use them in writing and in small-group discussions and to add more words to the wall as they continued reading *Hurry Freedom.*

When Debbi finished her Read Aloud, she asked students to reread the introduction on their own and complete a double-entry journal. In the column labeled "Text," they copied one or more excerpts that piqued their interest and raised questions, and in the column labeled "Personal Thoughts" they wrote their responses to items in the first column.

One benefit of using the double-entry journal is that when several students selected the same excerpt, which they often did, their responses were quite different. Those responses provided an interesting basis for discussion. Several students, for example, selected an excerpt about a black man named William Oliver who, because of his financial success during the gold rush, was able to buy his family's freedom. Figure 7.2 shows that excerpt and the responses of three students. While they all seem impressed by Oliver's feat, student #2 is dismayed that anyone would have to buy someone out of slavery in the first place.

Since the book contains only eight short chapters, students could read a chapter and prepare a double-entry journal each day. Most of our class time was set aside for discussion, but some of it was used for independent reading and journal writing. Figure 7.3 shows that from the start, students were able to select excerpts from *Hurry Freedom*'s introduction and respond to them. This type of journaling made the group discussions multifaceted and interesting.

One of the topics that we discussed was Mifflin Gibbs's motivation to find a better life by risking everything and heading to California. In *Hurry Freedom*, we learn that Gibbs was severely depressed about the quality of his life. "But instead of giving up, he had a talk with himself and he heard a voice from somewhere inside him. It commanded, 'What! Discouraged? Go do some great thing!'" (p. 6). Students were impressed by this, and for a few days this command was called out repeatedly in the classroom. Debbi also copied the quote and hung it in the front of the classroom, providing inspiration to all of us.

Students also reported feeling angry at the treatment Gibbs received. After reading that Gibbs was allowed to attend the opera but only in a section that was segregated from whites, one student wrote, "I felt that it was insulting to the black people that the white people have to put them separated like they were germs."

Text	Personal Thoughts
"William Oliver, an ex-slave from Maryland and cook for a wagon train, found gold and bought his wife and children out of slavery" (p. 16).	**Student #1:** I thought that it would be very rewarding to bring your family out of slavery. It's almost like how rewarding it is when you win a prize, except a greater accomplishment. **Student #2:** I realize how good it must feel to buy someone out of slavery but then why should you even have to do that?! You shouldn't have to buy someone out of slavery. **Student #3:** I feel happy and proud of William Oliver that he had luck finding gold and used it for a good cause.

Figure 7.2: *Three students respond to the same text excerpt with a mix of awe, pride, and indignation.*

Making Sense of History

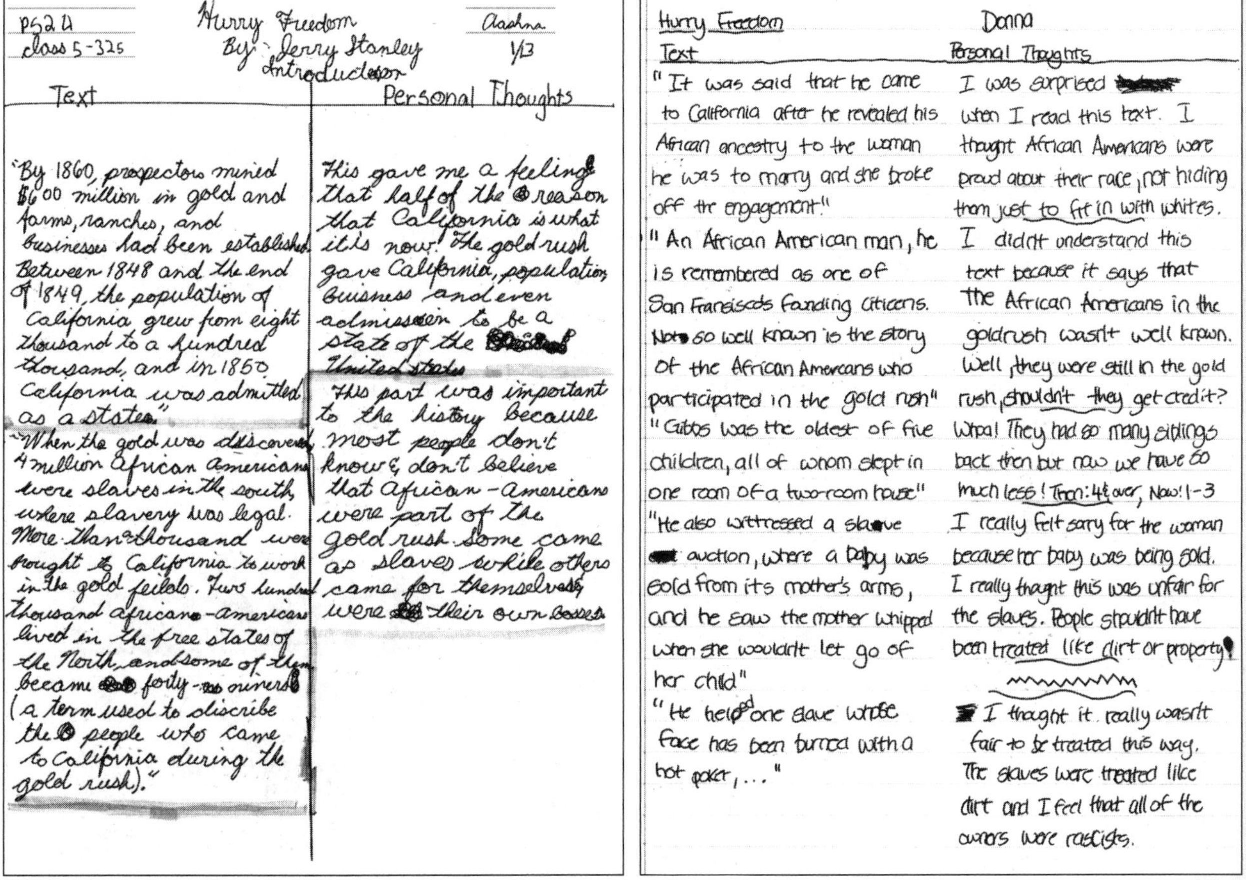

PS 24 class 5-325 — Hurry Freedom By: Jerry Stanley Introduction — Aashna 1/13

Text	Personal Thoughts
"By 1860, prospectors mined $600 million in gold and farms, ranches, and businesses had been established. Between 1848 and the end of 1849, the population of California grew from eight thousand to a hundred thousand, and in 1850 California was admitted as a state." "When the gold was discovered 4 million african americans were slaves in the south, where slavery was legal. More than a thousand were brought to California to work in the gold feilds. Two hundred thousand african-americans lived in the free states of the North, and some of them became forty-niners (a term used to discribe the people who came to California during the gold rush)."	This gave me a feeling that half of the reason that California is what it's now! The gold rush gave California, population, buisness and even admission to be a state of the United states. This part was important to the history because most people don't know & don't believe that african-americans were part of the gold rush. Some came as slaves while others came for themselves were their own bosses.

Hurry Freedom — Donna

Text	Personal Thoughts
"It was said that he came to California after he revealed his African ancestry to the woman he was to marry and she broke off the engagement!"	I was surprised when I read this text. I thought African Americans were proud about their race, not hiding them just to fit in with whites.
"An African American man, he is remembered as one of San Franciscos founding citicens. Not so well known is the story of the African Americans who participated in the gold rush"	I didn't understand this text because it says that the African Americans in the goldrush wasn't well known. Well, they were still in the gold rush, shouldn't they get credit?
"Gibbs was the oldest of five children, all of whom slept in one room of a two-room house"	Whoa! They had so many siblings back then but now we have so much less! Then: 4 & over, Now: 1-3
"He also witnessed a slave auction, where a baby was sold from its mother's arms, and he saw the mother whipped when she wouldn't let go of her child"	I really felt sorry for the woman because her baby was being sold. I really thought this was unfair for the slaves. People shouldn't have been treated like dirt or property!
"He helped one slave whose face has been burned with a hot poker, ..."	I thought it really wasn't fair to be treated this way. The slaves were treated like dirt and I feel that all of the owners were racists.

Figure 7.3: *Aashna and Donna's double-entry journals*

After reading that blacks were denied the right to testify in courts, another student wrote, "I felt so ANGRY! when I read this paragraph because I thought that this was unfair to every race in the world other than whites."

We received many responses of anger and outrage, but also of happiness and satisfaction. After reading that Mifflin Gibbs had many white customers and made many genuine friends, one student wrote, "This made me feel very happy because African Americans get along with the white(s)." As students completed the book, they were relieved that things worked out for Mifflin Gibbs in the long run.

By the end of the second week, Debbi and I were convinced that we had introduced students to an account that included evidence they were unlikely to find elsewhere. They were ready to grapple with an idea basic to the study of history: Not all accounts are the same.

WEEKS 3 AND 4: INSERTING INFORMATION INTO A MORE GENERAL ACCOUNT

My goal was to have students take what they had learned from *Hurry Freedom* and other books about the gold rush and add it to a simpler, less detailed account. I asked them to add information to the text, the illustrations, and even the captions of an existing account. This would be a concrete way to show students that not all accounts of the gold rush include the same evidence. They could modify a simple account with limited information by adding to it.

Before asking students to insert information into a second account, I modeled the process. Using the first page of Rhoda Blumberg's *The Great American Gold Rush* (1989), I read aloud to students, looking for places where I could add information. When I found places, I inserted a caret, numbered each place, and

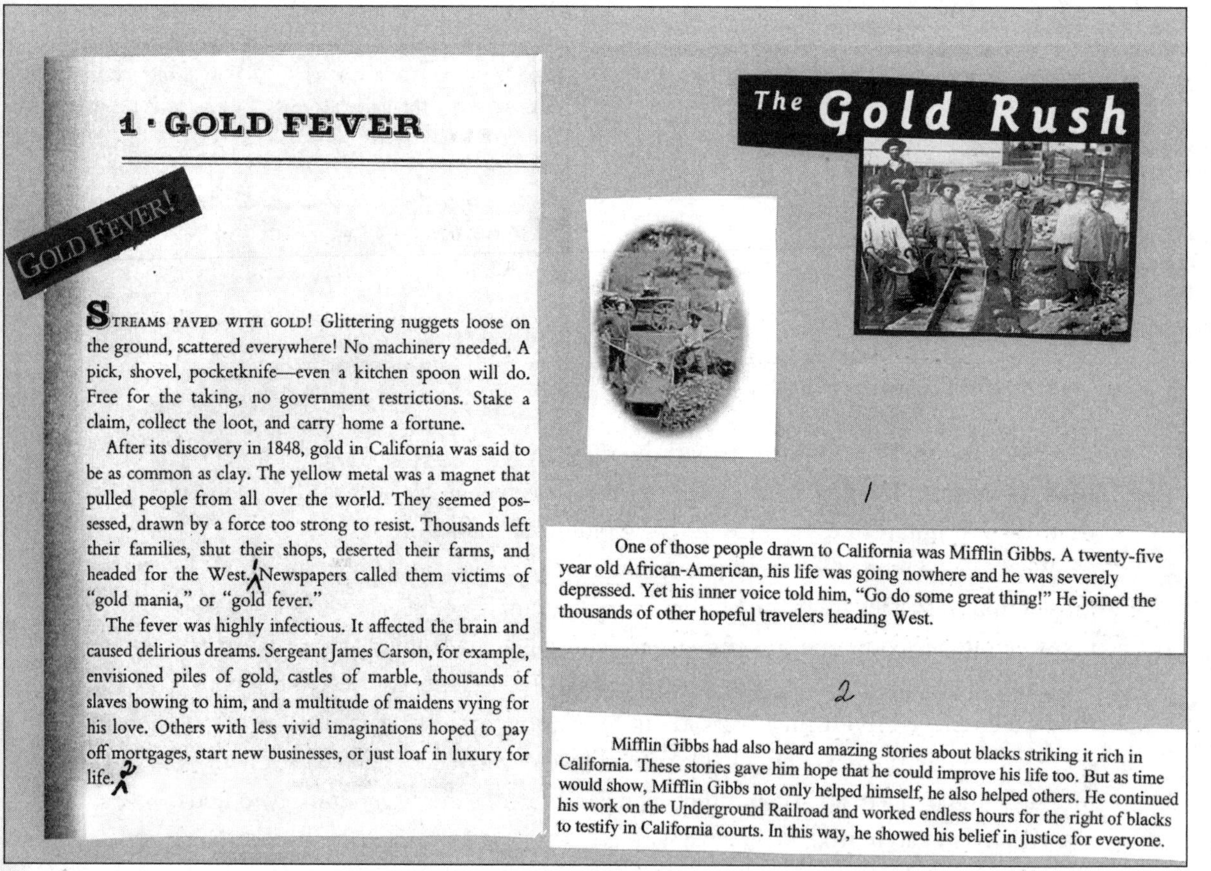

1 · GOLD FEVER

GOLD FEVER!

STREAMS PAVED WITH GOLD! Glittering nuggets loose on the ground, scattered everywhere! No machinery needed. A pick, shovel, pocketknife—even a kitchen spoon will do. Free for the taking, no government restrictions. Stake a claim, collect the loot, and carry home a fortune.

After its discovery in 1848, gold in California was said to be as common as clay. The yellow metal was a magnet that pulled people from all over the world. They seemed possessed, drawn by a force too strong to resist. Thousands left their families, shut their shops, deserted their farms, and headed for the West. Newspapers called them victims of "gold mania," or "gold fever."

The fever was highly infectious. It affected the brain and caused delirious dreams. Sergeant James Carson, for example, envisioned piles of gold, castles of marble, thousands of slaves bowing to him, and a multitude of maidens vying for his love. Others with less vivid imaginations hoped to pay off mortgages, start new businesses, or just loaf in luxury for life.

The Gold Rush

1

One of those people drawn to California was Mifflin Gibbs. A twenty-five year old African-American, his life was going nowhere and he was severely depressed. Yet his inner voice told him, "Go do some great thing!" He joined the thousands of other hopeful travelers heading West.

2

Mifflin Gibbs had also heard amazing stories about blacks striking it rich in California. These stories gave him hope that he could improve his life too. But as time would show, Mifflin Gibbs not only helped himself, he also helped others. He continued his work on the Underground Railroad and worked endless hours for the right of blacks to testify in California courts. In this way, he showed his belief in justice for everyone.

Figure 7.4: *Myra's model for adding to a historical account*

used stick-on notes to remind myself of the kind of information I wanted to add. Finally, I wrote out the information I wanted to add. See Figure 7.4.

Figure 7.5 shows the checklist I supplied to students to support their work. These directions encouraged them to look for gaps in information, gather information to fill those gaps, and write inserts. (See page 191 for a reproducible version of this checklist.)

We selected Bobbie Kalman's *The Gold Rush* (1999), which is part of the series Life in the West, as the second account to give students. In sharp contrast to *Hurry Freedom*, this book mentions African Americans only in passing—as slaves who might possibly find enough gold to buy their freedom. No free African Americans like Mifflin Gibbs are mentioned. The book is divided into short

Adding to a Historical Account

Step 1: Look for Gaps in Information

Read your account more than once. Look for places to add information. If you are reading a sentence, and you know more than what the author is telling you, this is a good spot to think about adding information. Ask yourself:

- Where can I add information?
- What can I add?

1. Put a caret (^) where you want to add information.
2. Use a stick-on note to answer the question, What can I add?

Step 2: Find Information and Take Notes

Look for information to add to your account. Begin with *Hurry Freedom*, but also use other books. Use the index to locate useful information. Ask yourself:

- What topics can I use to look up information in the index?
- What pages should I reread?
- What information do I want to include?
- What other books can I consult?

1. List your topics and the pages you will reread.
2. Take notes on each of your topics.

Step 3: Add to Your Account

Use the information you have gathered to add to your account. Write the inserts.

Figure 7.5: *Checklist for adding to a historical account*

stand-alone sections such as "Getting to the Gold Fields" and "Life at the Mines." We selected the ten sections that we felt would interest students the most. Debbi divided the class into small groups and assigned each group a section. We asked the groups to follow my directions and add to their section information they learned from *Hurry Freedom* and other books. Several students brought in books from the library to help with the research. Figure 7.6 lists books that were useful in supporting and supplementing this project. In addition to adding text, we also encouraged students to add illustrations and captions.

The results of this project were amazing! Figure 7.7 shows how Aashna and Richard added information to a two-page account entitled "Gold Strike." By comparing what the text said to what the students inserted, we see that Aashna and Richard engaged in some complex thinking:

* **Text:** The first paragraph in "Gold Strike" explains that many people, especially immigrants from Europe, wanted to escape the crowded conditions in the east.

  Insert #1: The students give specific information about one person, Mifflin Gibbs (who is not an immigrant), and explicitly tell why he wanted to leave. The students are adding new, more specific information.

Sources for Filling Information Gaps in Historical Accounts

The California Gold Rush by Jean Blashfield. Compass Point.

The California Gold Rush by Barbara Saffer. Mason Crest.

Gold: The True Story of Why People Search for It, Mine It, Trade It, Steal It, Mint It, Hoard It, Shape It, Wear It, Fight and Kill for It by Milton Meltzer. HarperCollins.

Gold Fever! Tales from the California Gold Rush by Rosalyn Schanzer. National Geographic.

The Gold Rush: A Primary Source History of the Search for Gold in California by Kerri O'Donnell. Rosen.

Gold Rush! The Young Prospector's Guide to Striking it Rich by James Klein. Illustrated by Michael Rohani. Tricycle.

The Gold Rush of 1849: Staking a Claim in California by Arthur Blake and Pamela Dailey. Millbrook.

The Wells Fargo Book of the Gold Rush by Margaret Rau. Atheneum.

Figure 7.6: *Books about the gold rush*

Making Sense of History

GOLD STRIKE

In the 1800s, most of the people in the United States and Canada lived in the eastern states and provinces. Communities, roads, and pastures marked the landscape. Eastern towns and cities were becoming crowded with newcomers from Europe and Britain. Land in the East was expensive. Many people wanted to have their own land and escape from the cramped conditions of city life.

The West

In the early 1800s, the western areas of the United States and Canada were mainly unsettled. Miles of grassy plains and steep mountains lay to the west of the busy, populated eastern cities. At first, only a small number of people made the long and difficult journey west. Most of them were men who went to start ranches or work as cowboys.

Mifflin Gibbs was one of those people

1) A black man from Philadelphia named Mifflin Gibbs was one of those people. He had a very depressing life. He was the sole supporter of his family since he was eight years old, when his dad died, and all he earned was $3.00 a month. However, he listened to a voice deep inside him that said, "Go do some great thing."

Mifflin Gibbs, a sad, depressed man.

Gold beckons

In the mid-1800s, gold was discovered in the rivers of western North America. It took time for people to learn of this discovery. When the news of gold findings traveled east, many people did not believe these reports to be true. When some of the gold was brought to the East, however, people quickly became interested! Rumors and newspaper headlines convinced people that there really was gold in the West. People across the continent were eager to make a claim and become rich. Thousands of people made the trip west in search of their fortune. A great **migration** of people to the West in search of gold was known as a **gold rush**.

The prospectors

The people who headed west to search for gold were called **prospectors**. When they arrived, there were plenty of opportunities for them to become **miners**. Anyone who came to the gold fields had a chance of striking gold.

1) Oregon trail - deaths
2) White have more chance they tried to stop blacks

2) One way to migrate to California was over the Oregon Trail. Many people used this trail. Some people froze to death, while many others got diseases such as cholera and dysentery. Still others were bitten or killed by wild animals. All this happened because at that time, the roads were new and people had extremely little experience in overland traveling. As a result, at least 1,200 people died. Skeletons and bones of horses and humans littered the trail.

3) Everyone had a chance to mine, but mainly it was the white men who did the mining. The whites had more chance to mine because they banned the blacks from entering gold fields such as Sierra Nevada. Also, the whites would beat up the blacks to keep them away from the fields.

In addition, the whites and mining associations worked together to build artificial channels, called sluice boxes, to stop the rivers from flowing.

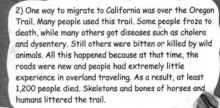

Abandoned wagons, dead horses, a couple of torn tents, poor tired men, and broken parts of wagons, were the consequences of little knowledge in overland traveling.

Figure 7.7: *Aashna and Richard's additions to "Gold Strike"*

Chapter 7: Historical Accounts

* **Text:** The account says that thousands of people migrated west to search for gold.

   Insert #2: The students give examples of specific hardships endured during the westward migration. These hardships include fierce weather conditions, diseases such as cholera and dysentery, and lack of travel experience. In effect, the students correct the account which seems to suggest—through omission—that migrating west was unproblematic.

* **Text:** The account says that anyone had a chance of finding gold.

   Insert #3: The students add information about the obstacles African Americans faced. They mention the efforts to ban blacks from some gold fields and threaten them physically. The students are correcting the account to show that not everyone had equal opportunity to find gold.

* **Text:** The illustration of wagons heading west has no caption.

   Caption Insert: The students correct the notion that travel was easy. They add their own illustrations of broken and abandoned wagons, dead horses, and tired men.

Over and over, Debbi and I found students enthusiastically engaged in this project. They had little or no trouble finding places to insert information. Nor did they have difficulty connecting specific information about Mifflin Gibbs to the more general information in *The Gold Rush*. Sometimes they had a great deal to say. Figure 7.8, for example, shows the lengthy inserts students wrote for the account of "Life in the Mines."

Students pasted their completed accounts and inserted materials on colored paper and made a class book. An introduction explained that, since historical accounts don't tell the whole story, the class expanded an existing account of the gold rush by adding information about the experience of African Americans.

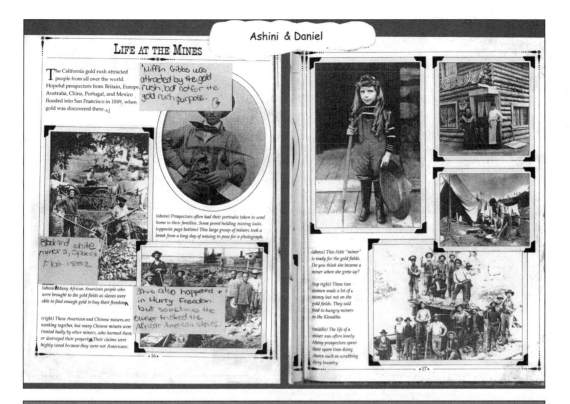

1. Mifflin Gibbs was one of the people attracted to the gold rush. He was heading for California, but not only for the purpose of finding gold. He wanted to work and start a new life. The idea came to him after his inner voice said, "What! Discouraged? Go do some great thing!"

When Mifflin Gibbs arrived in San Francisco, California with only ten cents, he was discouraged and wasted the ten cents on a cigar. Later on he got a job as a carpenter, at a house under construction. He only worked there for one week.

After that he polished shoes. Soon he had saved enough money to became partners with Peter Lester and they opened the Boot Emporium. They both sold shoes and boots for blacks and whites. While working in the Boot Emporium, they operated an 'Underground Railroad' in California. They used some of the money they earned to help other blacks escape to Mexico.

2. The slaves were brought to the Spanish Flat because they had to work and find gold for their freedom and for the freedom of their families. Sometimes the owners would lie to the slaves to get the gold the slaves found. Later, the owners would let the slaves go find more gold. Most of the people did not find gold, so it took time for the slaves to be able to buy their freedom or set their loves ones out of slavery.

3. Some white owners tricked their black slaves by telling them they were free. Then, after a while, the slaves collected enough money to buy rest of their family out of slavery. All of the sudden, the owner said the slave was a fugitive and took him back and kept the money the slave was going to use to buy his family out of slavery. This happened to many people including Sandy Jones. At the age 64, Sandy Jones's owner freed him. After working for 6 months he earned $3,000 to buy his wife and children out of slavery. Then his owner claimed Jones a fugitive and got him back as a slave. Jones's $3,000, which he was going to use to buy his family out of slavery, was gone too.

4. Sometimes Californians planned to do bad things to people of other races. One day, in November 1851, a white man wanted to buy a certain pair if boots from the Boot Emporium. He said he would come back later to purchase them and asked if they could be held for him. Peter Lester agreed. A second man came later and wanted to buy the same pair of boots. He was told they were being held for a customer. The second man left angry and came back with the first man. The first man used racial names when referring to Lester. Then, while one clubbed Lester to the ground, the other man pointed a gun at Gibbs, so he wouldn't move. In the end, the two men left laughing as Lester was left unconscious in a pool of blood.

Figure 7.8: *Lengthy additions to "Life at the Mines"*

WEEKS 5 AND 6: EXTENDING THE EXPERIENCE BY CREATING SCRAPBOOKS

To help students solidify their knowledge about Mifflin Gibbs, Debbi and I had them create scrapbooks based on Gibbs's life. Students wrote from Gibbs's point of view and included graphics and made souvenirs that captured his experience. One scrapbook's cover had a photograph of Mifflin Gibbs and his famous "Go do some great thing" quote. The contents included maps of where Mifflin Gibbs lived—first in Philadelphia and then in

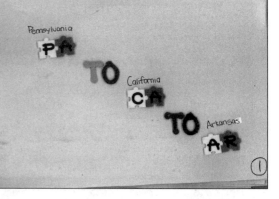

Cover and sample pages from a student-made scrapbook

Making Sense of History

San Francisco—the boat ticket for his ride to San Francisco, and some hair from the mule he rode across Panama. Students called it "a fun activity"; it was an upbeat way to end the study.

Concluding Thoughts

Inserting material from one or more accounts into another account is a concrete way of showing students that historians *select* their information. What one historian includes another might not. It all depends on the questions that are being asked. That's why we can always expect new history books and different ways of seeing the past. It's what keeps the discipline of history alive.

Final Thoughts

These are promising times for K–12 history teachers. Here in New York City, social studies is the new priority. Content is making a comeback. I suspect that this is true across the country and, as such, believe that now is the time to act—to grab the opportunity to try new things.

In this new climate, I urge you to try teaching history according to the historian's rules of the game. Teach your students about the historian's sense-making concepts, which are at the heart of Part Two of this book. At the same time, don't forget the three essential elements of good history teaching:

* Historical thinking

* Historical literature

* Hands-on experience

Putting these elements together will help you think about goals, materials, and activities. As a result, you will have a coherent teaching plan—a plan that is based on theory and research, but works in the real world with living, breathing students.

In this book, I provide you with ideas for how to do all this. Begin by trying out my ideas, but in time don't hesitate to adapt them to suit your needs and the needs of your students. I encourage you to do this. Above all, make history happen in your classroom.

Making Sense of History

Appendix 1: T-Chart for Examining Historical Context

What's Familiar? Past & Present (Me, Too!)	What's Unfamiliar? Past Only (Not Me!)

An explanation of how to use this chart appears on pages 58–60.

Appendix 2: Fact Pyramid and Because Box

An explanation of how to use this chart appears on pages 90–94.

Name: _____

What Do You Think?

Fill in the Fact Pyramid with four important pieces of information that you have read about (1—the most important—to 4—the least important). Next to each section, write a sentence explaining why you chose this fact as most or least important.

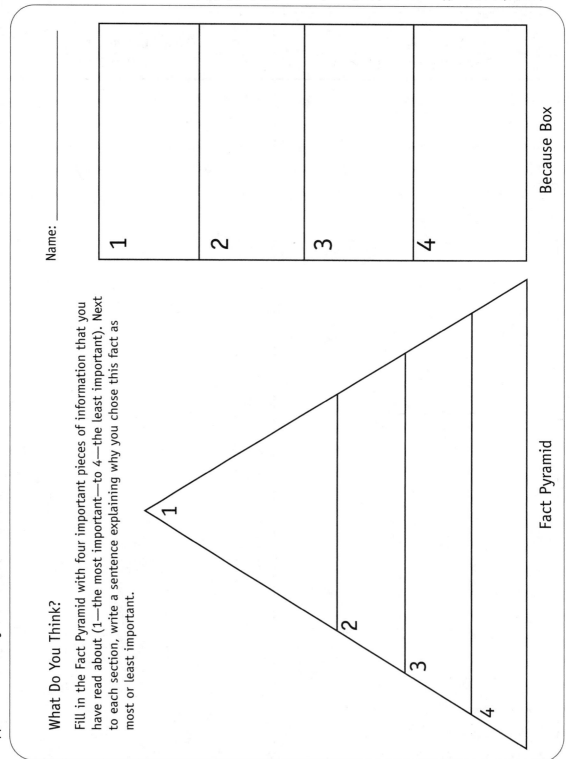

Fact Pyramid

Because Box

Planning Sheet

What would _____ say about _____?

1. _____

   _____

2. _____

   _____

3. _____

   _____

Final Comment:

_____

_____

Picture Ideas:

An explanation of how to use this sheet appears on pages 118–120.

Appendix 4: Chart for Sorting Fact and Fiction

Fact	Fiction	Not Sure

An explanation of how to use this sheet appears on pages 152–155.

Adding to a Historical Account

Step 1: Look for Gaps in Information

Read your account more than once. Look for places to add information. If you are reading a sentence, and you know more than what the author is telling you, this is a good spot to think about adding information. Ask yourself:

- Where can I add information?

- What can I add?

1. Put a caret (^) where you want to add information.

2. Use a stick-on note to answer the question, What can I add?

Step 2: Find Information and Take Notes

Look for information to add to your account. Begin with *Hurry Freedom*, but also use other books. Use the index to locate useful information. Ask yourself:

- What topics can I use to look up information in the index?

- What pages should I reread?

- What information do I want to include?

- What other books can I consult?

1. List your topics and the pages you will reread.

2. Take notes on each of your topics.

Step 3: Add to Your Account

Use the information you have gathered to add to your account. Write the inserts.

An explanation of how to use this sheet appears on pages 178–182.

Bibliography

Professional References Cited

Adhikari, M. (2002). History and story: Unconventional history in Michael Ondaatje's *The English Patient* and James A. Michener's *Tales of the South Pacific*. *History and Theory, 41*, 43–55.

Alleman, J., & Brophy, J. (1994). Teaching that lasts: College students' reports of learning activities experienced in elementary school social studies. *Social Science Record, 31*, 42–46.

Alleman, J., Brophy, J., & Knighton, B. (2003). Co-constructing classroom resources. *Social Studies and the Young Learner, 16*, 5–8.

Apol, L., Sakuma, A., Reynolds, T. M., & Rop, S. K. (2003). "When can we make paper cranes?": Examining pre-service teachers' resistance to critical readings of historical fiction. *Journal of Literacy Research, 34*, 429–464.

Bailyn, B. (1994). *On the teaching and writing of history*. Hanover, NH: University Press of New England.

Bain, R. B. (2005). "They thought the world was flat?" Applying the principles of how people learn in teaching high school history. In M. S. Donovan, & J. D. Bransford (Eds.), *How students learn: History in the classroom* (pp. 179–213). Washington, DC: National Academies Press.

Barton, K. C. (2005). "Best not to forget them": Secondary students' judgments of historical significance in Northern Ireland. *Theory and Research in Social Education, 33*, 9–44.

Barton, K. C., & Levstik, L. (1998) "It wasn't a good part of history": National identity and students' explanations of historical significance. *Teachers College Record, 99*, 478–513.

Barton, K. C., & Levstik, L. (2003). Why don't more history teachers engage students in interpretation? *Social Education, 67*, 358–361.

Barton, K. C., & Levstik, L. S. (2004). *Teaching history for the common good*. Mahwah, NJ: Erlbaum.

Berlin, I. (2004). American slavery in history and memory and the search for social justice. *The Journal of American History, 90*, 1251–1268.

Brooks, W., & Hampton, G. (2005). Safe discussions rather than first hand encounters: Adolescents examine racism through one historical fiction text. *Children's Literature in Education, 36*, 83–98.

Buehl, D. (2001). *Classroom strategies for interactive learning*. Newark, DE: International Reading Association.

Cercadillo, L. (2001). Significance in history: Students' ideas in England and Spain. In A. Dickinson, P. Gordon, & P. Lee (Eds.), *International review of history education: Vol. 3. Raising standards in history education* (pp. 116–145). Portland, OR: Woburn Press.

Coats, K. (2005). [Review of the book *Day of tears: A novel in dialogue*]. *The Bulletin of the Center for Children's Books, 58*, 497.

Cohen, P. (1998, July 18). A woman's worth: 1857 letter echoes still. *The New York Times*, pp. B7, B9.

Collier, C. (1999). *Brother Sam and all that*. Orange, CT: Clearwater Press.

Cowley, R. (Ed.). (1999). *What if? The world's foremost military historians imagine what might have been*. New York: Berkley Books.

Cunningham, D. (2004). Empathy without illusions. *Teaching History, 114*, 24–29.

Darnton, R. (1984). *The great cat massacre and other episodes in French cultural history*. New York: Basic Books.

Davis, J. B. (2003). Identifying with ancestors: Tracking the history of America. *Social Studies and the Young Learner, 16*(2), 13–16.

Davis, O. L., Jr. (2001). In pursuit of historical empathy. In O. L. Davis Jr., E. A. Yeager, & S. J. Foster (Eds.), *Historical empathy and perspective taking in social studies* (pp. 1–12). Lanham, MD: Rowan & Littlefield.

Donovan, M. S., & Bransford, J. D. (2005). Introduction. *How students learn: History in the classroom* (pp. 1–27). Washington, DC: National Academies Press.

Downey, M. T. (1996). *Writing to learn history in the intermediate grades*. Berkeley, CA: National Center for the Study of Writing and Literacy. (ERIC Document Reproduction Service No. ED 397422)

Dudziak, M. L. (June 2004). Brown as a Cold War case. *The Journal of American History, 91*. Retrieved July 2, 2004, from http://www.historycooperative.org/journals/jah/91.1/dudziak.html

Edinger, M. (2000). *Seeking history: Teaching with primary sources in grades 4–6*. Portsmouth, NH: Heinemann.

Ellis, J. J. (2004). *His excellency: George Washington*. New York: Knopf.

Ellis, J. J. (2005, July 31). [Review of the book *Thomas Paine and the promise of America*]. *The New York Times Book Review*, p. 15.

Engberg, G. (2002). Talking with Phillip Hoose. *Book Links, 11*, 11–13.

Engberg, G. (2002/2003). Talking with Ken Mochizuki. *Book Links, 12*, 7–10.

Epstein, T. (1998). Deconstructing differences in African-American and European-American adolescents' perspectives on U.S. history. *Curriculum Inquiry, 28*, 397–423.

Epstein, T. (2001). Racial identity and young people's perspectives on social education. *Theory into Practice, 40*, 42–47.

Evers, J. (2003). Review of the book *History makers: A questioning approach to reading and writing biographies. The Social Studies, 94,* 279.

Field, S. (2001). Perspectives and elementary social studies. In O. L. Davis Jr., E. A. Yeager, & S. J. Foster (Eds.), *Historical empathy and perspective taking in social studies* (pp. 115–138). Lanham, MD: Rowan & Littlefield.

Fischer, D. H. (2004). *Washington's crossing.* New York: Oxford.

Foner, E. (2003). *Who owns history? Rethinking the past in a changing world.* New York: Hill & Wang.

Foster, S. J. (1999). Using historical empathy to excite students about the study of history: Can you empathize with Neville Chamberlain? *The Social Studies, 90,* 18–24.

Foster, S. J. (2001). Historical empathy in theory and practice: Some final thoughts. In O. L. Davis Jr., E. A. Yeager, & S. J. Foster (Eds.), *Historical empathy and perspective taking in social studies* (pp. 167–181). Lanham, MD: Rowan & Littlefield.

Freedman, R. (1994). Bring 'em back alive: Writing history and biography for young people. *School Library Journal, 40,* 138–141.

Fresch, E. T. (2004). *Connecting children with children, past and present: Motivating students for inquiry and action.* Portsmouth, NH: Heinemann.

Furin, T. L. (2003). High-stakes testing: Death of our democracy? *Social Studies and the Young Learner, 15*(4), 32.

Gago, M. (2005). Children's understanding of historical narrative in Portugal. In R. Ashby, P. Gordon, & P. Lee (Eds.), *Understanding history: Recent research in history education: Vol. 4. International review of history education* (pp. 83–97). London: RoutledgeFalmer.

Gaines, K. (2004). Whose integration was it? An introduction. *The Journal of American History, 91.* Retrieved June 30, 2004, from http://www.historycooperative.org/journals/jah/91.1/gaines.html

Gallavan, N. P., & Kottler, E. (2002). After the reading assignment: Strategies for leading student-centered classroom conversations. *The Social Studies, 93,* 267–271.

Gerwin, D., & Zevin, J. (2003). *Teaching U.S. history as mystery.* Portsmouth, NH: Heinemann.

Giorgis, C., & Johnson, N. J. (2004). Talking with Russell Freedman. *Book Links, 13,* 43–45.

Gleick, J. (2003, August 16). Known to everyone and no one. *The New York Times,* pp. A15, A17.

Grant, S. G. (2001). It's just the facts, or is it? Teachers' practices and students' understandings of history. *Theory and Research in Social Education, 29,* 65–108

Grant, S. G. (2003). *History lessons: Teaching, learning, and testing in U.S. high school classrooms.* Mahwah, NJ: Erlbaum.

Greenblatt, S. (2004). *Will in the world: How Shakespeare became Shakespeare.* New York: Norton.

Gustin, G. (2004). [Review of the book *The voice that challenged a nation.*] *School Library Journal, 50,* 120.

Hakim, J. (1993). *A history of us: Vol. 3. From colonies to country.* New York: Oxford.

Harvey, S. (1998). *Nonfiction matters: Reading, writing, and research in grades 3–8.* York, ME: Stenhouse.

Holland, K. E., & Shaw, L. A. (1993). Dances between stances. In K. E. Holland, R. A. Hungerford, & S. B. Ernst (Eds.), *Journeying: Children responding to literature* (pp. 114–136). Portsmouth, NH: Heinemann.

Holt, T. (1990). *Thinking historically: Narrative, imagination, and understanding.* New York: College Entrance Examination Board.

Howard, R. W. (2003). The shrinking of social studies. *Social Education, 67,* 285–288.

Hsiao, Y. (2005). Taiwanese students' understanding of differences in history textbook accounts. In R. Ashby, P. Gordon, & P. Lee (Eds.), *Understanding history: Recent research in history education: Vol. 4. International review of history education* (pp. 54–67). London: RoutledgeFalmer.

Hunt, M. (2000). Teaching historical significance. In J. Arthur & R. Phillips (Eds.), *Issues in history teaching* (pp. 39–53). London: Routledge.

Hunt, M. (2003). Historical significance. *History Teacher* Supplement, 36, 33–36.

Hurst, C. (1999, November). [Review of the book *The Birchbark House*]. *Carol Hurst's Children's Literature Newsletter.* Retrieved July 3, 2005, from http:///www.carolhurst.com/titles/ birchbarkhouse/html

Janeczko, P. B. (1999). *How to write poetry.* New York: Scholastic.

Johnson, P. (2005). *George Washington: The founding father.* New York: HarperCollins.

Landorf, H., & Lowenstein, E. (2004). The Rosa Parks "myth": A third grade history investigation. *Social Studies and the Young Learner, 16,* 5–9.

Lee, M. (2004). *Promoting historical inquiry using secondary sources: Exploring the promise and possibilities in new genres of historical writing.* Paper presented at the annual meeting of the American Educational Research Association, San Diego, CA.

Lee, P. (1998). "A lot of guess work goes on": Children's understanding of historical accounts. *Teaching History, 92,* 29–36.

Lee, P. (2001). *Understanding history.* Centre for the Study of Historical Consciousness, University of British Columbia, Vancouver, B.C., http://www.cshc.ubc.ca.

Lee, P. (2005). Putting principles into practice: Understanding history. In M. S. Donovan, & J. D. Bransford (Eds.), *How students learn: History in the classroom* (pp. 31–77). Washington, DC: National Academies Press.

Lee, P., & Ashby, R. (2000). Progression in historical understanding among students ages 7–14. In P. N. Stearns, P. Seixas, & S. Wineburg (Eds.), *Knowing, teaching, and learning history: National and international perspectives* (pp. 199–222). New York: New York University Press.

Lee, P., & Ashby, R. (2001). Empathy, perspective taking, and rational understanding. In O. L. Davis Jr., E. A. Yeager, & S. J. Foster (Eds.), *Historical empathy and perspective taking in social studies* (pp. 21–50). Lanham, MD: Rowan & Littlefield.

Lee, P., Ashby, R., & Dickinson, A. (2001). Signs of the times: The state of history education in the UK. In A. Dickinson, P. Gordon, & P. Lee (Eds.), *International review of history education: Vol. 3. Raising standards in history education* (pp. 190–218). Portland, OR: Woburn Press.

Bibliography

Lee, P., & Shemilt, D. (2003). A scaffold, not a cage: Progression and progression models in history. *Teaching History, 113*, 13–23.

Lee, P., & Shemilt, D. (2004). "I just wish we could go back in the past and find out what really happened": Progression in understanding about historical accounts. *Teaching History, 117*, 25–34.

Levstik, L. S. (1997). "Any history is someone's history": Listening to multiple voices from the past. *Social Education, 61*, 48–51.

Levstik, L. S., & Barton, K. C. (2001). *Doing history: Investigating with children in elementary and middle schools.* (2nd ed.). Mahwah, NJ: Erlbaum.

Lindquist, T. (n.d.). *Why and how I teach with historical fiction.* Retrieved on June 21, 2005, from http://teacher.scholastic.com/lessonrepro/lessonplans/instructor/social1.htm

Lindquist, T. (2002). *Seeing the whole through social studies.* (2nd ed.). Portsmouth, NH: Heinemann.

Lomas, T. (1990). *Teaching and assessing historical understanding.* London: The Historical Association.

Lowenthal, D. (1985). *The past is a foreign country.* Cambridge, United Kingdom: Cambridge University Press.

Martin, D., & Brooke, B. (2002). Getting personal: Making effective use of historical fiction in the history classroom. *Teaching History, 108*, 30–35.

Mayer, R. H. (1998). Connecting narrative and historical thinking: A research-based approach to teaching history. *Social Education, 62*, 97–100.

Mayer, R. H. (1999). Use the story of Anne Hutchinson to teach historical thinking. *The Social Studies, 90*, 105–109.

McCormick, T. (2004). Letters from Trenton, 1776: Teaching with primary sources. *Social Studies and the Young Learner, 17*, 5–12.

Mccullagh, C. B. (2004). What do historians argue about? *History and Theory, 43*, 18–38.

McCullough, D. (2005). *1776.* New York: Simon & Schuster.

McKeown, M. G., & Beck, I. L. (1994). Making sense of accounts of history: Why young students don't and how they might. In G. Leinhardt, I. L. Beck, & C. Stainton, (Eds.), *Teaching and learning in history* (pp. 1–26). Hillsdale, NJ: Erlbaum.

Miksch, K. L., & Ghere, D. (2004). Teaching Japanese-American incarceration. *The History Teacher, 37*(2), 211–227.

Mosborg, S. (2002a). Recruiting history knowledge when reading the daily news: On background narratives and footing shifts. Paper presented at the International Conference of the Learning Sciences, Seattle, WA.

Mosborg, S. (2002b). Speaking of history: How adolescents use their knowledge of history in reading the daily news. *Cognition and Instruction, 20*, 323–358.

National Center for History in the Schools. (1994). *National standards for United States history: Exploring the American experience.* Los Angeles, UCLA. (available online at www.sscnet.ucla.edu/nchs)

National Council for History Education. (2003). *Building a history curriculum: Guidelines for teaching history in schools.* (2nd ed.). Westlake, OH: NCHE.

National Council for the Social Studies. (1994). *Expectations of excellence: Curriculum standards for social studies.* Washington, DC: National Council for the Social Studies.

Newmann, F. M., Marks, H. M., & Gamoran, A. (1996). Authentic pedagogy and student performance. *American Journal of Education, 104,* 280–312.

Newmann, F. M., & Wehlange, G. G. (1993). Five standards of authentic instruction. *Educational Leadership, 50,* 8–12.

Oja, M. F. (1988). Fictional history and historical fiction: Solzhenitsyn and Kis as exemplars. *History and Theory, 27,* 111–124.

Pace, D. (2004). The amateur in the operating room: History and the scholarship of teaching and learning. *American Historical Review, 109,* 1171–1192.

Parker, W. C. (2001). *Social studies in elementary education* (11th ed.). Upper Saddle River, NJ: Merrill/Prentice Hall.

Partington, G. (1980). The idea of an historical education. Slough, UK: NFER.

Paxton, R. J. (2003). Don't know much about history—never did. *Phi Delta Kappan, 85,* 265–273.

Percoco, J. A. (2001). *Divided we stand: Teaching about conflict in U.S. history.* Portsmouth, NH: Heinemann.

Power, C. L. (2003). Challenging the pluralism of our past: Presentism and the selective tradition in historical fiction written for young people. *Research in the Teaching of English, 37,* 425–466.

Rochman, H. (1999). [Review of the book *The Birchbark House*]. *Booklist, 95,* 1427.

Rochman, H. (2005). The Booklist interview: Alexandria LaFaye. *Booklist, 101,* 1673.

Routman, R. (2000). *Kids' poems: Teaching third and fourth graders to love writing poetry.* New York: Scholastic.

Scheurman, G. & Newmann, F. M. (1998). Authentic intellectual work in social studies: Putting performance before pedagogy. *Social Education, 62,* 23–25.

Seixas, P. (1994). Students' understanding of historical significance. *Theory and Research in Social Education, 22,* 281–304.

Seixas, P. (1997). Mapping the terrain of historical significance. *Social Education, 61,* 22–27.

Selwyn, D., & Maher, J. (2003). *History in the present tense: Engaging students through inquiry and action.* Portsmouth, NH: Heinemann.

Shaughnessy, J., & Haladyna, T. (1985). Research on student attitude toward social studies. *Social Education, 49*(8), 692–695.

Spiegel, D. L. (2005). *Classroom discussion: Strategies for engaging all students, building higher-level thinking skills, and strengthening reading and writing across the curriculum.* New York: Scholastic.

Staff of Social Education. (2003). No Child Left Behind: The impact on social studies classrooms. *Social Education, 67,* 291–295.

Steffy, S., & Hood, W. J. (Eds.). (1994). *If this is social studies, why isn't it boring?* York, ME: Stenhouse.

Strout, C. (1992). Border crossings: History, fiction and dead certainties. *History and Theory, 31,* 153–162.

Tally, S. (2000). *Almost America: From the colonists to Clinton: A "what if" history of the U.S.* New York: Quill/HarperCollins.

VanSledright, B. A. (1995). "I don't remember—the ideas are all jumbled in my head": 8th graders' reconstructions of colonial American history. *Journal of Curriculum and Supervision, 10,* 317–345.

VanSledright, B. A. (1997/1998). On the importance of historical positionality to thinking about and teaching history. *International Journal of Social Education, 12,* 1–18.

VanSledright, B. A. (2002a). Confronting history's interpretive paradox while teaching fifth graders to investigate the past. *American Educational Research Journal, 39,* 1089–1115.

VanSledright, B. A. (2002b). Fifth graders investigating history in the classroom: Results from a researcher-practitioner design experiment. *Elementary School Journal, 103,* 131–160.

VanSledright, B. A. (2004). What does it mean to think historically . . . and how do you teach it? *Social Education, 68,* 230–233.

VanSledright, B. A., & Afflerbach, P. (2005). Assessing the status of historical sources: An exploratory study of eight U.S. students reading documents. In R. Ashby, P. Gordon, & P. Lee (Eds.), *Understanding history: Recent research in history education: Vol. 4. International review of history education* (pp. 1–20). London: RoutledgeFalmer.

VanSledright, B. A., & Frankes, L. (2000). Concept- and strategic-knowledge development in history study: A comparative exploration in two fourth-grade classrooms. *Cognition and Instruction, 18,* 239–283.

Wineburg, S. (1999). Historical thinking and other unnatural acts. *Phi Delta Kappan, 80,* 488–499.

Wineburg, S. (2004). Crazy for history. *Journal of American History, 90*(4), 1401–1414.

Wineburg, S. S., & Fournier, J. (1994). Contextualized thinking in history. In M. Carretero & J. F. Voss (Eds.), *Cognitive and instructional processes in history and the social sciences* (pp. 285–308). Hillsdale, NJ: Erlbaum.

Yeager, E. A., & Foster, S. J. (2001). The role of empathy in the development of historical understanding. In O. L. Davis, Jr., E. A. Yeager, & S. J. Foster (Eds.), *Historical empathy and perspective taking in social studies* (pp. 13–19). Lanham, MD: Rowan & Littlefield.

Zarnowski, M. (1990). *Learning about biographies: A reading-and-writing approach for children.* Urbana, IL: National Council of Teachers of English.

Zarnowski, M. (1996). Constructing historical interpretations in elementary school: A look at process in product. In J. Brophy (Ed.), *Advances in research on teaching: Vol. 6. Teaching and learning history* (pp. 183–205). Greenwich, CT: JAI Press.

Zarnowski, M. (2002). Historical nonfiction and biography. In A. A. McClure & J. V. Kristo (Eds.), *Adventuring with books: A booklist for pre-k–grade 6* (13th ed.). Urbana, IL: National Council of Teachers of English.

Zarnowski, M. (2003). *History makers: A questioning approach to reading and writing biographies.* Portsmouth, NH: Heinemann.

Zarnowski, M. (2004). Biography from a variety of perspectives. *Social Studies and the Young Learner, 17,* 22–24.

Children's Books Cited

Adams, M. M. (2005). *The life and times of Cleopatra.* Hockessin, DE: Mitchell Lane.

Adler, D. A. (2000). *America's champion swimmer: Gertrude Ederle.* San Diego, CA: Harcourt.

Adler, D. A. (2004). *George Washington: An illustrated biography.* New York: Holiday House.

Allen, T. B. (2004). *George Washington, spymaster: How the Americans outspied the British and won the Revolutionary War.* Washington, DC: National Geographic.

Ammon, R. (2000). *Conestoga wagons.* New York: Holiday House.

Amstel, M. (2000). *Sybil Ludington's midnight ride.* Minneapolis, MN: Carolrhoda.

Anderson, L. H. (2000). *Fever 1793.* New York: Simon & Schuster.

Andryszewski, T. (1993). *The Dust Bowl: Disaster on the plains.* Madison, WI: Turtleback.

Armstrong, W. H. (1969). *Sounder.* New York: HarperTrophy.

Aronson, M. (2003). *Witch-hunt: Mysteries of the Salem witch trials.* New York: Atheneum.

Aten, J. (2001). *Our living Constitution: Then and now.* New York: Good Apple.

Atkin, S. B. (1993). *Voices from the fields: Children of migrant farmworkers tell their stories.* New York: Little, Brown.

Barasch, L. (2004). *Knockin' on wood: Starring Peg Leg Bates.* New York: Lee & Low.

Bartoletti, S. C. (1996). *Growing up in coal country.* Boston: Houghton Mifflin.

Bartoletti, S. C. (2000). *Coal miner's bride.* New York: Scholastic.

Bartoletti, S. C. (2001). *Black potatoes: The story of the great Irish famine, 1845–1850.* Boston: Houghton Mifflin.

Bausum, A. (2004). *With courage and cloth: Winning the fight for a woman's right to vote.* Washington, DC: National Geographic.

Bial, R. (1999). *One-room school.* Boston: Houghton Mifflin.

Bial, R. (2002). *Tenement: Immigrant life on the Lower East Side.* Boston: Houghton Mifflin.

Bial, R. (2004). *Where Washington walked.* New York: Walker.

Blake, A., & Dailey, P. (1995). *The gold rush of 1849: Staking a claim in California.* Brookfield, CT: Millbrook.

Blashfield, J. (2000). *The California gold rush.* Minneapolis, MN: Compass Point.

Blumberg, R. (1989). *The great American gold rush.* New York: Bradbury/Macmillan.

Blumberg, R. (2004). *York's adventures with Lewis and Clark: An African-American's part in the great expedition*. New York: HarperCollins.

Boling, K. (2006). *January 1905*. San Diego, CA: Harcourt.

Bradley, K. B. (2005). *The president's daughter*. New York: Delacorte.

Brill, M. T. (1997). *Women for peace*. New York: Watts.

Brooks, P. S. (1995). *Cleopatra: Goddess of Egypt, enemy of Rome*. New York: HarperCollins.

Bunkers, S. (Ed.). (2000). *A pioneer farm girl: The diary of Sarah Gillespie, 1877–1878*. Mankato, MN: Blue Earth Books.

Byrd, R. (2003). *Leonardo: Beautiful dreamer*. New York: Dutton.

Cherry, L. (1992). *A river ran wild: An environmental history*. San Diego, CA: Harcourt.

Christensen, B. (2003). *The daring Nellie Bly: America's star reporter*. New York: Knopf.

Coerr, E. (1993). *Sadako*. New York: Putnam.

Collier, J. L., & Collier, C. (1974). *My brother Sam is dead*. New York: Simon & Schuster.

Collins, M. (2003). *Airborne: A photobiography of Wilbur and Orville Wright*. Washington, DC: National Geographic.

Coombs, K. M. (2000). *Children of the dust days*. Minneapolis, MN: Carolrhoda.

Cooper, I. (2003). *Jack: The early years of John F. Kennedy*. New York: Dutton.

Cooper, M. L. (2002). *Remembering Manzanar: Life in a Japanese relocation camp*. New York: Clarion.

Cooper, M. L. (2004). *Dust to eat: Drought and depression in the 1930s*. New York: Clarion.

Crowe, C. (2003). *Getting away with murder: The true story of the Emmett Till case*. New York: Dial.

Cushman, K. (1994). *Catherine, called Birdy*. New York: Harper.

Cushman, K. (1996). *The ballad of Lucy Whipple*. New York: Clarion.

Cushman, K. (2003). *Rodzina*. Boston: Houghton Mifflin.

Daynes, K. (2005). *Cleopatra*. London: Usborne.

Devaney, J. (1991). *America goes to war, 1941*. New York: Walker.

Dudley, W. (Ed.). (1997). *Asian Americans: Opposing viewpoints*. San Diego, CA: Greenhaven.

Duncan, D. (1996). *People of the West*. Boston: Little, Brown.

Duncan, D. (1996). *The West: An illustrated history for children*. Boston: Little, Brown.

Erdrich, L. (1999). *The birchbark house*. New York: Hyperion.

Erdrich, L. (2005). *The game of silence*. New York: HarperCollins.

Forbes, E. (1943/1998). *Johnny Tremain*. Boston: Houghton Mifflin.

Fradin, D. B. (2000). *Bound for the North Star: True stories of fugitive slaves*. New York: Clarion.

Fradin, D. B., & Fradin J. B. (2000). *Ida B. Wells: Mother of the civil rights movement*. New York: Clarion.

Fradin, J. B., & Fradin D. B. (2004). *The power of one: Daisy Bates and the Little Rock Nine*. New York: Clarion.

Freedman, R. (1983). *Children of the Wild West*. New York: Clarion.

Freedman, R. (1987). *Lincoln: A photobiography*. New York: Clarion.

Freedman, R. (1994). *Kids at work: Lewis Hine and the crusade against child labor*. New York: Clarion.

Freedman, R. (1997). *Out of darkness: The story of Louis Braille*. New York: Clarion.

Freedman, R. (1999). *Babe Didrikson Zaharias: The making of a champion*. New York: Clarion.

Freedman, R. (2000). *Give me liberty!: The story of the Declaration of Independence*. New York: Holiday House.

Freedman, R. (2002). *Confucius: The golden rule*. New York: Scholastic.

Freedman, R. (2003). *In defense of liberty: The story of America's Bill of Rights*. New York: Holiday House.

Freedman, R. (2004). *The voice that challenged a nation: Marian Anderson and the struggle for equal rights*. New York: Clarion.

Freedman, R. (2005). *Children of the great depression*. New York: Clarion.

Garland, S. (2000). *Voices of the Alamo*. New York: Scholastic.

Garza, H. (1996). *Barred from the bar: A history of women in the legal profession*. New York: Watts.

Giblin, J. C. (1998). *George Washington: A picture book biography*. New York: Scholastic.

Giblin, J. C. (1999). *The mystery of the mammoth bones*. New York: HarperCollins.

Giblin, J. C. (2002). *The life and death of Adolph Hitler*. New York: Clarion.

Giblin, J. C. (2005). *Good brother, bad brother: The story of Edwin Booth and John Wilkes Booth*. New York: Clarion.

Giff, P. R. (2000). *Nory Ryan's song*. New York: Random House.

Grimes, N. (2002). *Talkin' about Bessie: The story of aviator Elizabeth Coleman*. New York: Scholastic.

Gulotta, C. (1999). *Extraordinary women in politics*. Danbury, CT: Children's Press.

Hamanaka, S. (1990). *The journey: Japanese Americans, racism, and renewal*. New York: Orchard.

Hansen, J., & McGowan, G. (2003). *Freedom roads: Searching for the Underground Railroad*. Chicago: Cricket.

Harness, C. (2000). *George Washington*. Washington, DC: National Geographic.

Hesse, K. (1997). *Out of the dust*. New York: Scholastic.

Hoose, P. (2001). *We were there, too! Young people in U.S. history*. New York: Farrar, Straus & Giroux

Hopkinson, D. (2003). *Shutting out the sky: Life in the tenements of New York, 1880–1924*. New York: Orchard.

Hurmence, B. (1997). *Slavery time when I was chillun*. New York: Putnam.

Jaffe, S. H. (1996). *Who were the Founding Fathers? Two hundred years of reinventing American history*. New York: Holt.

Jeffrey, G., & Watton, R. (2005). *Cleopatra: The life of an Egyptian queen*. New York: Rosen.

Kalman, B. (1998). *Homes of the West*. New York: Crabtree.

Kalman, B. (1998). *Life on the trail*. New York: Crabtree.

Kalman, B. (1999). *The gold rush*. New York: Crabtree.

Kalman, B. (1999). *Wagon train*. New York: Crabtree.

Kalman, B. (1999). *Who settled the West?* New York: Crabtree.

Kalman, B., & Lewis, J. (2000). *Women of the West*. New York: Crabtree.

Klein, J. (1998). *Gold rush! The young prospector's guide to striking it rich*. Berkeley, CA: Tricycle.

Kraft, B. H. (2003). *Theodore Roosevelt*. New York: Clarion.

Krull, K. (2000). *Lives of extraordinary women: Rulers, rebels (and what the neighbors thought)*. San Diego, CA: Harcourt.

Krull, K. (2004a). *The boy on Fairfield Street: How Ted Geisel grew up to become Dr. Seuss*. New York: Random House.

Krull, K. (2004b). *A woman for president: The story of Victoria Woodhull*. New York: Walker.

LaFaye, A. (2004). *Worth*. New York: Simon & Schuster.

Lanier, S., & Feldman, J. (2000). *Jefferson's children: The story of one American family*. New York: Random House.

Lasky, K. (2003). *The man who made time travel*. New York: Farrar, Straus & Giroux.

Lawlor, L. (1999). *Window on the West: The frontier photography of William Henry Jackson*. New York: Holiday House.

Lester, J. (2005). *Day of tears: A novel in dialogue*. New York: Hyperion.

Levine, E. (1992). *. . . If you traveled west in a covered wagon*. New York: Scholastic.

Levine, E. (1995). *A fence away from freedom*. New York: Putnam.

Littlefield, H. (1998). *Children of the trail west*. Minneapolis, MN: Carolrhoda.

Lyons, M. E. (Ed.) (2002). *Feed the children first: Irish memories of the great hunger*. New York: Atheneum.

MacDonald, F. (2001). *Cleopatra: Queen of kings*. New York: DK.

Mann, E. (2003). *Empire State Building: When New York reached for the skies*. New York: Mikaya Press.

Marrin, A. (1999). *Terror of the Spanish Main: Sir Henry Morgan and his buccaneers*. New York: Dutton.

Marrin, A. (2001). *George Washington and the founding of a nation*. New York: Dutton.

Marrin, A. (2002). *Dr. Jenner and the speckled monster: The search for the smallpox vaccine*. New York: Dutton.

Maurer, R. (2003). *The Wright sister: Katharine Wright and her famous brothers*. Brookfield, CT: Roaring Brook Press.

McArthur, D. (2002). *The Dust Bowl and the Depression in American history.* Berkeley Heights, NJ: Enslow.

McCully, E. A. (2004). *Squirrel and John Muir.* New York: Farrar.

McWhorter, D. (2004). *A dream of freedom: The civil rights movement from 1954 to 1968.* New York: Scholastic.

Meltzer, M. (1986). *George Washington and the birth of our nation.* New York: Watts.

Meltzer, M. (Ed.) (1987/1993). *The American revolutionaries: A history in their own words, 1750–1800.* New York: Crowell. [Reprint, Harper Trophy, 1993].

Meltzer, M. (Ed.). (1989/1992). *Voices from the Civil War: A documentary history of the great American conflict.* New York: Crowell. [Reprint, HarperCollins, 1992].

Meltzer, M. (1993). *Gold: The true story of why people search for it, mine it, trade it, steal it, mint it, hoard it, shape it, wear it, fight and kill for it.* New York: HarperCollins.

Meltzer, M. (1994). *Cheap raw material.* New York: Viking.

Meltzer, M. (2000). *Driven from the land: The story of the Dust Bowl.* Tarrytown, NY: Benchmark.

Meltzer, M. (2003). *Ten queens: Portraits of women in power.* New York: Dutton.

Morrison, T. (2004). *The coast mappers.* Boston: Houghton Mifflin.

Murphy, J. (1998). *Gone a-whaling: The lure of the sea and the hunt for the great whale.* New York: Houghton Mifflin.

Murphy, J. (2003). *An American plague: The true and terrifying story of the yellow fever epidemic of 1793.* New York: Clarion.

Nardo, D. (2005). *Cleopatra: Egypt's last pharaoh.* San Diego, CA: Lucent.

Nelson, R. (2003). *Communication then and now.* Minneapolis, MN: Lerner.

Nelson, R. (2003). *Home then and now.* Minneapolis, MN: Lerner.

Nelson, R. (2003). *School then and now.* Minneapolis, MN: Lerner.

Nelson, R. (2003). *Toys and games then and now.* Minneapolis, MN: Lerner.

Nelson, R. (2003). *Transportation then and now.* Minneapolis, MN: Lerner.

Nickles, G., & Fahey, K. (2001). *The Japanese.* New York: Crabtree.

Nixon, J. L. (1998). *Aggie's home.* New York: Dell.

Nixon, J. L. (1998). *David's search.* New York: Delacorte.

Nixon, J. L. (1998). *Lucy's wish.* New York: Dell.

Nixon, J. L. (1999). *Will's choice.* New York: Dell.

O'Brien, P. (2000). *The Hindenburg.* New York: Holt.

O'Connor, J. (2002). *The emperor's silent army: Terracotta warriors of ancient China.* New York: Viking.

O'Donnell, K. (2002). *The gold rush: A primary source history of the search for gold in California.* New York: Rosen.

Old, W. C. (2002). *To fly: The story of the Wright brothers.* New York: Clarion.

Partridge, E. (2002). *This land was made for you and me: The life and songs of Woody Guthrie*. New York: Viking.

Patent, D. H. (2002). *The Lewis and Clark trail then and now*. Photographs by William Muñoz. New York: Dutton.

Peterson, C. (1999). *Century farm: One hundred years on a family farm*. Honesdale, PA: Boyds Mills.

Pinkney, A. D. (2000). *Let it shine: Stories of black women freedom fighters*. San Diego, CA: Harcourt.

Rau, M. (2001). *The Wells Fargo book of the gold rush*. New York: Atheneum.

Reef, C. (2005). *Alone in the world: Orphans and orphanages in America*. New York: Clarion.

Rosen, M. (2001). *Shakespeare: His work and his world*. Cambridge, MA: Candlewick.

Ryan, P. M. (2002). *When Marian sang: The true recital of Marian Anderson, the voice of a century*. New York: Scholastic.

Saffer, B. (2002). *The California gold rush*. Broomall, PA: Mason Crest.

St. George, J. (2005). *Take the lead, George Washington!* New York: Philomel.

Sandler, M. (1994). *Pioneers: A Library of Congress book*. New York: HarperCollins.

Schanzer, R. (1999). *Gold fever! Tales from the California gold rush*. Washington, DC: National Geographic.

Schanzer, R. (2004). *George vs. George: The American Revolution as seen from both sides*. Washington, DC: National Geographic.

Schmandt-Besserat, D. (1999). *The history of counting*. New York: Morrow.

Stanley, D. (2002). *Saladin: Noble prince of Islam*. New York: HarperCollins.

Stanley, D., & Vennema, P. (1992). *Bard of Avon: The story of William Shakespeare*. New York: Morrow.

Stanley, D., & Vennema, P. (1994). *Cleopatra*. New York: Morrow.

Stanley, J. (1992). *Children of the Dust Bowl: The true story of the school at Weedpatch Camp*. New York: Crown.

Stanley, J. (1994). *I am an American: A true story of Japanese internment*. New York: Crown.

Stanley, J. (2000). *Hurry freedom: African Americans in gold rush California*. New York: Crown.

Stanley, J. (2003). *Cowboys and longhorns: A portrait of the long drive*. New York: Crown.

Taylor, M. D. (1976). *Roll of thunder, hear my cry*. New York: Dial.

Tunnell, M. O., & Chilcoat, G. W. (1996). *The children of Topaz*. New York: Holiday House.

Venezia, M. (2005). *George Washington: First president*. Danbury, CT: Children's Press.

Wadsworth, G. (2003). *Words west: Voices of young pioneers*. New York: Clarion.

Wallner, R. (2001). *Japanese immigrants, 1850–1950*. Mankato, MN: Capstone.

Warren, A. (1996). *Orphan train rider: One boy's true story*. Boston: Houghton Mifflin.

Warren, A. (1998). *Pioneer girl: Growing up on the prairie*. New York: Morrow.

Warren, A. (2001). *We rode the orphan trains*. Boston: Houghton Mifflin.

Welch, C. A. (2000). *Children of the relocation camps*. Minneapolis, MN: Carolrhoda.

Wilder, L. I. (1932). *Little house in the big woods*. New York: Harper & Row.

Willing, K., & Dock, J. (1994). *Quilting now and then*. New York: Now and Then Publications.

Winters, K. (2003). *Voices of ancient Egypt*. Washington, DC: National Geographic.

Worth, R. (2006). *Cleopatra: Queen of ancient Egypt*. Berkeley Heights, NJ: Enslow.

Yancey, D. (2004). *Life during the Dust Bowl*. San Diego, CA: Lucent.

Yolen, J. (1998). *House, house*. New York: Cavendish.

Zurlo, T. (2003). *The Japanese Americans*. San Diego, CA: Lucent.

Index

Index